Cuisine Niçoise

CUISINE NIÇOISE

Recipes from a Mediterranean Kitchen

Translated and edited by Peter Graham

Jacques Médecin

GRUB STREET · LONDON

This edition published in 2002 by Grub Street,
The Basement,
10 Chivalry Road,
London SW11 1HT
Email: food@grubstreet.co.uk
www.grubstreet.co.uk

Copyright this edition © 2002 Grub Street, London
First published as *La Cuisine du Comté de Nice* by Julliard 1972
Introduction and translation copyright © Peter Graham, 1983, 2002
First published in Great Britain
by Penguin Books Ltd, 1983

British Library Cataloguing in Publication Data
Medécin, Jacques
  Cuisine Niçoise: recipes from a Mediterranean kitchen
  1. Cookery, French
  I. Title II. Graham, Peter, 1939-
  641.5'944941

  ISBN 1-904010-08-3

Typeset by Pearl Graphics, Hemel Hempstead

Printed and bound in Great Britain by
Biddles Ltd, Guildford and King's Lynn

Contents

PREFACE

If I were asked why I wrote this book, I would reply:

because it seems to me that I belong to the last generation which has had
traditional recipes handed down to it;

because I love Nice, its surrounding countryside, its pretty girls and their
strapping young escorts, its arts, its flowers, fruit and vegetables, and, of
course, its cooking;

because genuine Niçois food simply cannot be found except in Niçois homes
and a handful of restaurants in Nice;

because, all over the world, I have had the most unpleasant experience of
being served up leftovers masquerading as salade niçoise;

because I love cooking for friends and watching them discover with delight
the subtlety of our Mediterranean traditions;

because in Nice and in my family, both men and women do the cooking,
passing on their skills from father to daughter and from mother to son;

because, in the 1880s, my dear grandmother took down a multitude of
centuries-old recipes dictated to her by an aged peasant woman, Tanta
Mietta, who lived on the beautiful hill of Gairaut, behind Nice;

and lastly because I would like to make this small contribution to the history
of Nice and its glorious culinary traditions.

It only remains for me to wish you *bon appétit*!

Jacques Médecin

INTRODUCTION

First, an explanation of this book's subtitle, 'Recipes from a Mediterranean Kitchen'. Why Mediterranean? you may be wondering. Why not French? The answer is simply that Nice has been part of France only since 1860. For almost 500 years before that (apart from a brief interlude under French rule from 1792 to 1814), Nice belonged to the House of Savoy, whose kingdom, known as the Kingdom of Sardinia, also included Savoy, Sardinia, and Piedmont (and, for part of the mid nineteenth century, almost the whole of Italy). Until 1860, there was little or nothing French about Nice's culture. And its culinary traditions, although showing some Provençal and Italian influences, have always been quite individual.

To the modern mind, Nice may conjure up an image of pleasure-seeking Edwardianism. As far as its cookery is concerned, any such image is quite irrelevant. The Promenade des Anglais, the gingerbread Hôtel Negresco, the casinos, and the swish suburbs of Cimiez are mere accretions that have made their appearance over the last 100 years or so, thanks to the attractions of sun and an average annual temperature of 18°C. They have little to do with the forces that made traditional Niçois cookery what it is.

Nice and its tiny province, the Comté de Nice (which extends along the Mediterranean coast from Antibes to Monaco, and northwards up into the Alps as far as Piedmont), have always been a backwater, an enclave hemmed in by mountain and sea. As there is little arable land, Nice has never been self-sufficient, and throughout its history has suffered from a chronic shortage of wheat. In the Middle Ages, its political alliances were governed by the need to ensure regular food supplies for its inhabitants.

This historical background goes a long way towards explaining the simplicity – frugality almost – of Niçois food. It is a far cry from the sumptuous cuisine of such rich farming provinces as Normandy or Burgundy. Herbs and other flavourings (particularly anchovy) are expertly used to enhance everyday products. Fish (readily available) and vegetables (easily grown in an ideal climate and needing little space) predominate over meat, and account for the two longest chapters in this book. And preserves of various kinds – salted and dried fish, salt pork, pickled and dried vegetables, bottled fruit, raisins, nuts and so on – still play the important role they did in the past, even though the eventuality of a serious food shortage has long since vanished.

The other great influence over Niçois cookery has been Italian (see pages 161-184), and more especially Genoese and Neapolitan. Historically, Genoa has always had strong ties with Nice, and this shows in several recipes such as *pistou*, a sauce derived from the Genoese *pesto*, and made of basil, garlic, olive oil, and Parmesan (some Niçois claim that *pistou* travelled the other way – from Nice to Genoa . . .).

Nice was always, until recently, an important centre of trade, both by sea and by land. It exchanged its fresh fruit, vegetables, and above all olive oil for preserves brought in by foreign boats. Prominent among such preserves were salt cod (*morue*) and wind-dried cod (stockfish) from Scandinavia (cod is not found in the Mediterranean). Indeed, stockfish was so enthusiastically adopted by the Niçois that it has become the symbol of traditional local gastronomy.

Such openness to outside influences also explains, no doubt, why the Niçois adopted such an 'outlandish' dish as English Christmas pudding. It was probably first introduced not by English traders, who had been doing business with Nice since the sixteenth century, but by the leisured classes who began wintering there in the mid eighteenth century. Jacques Médecin remembers his grandmother, when he was still a small boy, making what she called '*ploum-pudding*' for Christmas and the New Year. Set alight with lashings of rum, it was a long-anticipated treat that gave the younger members of the family a chance to taste a sweet with alcohol in it. Médecin long assumed the pudding to be a 'home-grown' speciality, and it was only much later that he learned of its English origins. Similarly, cheesecake can be found in Niçois *pâtisseries*: it was originally made at the request of Russian princes.

The best way to get an idea of what Niçois food is all about is to stroll into the old quarter of Nice. The narrow Rue du Marché and the streets that form its continuation are mainly lined with tiny food shops of every description. There you will see a fairly comprehensive range of local food (and choosy local shoppers): aged Parmesans, mature Goudas, and various Niçois cheeses piled teeteringly on top of each other; serried ranks of brilliant fresh fish; salted anchovies in tubs, slabs of *morue*, long, emaciated stockfish, barrels of olives and pickled red peppers; row upon row of green and white fresh *pasta* and *gnocchi*; strange cuttlebone-shaped *panisses*, made of chickpea flour; *socca*, a very thick pancake made of the same flour, sold in chunks by street vendors; uncooked tripe hanging from hooks like thick woolly rugs; colourful displays of fruit and vegetables; and a range of *charcuterie* that can only excite admiration – your gaze may even be returned by the spectacular *porchetta*, a boned, stuffed, reconstituted, and roasted piglet whose back end is cut up into huge slices (like the pig in Savignac's celebrated poster for ham).

If, on the other hand, you cannot get to Nice, Jacques Médecin's book is a pretty satisfactory surrogate.

Some Important Ingredients

Fish

Although Nice has never been a major fishing port like Marseilles or Sète, fish, not meat, has always formed the staple diet of its inhabitants. There is an old Niçois saying which goes: 'Fish are born in water and die in oil.' It is well worth visiting one of the colourful fish markets in Nice or in one of the neighbouring towns along the coast. Imposing fishwives, known as *répétiéra* in

Niçois, set the streets ringing with their cries of 'Où peï! Où peï!' ('Fish for sale! Fish for sale!').

In February, you are more likely to hear 'A la bella poutina! A la bella poutina!', when their barrows are laden with glistening *poutine* (anchovies and sardines in their larval state). The fishing of these tiny creatures (several hundred to the pound) is prohibited elsewhere in France. But it was decided in 1860, when the Comté de Nice was incorporated into France, to introduce special legislation permitting such fishing between Antibes and the Italian border. Legend has it that Empress Eugénie, who apparently liked to call the fishermen of Nice her 'good friends', had something to do with that decision. The fishing of *poutine* (recipes 117 and 118) is nowadays very strictly controlled: no boat may make a catch of more than 100 kg, and the authorized period is closed by the maritime authorities as soon as the fish begin to grow scales.

Anchovies and sardines that manage to survive until the next stage of their growth, when they are known as *palaïa*, form the basis of a strong fish paste called *pissala* (No. 260), which should be the dominant flavour in a genuine *pissaladière* (No. 48) – though nowadays *pissala* is almost always made with fully grown anchovies.

Salted anchovies are one of the most important ingredients in Niçois cookery, and so excellent are they that they are often served on their own in Niçois restaurants with either oil or vinegar (or sometimes both), a few capers, and a clove (which is used in the salting mixture and imparts a particularly subtle and distinctive flavour). If salted anchovies from a tub are not available, the next best are sold in glass containers. Tinned anchovies, though passable, come last on the list (their taste is sometimes affected by the corrosion of the metal by salt). If you are lucky enough to get hold of fresh anchovies, salt them yourself (No. 259).

Another fish preserve that is much consumed by the Niçois is tunny, though it is no longer sold in barrels, but in tins as in Britain. The most highly prized part of the fish, as in Italy and Spain, is the belly (*ventresca*), which has a softer consistency and smoother flavour than the dorsal muscle. Tinned *ventresca* can be bought in Britain from specialized shops. Salt cod (*morue*) is also eaten in Nice, but not as widely as in Provence.

Undoubtedly the most typically Niçois of all preserved fish is stockfish, which is wind-dried, but not salted, cod. As hard as wood, it keeps almost indefinitely under dry conditions and needs several days' soaking before becoming usable as food. It gives its name – and pungent flavour – to a stew that has become the symbol of authentic Niçois gastronomy, *estocaficada* (No. 119). There even exists an association called 'L'Estocaficada' aimed at promoting Niçois traditions in the kitchen. Its exclusively Nice-born members meet once a month for a feast of local specialities, with stockfish stew as the *pièce de résistance*.

The Niçois also consume vast quantities of fresh fish. The culinary characteristics of each species are described in the recipes of the Seafood chapter. Anyone wishing to explore the subject of Mediterranean fish more thoroughly is advised to consult Alan Davidson's comprehensive *Mediterranean Seafood*.

Vegetables

The second main characteristic of Niçois cookery is its imaginative use of vegetables. Although the soil of the Comté de Nice is not all that fertile, there is plenty of sun; and an extensive irrigation network makes up for lack of rainfall during the long, dry summer months. Most vegetables eaten in Nice are familiar to British readers. Others, and their varieties, need some explanation; often they will be unavailable in Britain, so your only opportunity of trying them is to buy them when on holiday in France – or to grow them in your garden (often much easier than one supposes).

Globe artichokes

Médecin has a single recipe calling for the most common globe artichoke, the large so-called Breton variety (No. 131). Otherwise, what is needed is one of the very small violet-leaved varieties, preferably the one with spiny tips; properly trimmed (when the tips and other tough parts of the leaves are cut off), it can be eaten raw in a *salade niçoise* (No. 32) or *pan-bagnat* (No. 33). There is also a so-called Roman variety, shaped like a very broad and flat brandy glass, which is ideal for grilling (No. 133).

Courgettes

Nice boasts two varieties of courgette that are scarcely ever found elsewhere in France: the round courgette, which is melon-shaped and especially suitable for stuffing – its halves sit obediently flat in the baking dish (No. 157); and the splendidly named *courge longue pleine de Naples coureuse*, which starts off life looking like a lighter-coloured version of the familiar dark-green courgette, then swells into a large 11-13 lb/5-6 kg) marrow the shape of a huge dog-bone, at which point it becomes a *courge rouge*. Its yellow-orange flesh at that stage is similar to that of a pumpkin, though tastier and less sweet. As both the vegetable and its seed are, as far as I know, unavailable in Britain, I have suggested pumpkin as an alternative in recipes where Médecin calls for *courge rouge* (Nos. 10, 11, 163 and 206). The *courge rouge* can be stored for several months, and in Nice replaces courgettes when they are no longer in season.

As in Italy, the flowers of all three varieties, taken from male stems (which do not bear fruit), are used in various recipes – in soup (No. 18), in fritters (No. 159), stuffed (No. 158), or as flavouring (No. 162).

Mesclun

This typically Niçois mixture of salad plants has risen to fame over recent years, and is now common, if not *de rigueur*, all over France on the menus of restaurants which have any '*nouvelle cuisine*' pretensions. But what you get on your plate almost never corresponds to what Médecin considers to be the authentic mixture – rocket, young dandelion, and young lettuce, with the possible addition of a little watercress and chervil (No. 182).

Packets of *mesclun* seed sold in Nice, on the other hand, may include any or all of the following plants: red Treviso chicory, white chicory (eaten unblanched, therefore bitter), Oak Leaf lettuce, Cos lettuce, and purslane, as well as rocket, dandelion, and chervil. Not surprisingly, the word *mesclun* comes from the Latin *miscellanea*.

At the turn of the century, *mesclun* grown by the Franciscan Fathers in Cimiez (the hill at the back of Nice) was highly esteemed as a gift from children to their elders; it would be specially presented in an *espourtoula*, a wicker basket with a handle.

Swiss chard

The Niçois eat so much Swiss chard (*bléa* in Niçois) that they sometimes crudely refer to themselves as *caga-bléa* (*caga* means 'cack'). This mild-tasting vegetable (and more particularly the green tops of its stalks) goes into a wide variety of recipes, from stuffings and omelettes to *tourte de blette* (No. 230), a sweet pie which is surely the greatest oddity in Niçois cookery. Swiss chard is not always readily available, and can, at a pinch, be replaced by spinach and/or lettuce. But neither the taste nor the consistency is quite the same. It is easily grown.

Mushrooms

Truffle-hunting goes on in some parts of the Comté de Nice. Black truffles (*Tuber melanosporum*) are found around Le Mas, while their highly aromatic lighter cousins, white truffles (*Tuber magnatum*), grow in the area of Tende and La Brigue near the Piedmont border. As both are extremely rare, they tend to be used as seasoning rather than as food. White truffles are cut with a special instrument into paper-thin shavings, which are then sprinkled on to any dish from vermicelli soup, pasta and rice to fish and even green salad.

Black truffles are either used to flavour scrambled eggs or, more extravagantly, cooked on their own in a tiny covered ramekin with a spoonful of meat stock.

Neither variety is found in Britain, though the related *Tuber aestivum* is said still to grow in the beechwoods of southern England where it was once extensively hunted.

The British, for some reason, seem to have a mental block against eating wild mushrooms (except for field or horse mushrooms), and every year millions of so-called 'toadstools' go to waste in woods and fields. Two such fungi are much eaten in Nice: the cèpe is an essential ingredient of *daube à la niçoise* (No. 54), while *Lactarius sanguifluus* is cooked both on its own (No. 149) and with other ingredients (No. 39). (*Lactarius sanguifluus* is not found in Britain, but can be replaced by its relative, *Lactarius deliciosus*, or Saffron Milk Cap.)

Dried cèpe, which is just as good as fresh in dishes such as a *daube*, is widely available in Britain, though of variable quality: avoid any packet whose contents look completely dark brown or black with no buff patches – they are probably mushrooms that were dried when past their prime, if not maggoty, and are very indigestible.

Herbs

Niçois recipes use herbs extensively, but with moderation. And they never call for *herbes de Provence*, that overfine mixture of stale dried herbs and, especially, their twigs (ground small to avoid detection) which so often smothers steaks in bad restaurants on both sides of the Channel. Herbs, as Médecin rightly says, should always be used with discretion so that the taste of the food itself is never disguised.

What he does not say (because he takes it for granted) is that, whenever possible, *fresh herbs should be used in preference to dried ones*. In some cases – thyme, marjoram, rosemary, bay leaf, winter savory, and fennel – the difference in flavour between the two is very slight. There are, however, other herbs, such as basil, tarragon, and chervil, that are but a shadow of themselves once they have gone through the drying process, while fresh sage, as anyone who has eaten in Italy will know, has an utterly different flavour from that of the dried herb, whose overpowering mustiness was the bane of British stuffings. Recipes such as Nos. 1, 16, 63, 64 and 67 (one of the most deliciously original in the book) are to my mind not worth attempting unless fresh sage can be obtained. The strength of sage varies, so it is best to experiment with quantities if you have a plant in your garden.

Certain other herbs are always difficult to come by in Britain, whether fresh or dried, and cooks in search of authenticity will have either to grow them from seed themselves (borage, purslane – though the latter is sometimes available from Greek-Cypriot greengrocers under the name of *glystiridha*), or to scour the countryside, field guide in hand, for wild thyme, wild marjoram (the commercially available *origano* is a stronger version of the same herb), poppy, and smooth sow-thistle. The last two ingredients, along with borage and purslane, make up a curious, specifically Niçois concoction of herbs known as *réfrescat* (Nos. 13, 14, and 15) though Médecin does add, mercifully, that one or more of the herbs, if unavailable, may be omitted without too much detriment to the flavour of the dish.

When a *bouquet garni* is called for, it is understood to mean a sprig of thyme, a bay leaf, and a bunch of parsley tied together with string or enclosed in a muslin bag, except when extra ingredients are expressly indicated.

Parmesan

When Médecin calls for grated Parmesan, he naturally means *freshly* grated Parmesan. Its flavour is in quite a different league from that of the powdered stuff sold in plastic packets (which contains a large proportion of grated

Parmesan rind). I have not reduced the usually very generous amounts of Parmesan indicated by Médecin, despite the high cost of the cheese: do as your conscience and purse-strings dictate, but please prefer half quantities of the real cheese grated at the last moment to the full weight of stale powder.

Olive Oil

For Médecin, there is only one acceptable type of oil for cooking or for salads: olive oil. And not just any old olive oil. It has to be Niçois and, if possible, pressed by the firm of Nicolas Alziari. I can see why. Alziari's product is a lively yellow colour, like undiluted Pernod. And although the flavour of olives is always subtly present, it is smooth and mild enough to be used for making mayonnaise (whereas normally a mixture of olive oil and a neutral salad oil produces the best result). Again, Médecin's lavish quantities have been left untouched, except in the case of deep-frying, where I have simply specified 'deep-frying oil' instead of olive oil. However, if you want to experience the genuine flavour of Niçois fritters or doughnuts, whether sweet or savoury, you will have to damn expense and use olive oil.

Pine-Nuts

Another expensive ingredient – but they impart an essential flavour to the dishes in which they are called for. The best is brought out of pine-nuts if they are heated very gently in a pan or, better, in an oven dish until they begin to sweat their oil and turn very slightly darker (from creamy white to the colour of roasted peanuts).

Petit Salé

This form of salt pork features very often in Niçois recipes. Very few butchers in Britain make salt streaky pork, and when they do it is not much like the French version. *Petit salé* is not unsmoked bacon (though in a real emergency it could be replaced by it). So, for those in search of the real thing, here is a recipe for *petit salé* from Jane Grigson's *Charcuterie and French Pork Cookery* (Grub Street 2001), reproduced with the kind permission of the publisher:

'Flavoured salt (*sel aromatisé*) is the first requirement:
To every 2½ lb/1.25 kg salt (enough for 12 lb/6 kg meat in fact)
1 oz/25 g saltpetre (now no longer available in Britain)
1 oz/25 g granulated sugar
1 teaspoon peppercorns
1 oz/25 g juniper berries
4 bay leaves, crushed
thyme leaves from two sprigs, crushed
4 cloves

'Mix it all well together. Put about ¾ lb/300 g in the bottom of a stoneware pot.

'Take the piece of belly of pork and rub a good handful of salt firmly into the skin side. Turn it over and rub some more into the flesh side, but not so vigorously. Lay it on the layer of salt, flesh side down, skin side up, and pack the rest of the salt round the sides and over the top. Put a piece of boiled wood on top (or a scrupulously clean plate) and a light weight.

'Leave in a cool, dark place for at least four days per inch thickness of meat. You can leave the *petit salé*, on the other hand, in salt for much longer – one handbook recommends two months. You will find that the meat juices turn the salt to brine.'

Petit salé should be cut up to the required size and blanched before use.

A Note on Conversions

Please stick to *either* imperial *or* metric measurements. While the proportions remain the same within the two sets of measurements, the actual quantities may vary slightly.

A Note on Utensils

There are two typically Niçois kitchen utensils, the *pignata* and the *tian*. The *pignata* is an earthenware dish with a hollow handle, used like a casserole (it is more generally known under its Provençal name, *poêlon*). The *tian* is a deepish earthenware gratin dish which, like the word casserole, has given its name to its contents (Nos. 103, 114, 162, and 198).

When Médecin tells you to use a wooden spoon, he in fact means a box-wood spoon, which is far more expensive, but also much longer-lasting, than the ordinary article.

Acknowledgement

Some of the material in this Introduction is based on Jacques Médecin's own introduction to the French edition, and on information kindly supplied by Elizabeth David.

Peter Graham

SOUPS

1 Garlic and Sage Soup
L'aiga Saou / L'Eau Salée

For 4

6 cloves garlic	salt, pepper
1/4 lb/100 g vermicelli	2 tbs olive oil
2 leaves sage (see page xii)	2 oz/50 g grated Parmesan

1. Put the whole, peeled cloves of garlic into 3½ pints/2 litres of water and bring to the boil.

2. Lower heat and simmer for 20 minutes. Add the vermicelli, crushing it slightly between the fingers. Season with salt and pepper to taste. Add the sage.

3. Simmer for a further 10 minutes. Remove the cloves of garlic and, placing them individually in a tablespoon, crush them with a fork to the smoothest paste possible.

4. Remove the liquid from heat, and stir in the garlic paste and olive oil. Serve hot with generous pinches of grated Parmesan.

● This soup is equally good when the vermicelli is replaced by tapioca, semolina, or *couscous* grain.

2 Stuffed-Cabbage Soup

Lu Capoun Rout / Les Choux Farcis Cassés

In the old days, this soup was quite simply the water in which stuffed cabbages (No. 152) had been boiled. During cooking, one or two of the cabbages would become untied, spilling their delicious contents into the water in which they were being boiled. Nowadays, this subtly-flavoured soup is made for its own sake with the ingredients that go into stuffed cabbage.

For 6

2 oz/60 g rice	2 eggs
salt	30 tender cabbage leaves taken
5 sprigs parsley	from the heart, or 30 broccoli
1/4 bay leaf	sprouts
2 leaves sage	5 oz/150 g lean *petit salé*
1 sprig thyme	(see page xiii)
2 medium onions	2 tbs olive oil
2 cloves garlic	pepper

1. Wash the rice and drain well. Bring 5 pints/3 litres of water to the boil. Let the rice fall into it in a steady rain. Salt slightly.

2. Make a small *bouquet garni* with the parsley, bay leaf, sage, and thyme, and drop it into the boiling water along with the whole, unpeeled onions and the whole, peeled cloves of garlic.

3. Simmer for 15 minutes. Meanwhile, separate the whites from the yolks of the eggs, and whip until stiff. Cut the cabbage or broccoli into strips, dip in the white of egg, and add to the soup along with the finely diced *petit salé*.

4. Simmer for a further 10 minutes. Put the egg yolks and olive oil into a soup tureen and mix well. Remove the onions, garlic, and *bouquet garni* from the soup, then pour it into the tureen, stirring all the time. Season with plenty of pepper.

● The cabbage or broccoli may be replaced by Swiss chard tops or any variety of green salad vegetable; if so, 2 tablespoons of grated Parmesan and a large pinch of grated nutmeg should be mixed in with the egg yolks and olive oil in step 4.

3 Fish Soup

La Soupa dé Peï / *La Soupe de Poisson*

There is an infinite variety of fish soups to be found along the northern Mediterranean coast from Genoa, in Italy, to the small French port of Collioure, by the Spanish border. The *bourride* of Toulon is made with white fish only and is almost milky in appearance. *Bouillabaisse* is a very liquid soup in which the fish (mainly small ones) should if possible remain whole. The fish soup of Nice is a smooth, creamy purée of rockfish, and owes its consistency to the incomparably tasty flesh of the conger eel. It is eaten with toasted French bread, Parmesan, and *rouille* (No. 24). Some Niçois prefer spaghetti or coarse vermicelli instead of bread. But in any case the soup is always made the same way. It only really succeeds when made for at least a dozen people. Allow at least 3 hours to prepare it.

For 12 or more

13 lb/6 kg very small, fresh rockfish, including, if possible, *rascasse* (scorpion fish), wrasse, and the small green crabs known as *charlatans* or *charloù* in Niçois dialect (shore crabs will do)	6 cloves garlic, peeled
	4 fl oz/100 ml cognac
	4 lb/2 kg tomatoes
	bouquet garni
	scant ¼ tsp saffron
2 lb/1 kg conger eel *or* moray eel, from the head *or* tail end	salt
	cayenne pepper
7 fl oz/200 ml olive oil	5 oz/150 g grated Parmesan
6 large onions, peeled	40 slices toast *or* 2-5 oz/50-150 g coarse vermicelli

1. Wash the fish very carefully to remove all traces of seaweed, sand, etc., but do not gut. Heat the olive oil in a stainless-steel frying pan until it is just beginning to smoke. Fry the fish in it until slightly browned, beginning with the sliced conger eel and larger fish. Remove the fish with a fish-slice and place in the bottom of a *very* large enamelled or stainless-steel saucepan, which should be kept warm on a hotplate.

2. When all the fish and crabs have been sealed in the frying pan, cook the sliced onions and finely chopped garlic in the same oil till golden. Add to the fish. Deglaze the pan with the cognac and add to the rest of the ingredients.

3. Place the saucepan over a moderate heat and pour in 7 quarts/8 litres of cold water. Add the peeled, seeded, and coarsely chopped tomatoes. Lastly, add the *bouquet garni* and the saffron.

4. Boil over a moderate heat for 1 hour.

5. Remove the soup from the stove and purée it, a ladleful at a time, until well broken up but not oversmooth. Put through a fairly fine sieve. (By the way, if you or your neighbours have chickens, give the birds the debris in the sieve – and see what gourmets they are!)

6. Put the sieved soup into a large flame-proof pot that can be used to serve the soup, and bring back to the boil. Correct seasoning carefully. Fish soup is the only Niçois dish that needs plenty of salt, though it should not, of course, be oversalted. It should also be quite fiery, so add the necessary amount of cayenne pepper, while remembering that the *rouille* with which the soup will be served will add plenty of punch.

7. If the soup is not to be served immediately, remove it from the stove and keep it at room temperature (you can even freeze it). Indeed, it will be all the tastier for being reheated gently for 30 minutes. It should be served with *rouille* (No. 24), grated Parmesan, and toast on the side (the toast can be replaced by vermicelli, which should be added to the soup during the last 20 minutes of cooking).

• • •

4 Aire Saint-Michel Soup

La Soupa dé L'airé San Michéù / Le Potage Aire Saint-Michel

This soup was invented by my father when he was a small child: in the district of Nice called the Aire Saint-Michel, he and his brothers and sisters would repair to a hut they had made of branches and play at being chefs. The dish has become something of a tradition in our family. The trouble is that it can be made only in spring-time.

For 6

20 small globe artichokes	1/4 lb/100 g fine vermicelli
6 spring onions	2 eggs
5 oz/150 g young broad beans, shelled	2 tbs olive oil
salt, pepper	4 tbs grated Parmesan

1. Cut the whole of the artichokes, including even the top of the stem, into thin slices. Slice the spring onions.

2. Place the vegetables in 3 quarts/3½ litres of cold water, seasoned with salt and pepper, and bring to the boil. Simmer very gently (200°F/95°C) for 20 minutes.

3. Turn up the heat until the soup is boiling furiously. Add the vermicelli and cook for another 10 minutes.

4. Break the eggs into a soup tureen and beat them. Mix in the grated Parmesan and olive oil. Dilute this mixture with spoonfuls of hot soup, beating energetically all the time with a fork, until it is perfectly liquid, then pour in the rest of the soup in one go. Add plenty of pepper, check the seasoning, and serve.

5 Tomato Soup

La Soupa dé Toùmati / La Soupe de Tomates

There are an infinite number of ways of making tomato soup. Cream of tomato soup is greatly appreciated in the Anglo-Saxon countries and in Germany; the Niçois version is not so thick, but is stronger tasting.
The following excellent recipe for tomato soup is the one most commonly encountered in the Comté de Nice, though I have tasted many variants of it.

For 10

4 large onions, peeled	10 leaves basil
2 cloves garlic, peeled	1 sprig thyme
4 tbs olive oil	1 clove
13 lb/6 kg tomatoes	1/2 bay leaf
salt	cayenne pepper
2 lumps of sugar	3 sprigs parsley

1. Slice the onions and chop finely 1 clove of garlic. Brown them in 3 tablespoons of olive oil.

2. Scald and peel the tomatoes, cut into quarters, salt, and put into a very large saucepan with the sugar and the browned onions and garlic. Add the basil, thyme, clove, bay leaf, and cayenne pepper (a pinch). Bring to the boil, and simmer for 15 minutes.

3. Purée until smooth. If the resulting purée looks too thick, dilute with a little boiling water until the desired consistency is obtained. Put back over a very gentle heat and simmer for another 15 minutes.

4. Pound the second clove of garlic in a mortar with the parsley.
Mix 1 tablespoon of olive oil into the paste. Check the seasoning of the soup and remove it from the stove. Add the garlic, parsley, and olive oil paste, and serve immediately.

● This tomato soup can, if desired, be thickened or made more filling with the addition of mashed potatoes, fine semolina, very fine *pasta*, tapioca, or toast (the last two being particularly common in Nice).

6 Vegetable Soup
La Soupa dé Lieumé / La Soupe de Légumes

For 8

1/4 lb/100 g carrots, peeled	3 tbs olive oil
2 oz/50 g turnip, peeled	5 oz/150 g haricot beans (fresh if
5 small courgettes (in winter,	possible), green peas *or* broad
1 lb/500 g pumpkin – see page x)	beans, shelled
1/2 lb/200 g potatoes, peeled	2 tbs chopped parsley
10 Swiss chard tops	2 leaves sage
1 large leek	2 leaves basil
5 cloves garlic, peeled	salt, pepper
5 large onions, peeled	3 oz/80 g rice *or* macaroni
3/4 lb/300 g tomatoes	3 oz/75 g grated Parmesan

1. Cut the carrots, turnip, courgettes, and potatoes into small dice. Slice the Swiss chard tops, leek, garlic, and onions. Peel and seed the tomatoes, chop coarsely, and leave to drain.

2. Put the olive oil into a deep saucepan and brown the onions. When they are just turning golden, add the leek, garlic, and tomatoes. Reduce over a moderate heat by at least a third. Add the rest of the vegetables (but not the peas or broad beans if these are being used) and the chopped herbs. (If dried haricot beans are being used, soak as indicated on the packet, and boil for 20 minutes before putting them in the soup.) Dilute with 3 quarts/3½ litres of hot water, and bring back to the boil. Add salt and pepper to taste.

3. After 25 minutes' cooking, add the rice or macaroni, and the green peas or broad beans if they are being used instead of haricot beans. Correct seasoning. If the liquid seems to have reduced too much, add some boiling water.

4. Cook for another 20 minutes, and serve with grated Parmesan.

● ● ●

7 Pistou
Lou Pistou / Le Pistou

This is undoubtedly the most popular soup in the Nice area. The word *pistou* means 'pounded' in Niçois, and strictly speaking describes not the soup itself but the sauce that goes into it – a mixture of garlic, basil, olive oil, and Parmesan pounded together in a mortar.

It is sometimes erroneously supposed that *pistou* is the Niçois word for basil; the word is in fact *balico*.

The soup itself is basically the same as No. 6, though the rice or macaroni must be replaced by coarse vermicelli. Not all the ingredients listed in the previous recipe need to be included, but there are three absolute musts: tomatoes, courgettes, and fresh haricot beans. So it is a soup that really comes into its own from late spring to early autumn. *Pistou* may be a simple soup, but it is also extraordinarily subtle – as you will discover if you follow my recipe.

For 8

5 pints/3 litres vegetable soup (No. 6)   6 tbs grated Parmesan
3 cloves garlic, peeled   3 tbs olive oil
10 large basil leaves

1. Pound the garlic to a fine paste in a mortar. Avoid using hand-operated or electric garlic crushers, as they separate the pulp from the juice, thus spoiling the taste of the garlic. It is encouraging to note that those noblest of utensils, pestle and mortar, have recovered their rightful place in the modern kitchen and dining-room.

2. Wash the basil, dry well, add to the mashed garlic, and pound to a fine paste.

3. Pour the grated Parmesan into the mortar and incorporate carefully with a fork.

4. Give the *pistou* a creamy consistency by gradually adding the olive oil and mixing with a fork.

5. *Pistou* must never cook. It should be added to the soup at the very last moment, away from the heat, just before serving.

● The fact that *pistou* must never cook means, of course, that any tinned form of *pistou* soup, heated up at the last minute, can only cut a very sorry figure compared with the real thing. This probably explains why many a gourmet has been turned off *pistou* – through tasting the tinned version. The genuine Niçois recipe should, however, reveal the soup in all its delicious splendour.

● *Pistou* sauce is greatly appreciated all along the Ligurian coast (it is known as *pesto* in Italian). I will make no attempt to settle the question as to whether *pistou* migrated from Nice to Genoa, or vice versa, but let me simply say that the Ligurians like to add ¼ lb/100 g of pine-nuts to the ingredients pounded in the mortar. In Portofino, this form of *pistou* with pine-nuts is eaten as an accompaniment to spaghetti and *lasagne*.

● In the north of the Alpes-Maritimes *département*, *pistou* sauce is often eaten with mutton.

8 Cream of Broad Bean Soup

Lou Vélutat dé Fava / Le Velouté de Fèves

For 8

3¹/4 lb/1¹/2 kg dried, *or* 4¹/2 lb/2 kg fresh broad beans, shelled
1 onion, peeled
4 tbs olive oil
10 Swiss chard tops *or* leaves of 2 large lettuces.

bouquet garni
salt, pepper
¹/4 lb/100 g bread
2 oz/50 g lean *petit salé* (see page xiii)

1. Put the broad beans (if they are dried broad beans, they should first be soaked for at least 3 hours), sliced onion, 2 tablespoons of olive oil, Swiss chard tops or lettuce leaves cut into coarse strips, and *bouquet garni* into 5 pints/3 litres of water. Add salt and pepper, and bring to the boil. Cook over a moderate heat for 45 minutes.

2. Purée. Return to a very gentle heat.

3. Cut the bread into small dice (¹/4 inch/¹/2 cm) and fry in 2 tablespoons of olive oil until golden brown.

4. Cut the *petit salé* into similarly small dice and fry until crisp.

5. Just before serving, drop the *petit salé* into the soup. Put the fried bread into a bowl, and serve on the side.

9 Spring Soup

La Soupa dé Prima / Le Potage Printanier

For 8

1/2 lb/200 g small globe artichokes	1/2 lb/200 g peas, shelled
1/2 lb/200 g spring onions	2 eggs
1/2 lb/200 g Swiss chard tops	2 tbs olive oil
1/2 lb/200 g broad beans, shelled	salt, pepper
1/2 lb/200 g new potatoes	4 oz/100 g grated Parmesan

1. Cut the artichokes (all except the green tips of the leaves), spring onions, and Swiss chard tops into thin slices. Put them, with the broad beans, into 5 pints/3 litres of cold water and bring to the boil over a moderate heat. Allow to cook for 20 minutes.

2. Add the potatoes, finely diced, and the peas. Boil for another 20 minutes.

3. Just before serving, and away from the heat, add the eggs, beaten thoroughly with the olive oil. Correct seasoning, and serve with a bowl of grated Parmesan on the side.

• • •

10 Courgette or Pumpkin Soup

La Soupa dé Cougourda / La Soupe de Courge

For 8

10 small courgettes *or*	1 leaf sage
31/4 lb/11/2 kg pumpkin	salt, pepper
(see page x)	2 tbs olive oil
4 large onions, peeled	3 oz/80 g rice
1 clove garlic, peeled	4 oz/100 g grated Parmesan
bouquet garni	

1. Cut the courgettes or pumpkin into 1-inch/3-cm dice. Slice the onion and chop the garlic finely.

2. Place these ingredients, along with the *bouquet garni* and sage, in 5 pints/3 litres of boiling water. Add salt and pepper. Pour in the olive oil.

3. When the soup has simmered for 45 minutes, purée and return to the saucepan. Bring back to the boil.

4. Add the rice and boil for a further 15 minutes. Serve with a bowl of grated Parmesan on the side.

11 Poutine or Nonat Soup

La Soupa dé Poutina o dé Nounat
La Soupe de Poutine ou de Nonats

For 4

2 small onions, peeled
1 clove garlic, peeled
1 tbs olive oil
2 tomatoes
1 clove

½ bay leaf
¾ lb/300 g *poutine or nonats*
    (see page ix and No. 113)
salt, pepper

1. Slice the onions and crush the garlic. Put them in a frying pan with the olive oil and brown.

2. Add the peeled, seeded and coarsely chopped tomatoes, the clove, and the bay leaf. Cook for another 5 minutes.

3. Pour into a deep saucepan. Cover with 3½ pints/2 litres of boiling water.

4. After boiling the soup for 15 minutes, purée, return to the saucepan, and bring back to the boil.

5. Plunge the *poutine* or *nonats* into the liquid, and remove from heat immediately. Season with salt and pepper. Leave for 5 minutes before serving, but no longer, otherwise the fish will completely disintegrate.

12 Mussel Soup

La Soupa aï Musclé / La Soupe aux Moules

For 4

5 pints/3 litres mussels (discard
   any that are not tightly shut)
1 onion, peeled
1 clove garlic, peeled
bouquet garni (consisting of
   fennel and celery leaves as well
   as thyme, parsley, and bay leaf

2 tbs olive oil
1/2 lb/200 g tomatoes
1 pinch saffron
salt, pepper
4 oz/125 g rice *or* 4 oz/125 g
   vermicelli

1. Scrub and beard the mussels, put into a saucepan with 2½ pints/1½ litres of water, and boil uncovered for 3 or 4 minutes until they open; shake the saucepan frequently during the process. Discard any that refuse to open.

2. Remove the mussels from their shells and put them back in their own cooking liquid, which should have been carefully poured off into another receptacle so as to remove any sand.

3. Put the finely sliced onion, chopped garlic, and *bouquet garni* in a large saucepan, and brown in the olive oil. Add the peeled, seeded, and coarsely chopped tomatoes, cook over a high heat for 3 minutes, and cover with the mussels' cooking liquid.

4. Bring to the boil, add a small pinch of saffron, pepper, and salt (not much, as the mussels are already salty), and cook the rice or vermicelli in the soup for 15 minutes.

5. Just before serving, add the mussels to the soup. Do not allow them to boil, as further cooking would make them tough.

● This soup is sometimes thickened with 4 tablespoons of double cream or very firm mayonnaise.

13 Dried Broad Bean Soup with Réfrescat

La Soupa dé Fava Sécagna où Réfrescat
La Soupe de Fèves Sèches Réfrescat

For 6

2 large carrots, peeled
4 Swiss chard tops
1 leek
10 leaves each of
  borage, purslane,
  poppy, smooth } the *réfrescat*
  sow-thistle, and (see page xii)
  dandelion
1¼ lb/600 g dried broad beans
2 onions, peeled

1 clove garlic, peeled
1 sprig thyme
½ bay leaf
½ pint/250 ml meat stock
  (optional)
20 chard tops *or* large
  lettuce leaves
salt, pepper
3 tbs olive oil

1. Prepare the *réfrescat*: slice the carrots, cut the 4 Swiss chard tops into strips, cut up the leek finely, and tie the herbs into little bundles.

2. Put the broad beans, which should previously have been soaked for 2 hours, in a large saucepan containing 4½ pints/2½ litres of cold water along with the ingredients of the *réfrescat*, the finely sliced onions, and the garlic, thyme, and bay leaf. Bring very slowly to the boil.

3. When the soup has been boiling genfly for 1½ hours, purée it, return to the saucepan, and dilute with about ½ pint/250 ml of boiling water or stock, as desired. Bring back to the boil, add the 20 Swiss chard tops or lettuce leaves, cut into strips, and boil for 3 minutes. Season to taste, remove from heat, add the olive oil, and serve.

● ● ●

14 Lentil Soup with Réfrescat

La Soupa dé Lentilha où Réfrescat
La Soupe de Lentilles Réfrescat

This soup is made in exactly the same way as No. 13, except that the dried broad beans are replaced by an equal amount of lentils, and 4 oz/100 g of lean *petit salé* (see page xiii), cut into small dice, are added to the ingredients in step 2.

15 Haricot Bean Soup with Réfrescat

La Soupa dé Faïoù Fava où Réfrescat
La Soupe de Haricots Blancs Réfrescat

For 6

1 lb/500 g haricot beans
2 onions, peeled
1 clove
1 clove garlic, peeled
2 leaves sage
1 sprig thyme
réfrescat (ingredients and
   quantities as described in No. 13)

½ lb/200 g pumpkin (*or courge
   rouge* – see page x)
20 Swiss chard tops *or* large
   lettuce leaves
salt, pepper
3 tbs olive oil

1. Put the haricot beans, previously soaked for 4 hours, in a large saucepan containing 3½ pints/2 litres of cold water along with the whole onions, clove (stuck into one of the onions), garlic, sage, thyme, and *réfrescat* (prepared as described in No. 13). Bring slowly to the boil.

2. When the soup has been boiling for 1 hour, add the pumpkin cut into 1-inch/2-cm dice. Bring back to the boil.

3. After 20 minutes, add the Swiss chard tops or lettuce leaves, cut into strips. Boil for a further 10 minutes. Season to taste, remove from heat, add the olive oil, and serve.

16 Chickpea and Sage Soup

La Soupa dé Cêê a la Saùvia
La Soupe de Pois Chiches à la Sauge

For 6

1 lb/500 g chickpeas
2 onions, peeled
1 clove garlic, peeled
½ lb/200 g carrots, peeled
5 large lettuce leaves

10 leaves sage (see page xii)
1 sprig thyme
salt, pepper
1 tbs olive oil

1. Put the chickpeas (previously soaked as indicated on the packet), onions, garlic, sliced carrots, lettuce leaves cut into strips, sage, and thyme into a large saucepan with 4½ pints/2½ litres of water, and bring to the boil.

2. When the soup has simmered steadily for 3 hours, much of it will have evaporated; so add water as necessary, and season with salt and pepper. Pour in the olive oil, stir, and serve.

● You can, if you prefer, purée the chickpeas. In this case, remove the sage, onion, and lettuce before doing so. Then return the lettuce to the soup, add water, season, add olive oil, and serve.

17 Pea Soup

La Soupa dé Péou / Le Potage de Petits Pois

For 6

2-3 tbs olive oil
2 onions, peeled
2 carrots, peeled
bouquet garni
5 oz/150 g lean *petit salé*
  (see page xiii)

20 pea pods
¾ lb/300 g shelled peas
salt, pepper
1 lump sugar
croûtons

1. Put 2 tablespoons of olive oil into a saucepan, and brown the sliced onions and carrots, *bouquet garni*, diced *petit salé* and pea pods (well washed).

2. Add the peas and cover with 3½ pints/2 litres of cold water. Bring to the boil and simmer for 45 minutes.

3. Season with salt, pepper, and sugar. Remove the *bouquet garni* and the pea pods. Purée.

4. Dilute the purée with water (or stock if you like) till the desired consistency is obtained. Stir in a tablespoon of olive oil (optional), and serve with *croûtons*.

18 Courgette-Flower Soup

La Soupa dé Flou dé Cougourdéta
La Soupe de Fleurs de Courgette

For 6

½ lb/200 g courgettes
½ lb/200 g potatoes, peeled, *or*
   2 oz/50 g rice
1 onion, peeled
1 clove garlic, peeled
2 large leaves basil

1 tbs olive oil
2 tomatoes
bouquet garni
salt, pepper
30 courgette flowers (see page x)
4 oz/100 g grated Parmesan

1. Cut the courgettes into slices and the potatoes in quarters, and put them in 3½ pints/2 litres of cold water in a large saucepan. Bring to the boil and simmer for 45 minutes. (If rice is preferred instead of potatoes, do not cook yet.)

2. Brown the sliced onion, finely chopped garlic, and basil in the olive oil.

3. Transfer them, along with the peeled, seeded, and coarsely chopped tomatoes and *bouquet garni*, to the saucepan.

4. Cook for 20 minutes, purée, return to the saucepan, and bring back to the boil. Season with salt and pepper. Cut the courgette flowers crosswise into rings ½ inch/1 cm wide, after removing their stems and pistils, and add to the soup. Cook for a further 3 minutes and serve with grated Parmesan on the side.

5. If rice is used, purée the courgettes at the beginning of step 3 and add the rice for the last 20 minutes. As rice does not give as much consistency as potato, the courgette flowers are sometimes dipped in beaten egg before being added to the soup.

19 Purslane Soup

La Soupa dé Porcellana / La Soupe de Pourpier

For 6

1 lb/500 g potatoes	2 egg yolks
2 onions, peeled	1/2 pint/250 ml double cream
1/2 lb/250 g purslane (see page xii)	2 tbs chopped chervil
salt, pepper	*croûtons*

1. Peel the potatoes, rinse, cut into large dice, and put in 4½ pints/2½ litres of cold salted water along with the sliced onions and all the purslane except for 40 or so of the larger leaves. Bring to the boil.

2. Cook for 20 minutes, purée, and bring back to the boil. Correct seasoning. Thicken the soup by pouring it into a soup tureen in which the egg yolks have been beaten up with the cream.

3. Blanch the rest of the purslane for 3 minutes, drain, rinse in cold water, and add to the soup just before serving. Sprinkle with finely chopped chervil.

4. Serve with *croûtons*.

SAUCES

20 Tomato Sauce

Lou Saoussoun / La Sauce Tomate

Saoussoun accompanies a variety of dishes, including gratins and especially *pasta*. It is also used to deglaze frying pans or to give stocks a tomato flavour. So it is always worth making a considerable amount of the sauce at a time, even if one is cooking for only a few people.

To make 3½ pints/2 litres

11 lb/5 kg very ripe tomatoes	1 sprig thyme
2 tbs olive oil	1 bay leaf
4 onions, peeled	6 lumps sugar
4 cloves garlic, peeled	salt, pepper
10 leaves basil	cayenne pepper
1½ tbs chopped parsley	

1. Peel, seed and chop the tomatoes.

2. Put the olive oil into a large frying pan and brown the finely chopped onions, 3 cloves of garlic, chopped, 8 leaves of basil, the parsley, thyme, and bay leaf.

3. Put the tomatoes in a deep saucepan with the sugar and bring to the boil. Cook for 10 minutes, then strain off excess liquid through a fine sieve. Cook for another 5 minutes or so to dry out the tomatoes a little more.

4. Remove from heat and incorporate the contents of the frying pan. Add 1 clove of garlic and 2 leaves of basil, all finely chopped. Add salt, pepper, and cayenne pepper to taste.

● This sauce can easily be kept in the refrigerator for 5 or 6 days; but be careful not to leave it out in a hot kitchen, as tomato ferments without much prompting.

21 Uncooked Tomato Sauce
Lou Saoussoun Crut / La Sauce Tomate Crue

This recipe comes from Saint-Jean-Cap-Ferrat, a few miles from Nice.
For many years, this little village had a relationship with Nice similar to that
between Versailles and Paris. Now inhabited by a mixture of millionaires, film
personalities, and genuine fishermen, Saint-Jean-Cap-Ferrat still has enormous
charm.

This highly original sauce is always eaten cold – on a piece of toast rubbed
with garlic, with cold stuffed vegetables, with cold fish, or with virtually any
other cold dish. It can even turn an *assiette anglaise* (a plateful of cold meats)
into a typically Niçois speciality.

To make 3½ pints/2 litres

6½ lb/3 kg very ripe tomatoes	3 sprigs parsley
2 spring onions	salt, pepper
2 cloves garlic, peeled	cayenne pepper
5 leaves basil	2 tbs olive oil

1. Peel and seed the tomatoes, then crush them with a pestle in a large,
stoneware bowl.

2. Add the spring onions, garlic, basil, and parsley, all finely chopped.
Season with salt, pepper, and cayenne pepper to taste.

3. Pour in the olive oil and beat vigorously with a wooden spoon.

● In the refrigerator, most of the olive oil will rise to the surface, forming a
film that will protect the sauce against contact with the air. But it should not be
kept for more than 5 to 6 days (see remarks at the end of the preceding recipe).

22 Salad Dressing
La Bagna Rotou / La Sauce de Salade

Bagna rotou is a salad dressing containing plenty of olive oil and a number of ingredients aimed at giving it pungency. It is usually eaten with the raw vegetables (both sliced and whole) that form the basis of the Niçois diet during the hot summer months.

For 4

4 anchovy fillets *or* 1 tbs *pissala* (No. 260)	2 leaves basil
	1 tbs vinegar
1 spring onion	5 tbs olive oil
1 clove garlic, peeled	cayenne pepper
3 sprigs parsley	

1. Wash all the salt off the anchovies, and chop them finely along with the spring onion, garlic, parsley, and basil. Mix into the dressing (vinegar, olive oil, and cayenne pepper to taste).

2. Emulsify thoroughly with a fork.

23 Hot Sauce
La Bagna Caouda / La Sauce Chaude

It is odd how often modern fashion turns out to be a throwback to ancient tradition. Fondues of all kinds – whether with cheese (*savoyarde*), meat (*bourguignonne*), chocolate, or caramel – have become a great favourite with all sections of society: the opportunity guests have of dipping their forkfuls of food into a communal dish (whether to cook or to coat them) is clearly appreciated as a refreshing change from the routine of the traditional meal. But the technique was nothing new to the Niçois, who for centuries have been plunging their vegetables into *bagna caouda*. Here is the authentic recipe.

For 6

6 anchovy fillets *or* 2 tbs *pissala* (No. 260)	2 cloves garlic, peeled
4 tsp white breadcrumbs soaked in milk *or* cream	2 pints/1 litre olive oil

1. Put the crushed anchovy fillets or *pissala*, soaked breadcrumbs, and crushed garlic into a *fondue* saucepan (thick-bottomed, and presentable enough to appear on the table); cover with the olive oil and heat until very hot (though not smoking), stirring well.

2. Transfer to the table and keep hot (on a hot-plate, over a candle, etc.). The raw vegetables served with *bagna caouda* include the following (depending on the time of year): radishes, celery, small globe artichokes (quartered), broccoli, cauliflower, lettuce, carrots, mushrooms, chicory (quartered), and bulb fennel.

● Guests can dip the vegetables in the *bagna caouda* with their fingers if they like, but a fork is more efficient as each piece can be completely submerged and swirled around in the sauce. But as the fork that has been in contact with the hot oil can give the lips a nasty burn, another one should be provided for actual eating. Note the parallel with Chinese cooking: the vegetables are eaten hot, yet almost raw, with a subtly flavoured sauce.

24 Rouille

La Rouïa / La Rouille

This is the sauce that goes with fish soup (No. 3). The Niçois recipe differs slightly from the Provençal version, and is less complicated.

For 6

4 cloves garlic, peeled	2 egg yolks
1 sachet of saffron powder *or* a large	½ pint/250 ml olive oil
pinch of saffron filaments infused	1 tsp cayenne pepper
in a scant tablespoon of lemon juice	

1. Crush the garlic to a fine purée in a mortar. Add the saffron powder or the infusion. Add the egg yolks and emulsify into a mayonnaise with the olive oil.

2. When the mayonnaise (in fact an *aïoli* [No. 26]) is nice and firm, incorporate the cayenne pepper.

● *Rouille* will keep easily in the refrigerator for 24 hours. It goes well not only with fish soup, but with any kind of fish (preferably poached) and with steamed potatoes.

● A variation on this Niçois version of *rouille* can be obtained by putting 1 hard-boiled egg yolk and 1 raw egg yolk in with the garlic before adding the olive oil. It is claimed by some that this adds an extra creaminess to the *rouille*; I myself find that this is true only in the case of *aïoli*.

● In Provence, *rouille* is sometimes emulsified without any egg yolk at all. There is one school of thought which holds this to be a lighter concoction. But I do not think that *rouille* is made any heavier by the addition of egg yolks, as long as they are very fresh.

● Lastly, there exists a typically Marseillais version of *rouille*, which includes breadcrumbs previously soaked in water (or in milk, if the *rouille* is to accompany a *bourride* or Provençal fish stew).

25 Anchoïade

L'amplouada / L'Anchoïade

There are two types of anchovy sauce in Niçois cookery:

First version

4 anchovy fillets	7 fl oz/200 ml olive oil

Pound the anchovy fillets in the olive oil until smooth. Strain the oil through muslin: it can then be used to flour a number of dishes.

Second version

This is altogether a more sophisticated sauce, which goes wonderfully with meat or fish *meunière*.

2 large cloves garlic, peeled	½ pint/250 ml olive oil
4 anchovy fillets	1 oz/25 g capers
2 egg yolks	

1. Pound the garlic to a very fine paste in a mortar. Add the anchovy fillets and pound until blended. Incorporate the egg yolks and emulsify into a mayonnaise with the olive oil.

2. When the sauce is nice and firm, energetically beat in the finely chopped capers – they will make the sauce slightly more liquid, but this does not matter.

● A really tasty hors-d'oeuvre can be made from halved tomatoes garnished with quarters of hard-boiled egg and *anchoïade*.

26 Aïoli

L'Aïoli / L'Aïoli

Although typically Provençal, *aïoli* is often eaten in the Nice area. But my compatriots do not surround the consumption of it with anything like the pomp and circumstance that has become part of Provençal lore.

In Nice, *aïoli* is often simply served with cold mutton, cold salt cod, or even potatoes steamed in their jackets. I will leave it to the gurus of Provençal cuisine to list the procession of ingredients that should be eaten with *aïoli*, and merely describe the straightforward Niçois version of the dish.

For 8-10

10-15 cloves garlic, peeled	salt
1 raw egg yolk	2 pints/1 litre olive oil
1 hard-boiled egg yolk	

1. Pound the garlic to a fine paste in a mortar and add the egg yolks. Blend well. Add a pinch of salt, then gradually incorporate the olive oil as for a mayonnaise.

2. If the resulting consistency seems too firm, it can be made creamier by the addition, at the last moment, of 1 or 2 tablespoons of lukewarm water.

● If the oil is too cool compared with the temperature of the kitchen, or if too much is put in at a time, the dreaded accident may occur – a curdled *aïoli*. You can 'save' it by transferring it to another bowl and proceeding as follows: wash and wipe dry the pestle and mortar, pound another clove of garlic, add a small pinch of salt and another raw egg yolk, and little by little beat in your original curdled *aïoli*. Another way of getting the mayonnaise back to normal is to pour in 1 tablespoon of boiling water and beat vigorously.

27 Fishermen's Sauce

La Saoussa daï Pescaïré / La Sauce des Pêcheurs

Here again there are two types of sauce, one to go with grilled fish, whether hot or cold, and the other to accompany cooked seafood.

First version

8 tbs olive oil	2 tbs strong Dijon mustard
2 tbs vinegar	1 large crab *or* 1 large tin crabmeat

Make a dressing with the oil, vinegar and mustard. Incorporate the pounded meat of a crab or the contents of a tin of top-quality crabmeat. The sauce should be served cold.

Second version
For 2 lb/1 kg seafood

1 egg yolk	seafood *court-bouillon or* cooking
1 tsp Dijon mustard	liquid
¹/₂ pint/250 ml olive oil	2 tbs chopped parsley

1. Make a mayonnaise by mixing together the egg yolk and mustard, then gradually incorporating the olive oil.

2. Dilute the mayonnaise with just enough of the cooking liquid or *court-bouillon* of the mussels, crab, lobster, or fish to give the sauce the consistency of double cream. Incorporate the finely chopped parsley at the last moment.

28 Piquant Sauce

La Saoussa Picanta / La Sauce Piquante

This sauce goes well with stuffed breast of veal (No. 59).

For 4

1 clove garlic, peeled	1/2 pint/250 ml olive oil
2 anchovy fillets	1 tbs capers
1 oz/20 g breadcrumbs	2 gherkins
vinegar	1 tbs chopped parsley
2 egg yolks	salt, cayenne pepper

1. Rub the mortar with a clove of garlic. Put in the anchovy fillets and pound to a paste. Add the breadcrumbs, previously soaked in vinegar and squeezed dry. Mix well. Add the egg yolks and make a mayonnaise by gradually incorporating the olive oil.

2. Mix in the capers, gherkins, and parsley, all finely chopped.

3. Add salt and cayenne pepper to taste.

● This sauce should be really fiery.

● ● ●

29 Anchovy Butter

Lou Burré d'Amploua / Le Beurre d'Anchois

Grilled meat goes very well with the first version of *amplouada* (No. 25). However, it makes an equally happy marriage with the classical French recipe for anchovy butter; and as salted anchovies are one of the staple ingredients of Niçois cookery, it is only normal that anchovy butter, despite the fact that it is not specifically a Niçois recipe, should play a prominent role in our gastronomy.

For 6

6 anchovy fillets *or* 1 1/2 tbs *pissala*	juice of 1/2 lemon
made with anchovies (No. 260)	pepper
4 oz/100 g butter	

Wash the anchovy fillets well, chop them finely, and mix to a paste with the warmed butter. Add the lemon juice, and pepper to taste.

● Anchovy butter can be kept in the refrigerator for 4 or 5 days.

● If you have been unable to obtain anchovies that have been salted *à la niçoise* (i.e. flavoured with cloves), you can produce almost as good a result by leaving your anchovy fillets to soak in a bowl of water with 4 cloves.

30 Spiny Lobster, Lobster, Shrimp, or Crayfish Butter

Lou Burré dé Lingousta, dé Lingoustas, dé Ligouban, o dé Grita

Le Beurre de Langouste, de Homard, de Crevettes, ou d'Écrevisses

This naturally accompanies the shellfish that has flavoured it.

For 8

Shells of any of the following:	**7 oz/200 g butter**
spiny lobster, lobster, shrimps,	
or **crayfish**	

1. Pound the shells in a mortar as finely as you can (this operation is easier if you dry them first for 20 minutes in a gentle oven).

2. Incorporate the butter and continue pounding until a paste is obtained.

3. Put the paste into a saucepan three-quarters full of boiling water. As the butter rises to the surface, remove with a spoon and transfer to a small saucepan over a low heat. Simmer until the bubbles produced by the water cease, then remove immediately.

4. Strain the butter through muslin into a pot, and keep in the refrigerator.

31 Sauce for Grilled Spiny Lobster

La Saoussa per Lingousta Rimadi

La Sauce pour les Langoustes Grillées

All too many Niçois restaurateurs, intelligent enough at the start of their careers to serve grilled spiny lobster with the most natural sauce of all, have since lapsed into the production of complicated concoctions which have nothing to do with Niçois cookery, and which often interfere with the delicate flavour of a sublimely simple dish.

Fortunately there are still one or two pleasant restaurants in Nice where the sauce is prepared at the same time as the lobster – a precondition for the success of the dish.

---

4 oz/100 g spiny lobster coral and tomalley	1 tbs cognac
7 oz/200 g butter	pepper

---

1. For this recipe you will need hen lobsters, which can be recognized by the presence of large swimmerets under the tail (these are virtually atrophied in the case of the cock lobster); also, the hen's two back legs have pincers, for manipulating her eggs, whereas the cock's have only a hook at the end. When the lobster is cut in half, some soft brownish matter (tomalley) and orange roe (coral) are revealed. Remove them to a thick-bottomed, stainless-steel saucepan. Remove any lumps with your fingers – no kitchen utensil really does the job so well. It is not a very pleasant job, but vital if the sauce is to be a success.

2. Incorporate the warmed butter carefully and put over an extremely low heat. The temperature of the sauce must on no account exceed 86°F/30°C.

3. A brisk stir with a wooden spatula will soon produce a smooth cream, which does not need to be kept at more than 77° to 86°F/25° to 30°C.

4. Flavour with cognac and pepper to taste. Serve in a warmed sauceboat.

Hors-d'Oeuvre

32 (Genuine) Salade Niçoise
La Salada Nissarda / La (Vraie) Salade Niçoise

Salade niçoise is one of those dishes that is constantly traduced. At its most basic – and genuine – it is made predominantly of tomatoes, consists exclusively of raw ingredients (apart from hard-boiled eggs), and has no vinaigrette dressing: the tomatoes are salted three times and moistened with olive oil. However, nowadays even the Niçois often combine anchovies and tunny fish in the same salad, though traditionally this was never done – tunny used to be very expensive and was reserved for special occasions, so the cheaper anchovies filled the bill.

But whatever you do, if you want to be a worthy exponent of Niçois cookery, never, never, I beg you, include boiled potato or any other boiled vegetable in your *salade niçoise*.

For 6

10 medium tomatoes	(depending on the time of year,
3 hard-boiled eggs	either one *or* the other, *or*
12 anchovy fillets *or* 12 oz/300 g	neither, but not both)
tinned tunny fish	1 clove garlic, peeled and cut in
1 large cucumber	half
2 green peppers	4 oz/100 g black olives
6 spring onions	6 tbs olive oil
1/2 lb/200 g small broad beans *or*	6 leaves basil
12 small globe artichokes	salt, pepper

1. Quarter the tomatoes and salt them slightly on the chopping board. Quarter or slice the hard-boiled eggs. Cut each anchovy fillet into 3 or 4 pieces, or shred the tunny fish. Peel the cucumber and slice finely. Cut the peppers, onions, and artichokes or broad beans into very thin slices.

2. Rub a large salad bowl thoroughly with the two halves of the clove of garlic, put in all the above ingredients except the tomatoes, and add the olives.

3. Drain the tomatoes, salt them again slightly, and add to the bowl.

4. Make a dressing with the olive oil, the finely chopped basil, pepper, and salt. Pour on to the salad, which should be chilled before serving.

● As the various ingredients that go into *salade niçoise* are of bright and contrasting colours, they can be arranged most decoratively in the salad bowl.

33 Pan-Bagnat
Lou Pan-Bagnat / Le Pan-Bagnat

Originally, *pan-bagnat* (which literally means 'wet bread') was simply a *salade niçoise* (No. 32) to which had been added, an hour or so before serving, stale country bread broken into negotiable mouthfuls with a hammer or a pestle. The bread soaked up the olive oil and the juice of the tomatoes, making a delicious accompaniment to the salad. So delicious was it, in fact, that our grandmothers devised a more practical way in which country bread could be combined with *salade niçoise*. It caught on, and resulted in the modern *pan-bagnat* – a small round loaf, about 8 inches/20 cm across, which is now specially produced for that purpose by bakers in the Nice area. But any bread of any shape will do equally well.

1. Cut the bread in half horizontally and scoop out some of the white part.

2. Rub the inside of each half with a clove of garlic, sprinkle with a few drops of vinegar and a generous amount of olive oil, and add salt and pepper. Put a serving of *salade niçoise* between the two halves of the sandwich, and press firmly together.

3. Cool for at least an hour before serving.

● *Pan-bagnat* is most commonly eaten as a *mérenda*, the mid-morning (9 a.m.) snack consumed by early-risers; but it also makes a wonderful summer hors-d'oeuvre, an excellent and practical component of the picnic basket, or even a complete meal if you are out fishing or if the weather is very hot and your appetite is flagging.

● ● ●

34 Cold Ratatouille
La Ratatouïa Fresca / La Ratatouille Froide

This is simply an ordinary *ratatouille* (No. 197) seasoned with saffron (1 small pinch per ½ lb/250 g of *ratatouille*) and served very cold.

Allow 4 tablespoonfuls of *ratatouille* per person.

● ● ●

35 Stuffed Sardines
Li Sardina Farcit / Les Sardines Farcies

The stuffed sardines described as a main course (No. 102) can also be eaten cold or lukewarm as an hors-d'oeuvre with *saoussoun* or *saoussoun crut* (Nos. 20 and 21).

36 Stuffed Anchovies

Li Amploua Farcit / Les Anchois Farcis

Similarly, fresh anchovies prepared liked stuffed sardines (No. 102) or else marinated (No. 107) can also be served as an hors-d'oeuvre. But in the case of anchovies it is better to season the stuffing not with salt, but with a little anchovy butter, which should be mixed in with the Swiss chard leaves when they have cooked.

• • •

37 Anchovy Fritters

Li Bignéta d'Amploua / Les Beignets d'Anchois

For 6

4 eggs	1 small clove garlic, peeled
4 oz/100 g flour	12 large fresh anchovies
salt, pepper	oil for deep frying
2 lemons	12 sprigs parsley

1. Break the eggs into a bowl and beat thoroughly. Mix in the flour until a liquid batter is obtained. Season with salt, pepper, the juice of half a lemon, and the garlic, crushed.

2. Behead, clean, and bone the anchovies. Dip them individually in the batter and fry in very hot oil.

3. The fritters are cooked once they turn golden. Drain them all together on kitchen tissue. Fry the parsley in the oil for a few seconds until crisp. Serve the anchovies heaped on a plate and garnish with the parsley and the lemons, cut into quarters.

38 Tomatoes with Tunny
Lu Toùmati où Toun / Les Tomates au Thon

For 6

First version

3 eggs	4 oz/125 g tinned tunny
2 anchovy fillets	6 tomatoes
2 oz/50 g capers	

1. Hard-boil the eggs and cool them under running water so their shells can be removed easily.

2. Pound the eggs, anchovies, and half the capers to a paste.

3. Incorporate the tunny into the mixture.

4. Halve the tomatoes, and garnish with the mixture. Decorate with the remaining capers.

Second version

1 egg yolk	4 oz/125 g tinned tunny
1 tbs strong Dijon mustard	6 tomatoes
7 fl oz/200 ml olive oil	paprika

1. Make a mayonnaise by mixing the egg yolk with the mustard and pouring in a thin trickle of olive oil, beating all the time.

2. Incorporate the tunny into the mayonnaise.

3. Halve the tomatoes, and garnish with the mixture. Add paprika to taste.

39 Celery, Artichokes, Onions, Mushrooms, or Leeks as an Hors-d'Oeuvre

Api, Archicota, Céba, Boulet Sanguin, Pouaré en Antipast /
Céleri, Artichaut, Oignon, Champignons Sanguins,
Poireaux en Hors-d'Oeuvre

There are countless ways of eating the above vegetables as an hors-d'oeuvre, the commonest, at least in the case of artichokes, whether cooked or raw, being with a vinaigrette dressing. Here is a recipe that was much in vogue at the Palace Hotel in Nice between the wars. It remains an altogether excellent way of cooking the vegetables.

For 6

2 oz/50 g Malaga raisins	Milk Cap) (see page xi), *or*
12 pickling onions, peeled	18 small leeks, *or*
4 tbs olive oil	18 small globe artichokes, *or*
10 peppercorns	36 pickling onions, *or*
2 tomatoes	12 branches celery
30 medium-sized cultivated	1 large pinch thyme
mushrooms *or*, better, 18 fresh	7 fl oz/200 ml dry white wine
specimens of *Lactarius sanguifluus*	2 lemons
or *Lactarius deliciosus* (Saffron	salt

1. Soak the raisins in warm water.

2. Put 12 pickling onions into a stainless-steel saucepan with 1 tablespoon of olive oil, cover, and simmer very gently until the onions are transparent.

3. Remove the lid and continue cooking until the onions turn golden. Add the peppercorns, drained raisins, and peeled, seeded, and coarsely chopped tomatoes. Reduce, stirring all the time, until most of the liquid has evaporated.

4. Add the rest of the olive oil, or just enough to cover the contents of the pan, turn up the heat, and, stirring gently all the time, add the vegetables – mushrooms, leeks, artichokes (with the tips of their leaves cut off), celery, or peeled pickling onions – along with the thyme.

5. Cook briskly for 10 minutes, then add the white wine and the juice of the lemons. Turn down the heat, allow to come back to the boil, and simmer uncovered for 30 minutes.

6. Remove from heat, and add salt to taste. Serve cool or well chilled.

● Vegetables cooked in this way will keep for at least a fortnight in the refrigerator.

40 Raw Vegetables
Li Crudita / Les Crudités

The Niçois often grow vegetables in their gardens, and like to eat them raw at all times of the year. They constitute the commonest form of hors-d'oeuvre, though they are never eaten in the massive quantities offered by all too many restaurants.

The right amount to allow for is about 7 to 8 mouthfuls of raw vegetables, cut into chunks, per person. For the various accompanying sauces, see Nos. 22, 23, 25, and 26.

● ● ●

41 Niçois Caviare
La Fachoira / Le Caviar Niçois

This paste, which goes well with toast, is similar to the Provençal *tapénade*.

For 6

1 lb/500 g black olives	2 tbs capers
1 clove garlic, peeled	7 fl oz/200 ml olive oil
2 anchovy fillets	pepper
2 leaves basil	

1. Stone the olives and chop finely.

2. Incorporate the garlic, anchovy, basil, and capers, all chopped very finely.

3. Gradually pour in the olive oil, stirring all the time, until a light, smooth paste is obtained. Add pepper to taste.

42 Fishermen's Mussels

Lu Mùsclé daï Pescaïré / Les Moules des Pêcheurs

For 6

2 large onions, peeled and chopped	6 quarts/3 litres mussels (discard any that are not tightly shut)
2 cloves garlic, peeled and chopped	2 egg yolks
6 sprigs parsley	1 tbs strong Dijon mustard
pepper	3/4 pint/400 ml olive oil
	2 fl oz/50 ml double cream

1. Put the onions, garlic, two thirds of the parsley, and plenty of pepper (10 turns of the mill) into about 1 pint/½ litre of water in a large saucepan and boil for 30 minutes.

2. This *court-bouillon* will be ready when there are no more than 4 tablespoons of liquid left after evaporation. Turn up the heat and put in the scrubbed and bearded mussels until they open, shaking the pan vigorously all the time. On no account should the mussels cook for more than 3 minutes.

3. Drain the cooking liquid off into a bowl.

4. Remove the mussels from their shells, discarding any that have refused to open, and set them aside in a salad bowl.

5. Make a mayonnaise by mixing the egg yolks with the mustard and pouring in the olive oil in a thin trickle. Add the rest of the parsley, chopped. Do not salt.

6. Dilute the mayonnaise, which should be very firm, with the cold cooking liquid until it has a creamy consistency and tastes strongly of mussels. Then add the cream.

7. Pour this sauce over the mussels and put into the refrigerator. Serve chilled.

43 Octopus, Cuttlefish, or Squid Salad

La Salada dé Pourpré, Supioun, o Taout
La Salade de Poulpes, Seiches, ou Encornets

For 6

3 lb/¹/₂ kg small octopus, cuttlefish, *or* squid	4 lemons
4 tbs olive oil	pepper

1. Clean the fish and cut them into pieces 1 inch/2 cm long. Put them into a non-stick pan.

2. Get the fish to release their liquid by cooking for 15 minutes over a moderate heat, with a lid or plate covering the pan. When the pieces of fish are completely submerged by the reddish liquid, remove the lid, turn down the heat, and reduce until the liquid has entirely evaporated.

3. Pour in 3 tablespoons of olive oil and fry for a few minutes over a high heat. Remove from the stove, add the juice of the lemons and pepper to taste, and leave to cool. Put into the refrigerator.

4. This dish should be served when it has become very cold (by which time a delicate and transparent pink jelly will have set round the fish), with chilled Persian-style rice (No. 224, Method 3) and a sprinkling of olive oil.

● There exist two variations on this recipe:

(a) 1 g (a pinch) of saffron is added to the pan at the point when the cooking liquid submerges the fish;

(b) 3 raw tomatoes are peeled, seeded, puréed, and added to the salad once It is cold.

44 Young Broad Beans with Raw Ham

Li Favéta où Jamboun Crut / Les Févettes au Jambon Cru

For 6

60 young broad beans	6 spring onions
6 slices raw ham	4 sprigs parsley
3 tbs olive oil	

Arrange 10 broad beans lengthwise along each slice of raw mountain ham (or San Daniele ham). Pour ½ tablespoon of olive oil over them, and sprinkle with very finely chopped spring onion and parsley. Roll up each slice, and serve.

● ● ●

45 Baked Peppers

Lu Pébroun où Fourn / Les Poivrons au Four

For 6

6 large red *or* yellow peppers	1 clove garlic, peeled
3 tbs olive oil	salt, pepper
3 tbs chopped parsley	

1. Wash the peppers whole, leaving their stems on, dry them, and smear with 1 tablespoon of olive oil. Lay them out on a grill pan and place under a very hot grill, or on a barbecue.

2. Let them blacken a little, turning when necessary to avoid burning.

3. When the skin of the peppers is well blistered, remove them and leave to cool.

4. Meanwhile, chop the parsley and garlic very finely, and keep aside.

5. Cut the stems off the peppers, slice in half, and carefully remove all the seeds. Pick off all their skin with a pointed and very sharp knife.

6. Slice the peppers into strips and lay in a deepish flat serving dish. Sprinkle with the chopped parsley and garlic, cover with 2 tablespoons of olive oil, salt slightly, and add pepper to taste.

● This salad can be eaten with ham, Italian *coppa*, or the Corsican *lonzo*. But it is, I think, best of all by itself, on country bread with a few drops of vinegar.

46 Baked Tomatoes

Lu Toùmati où Fourn / Les Tomates au Four

For 6

6 large tomatoes	5 sprigs parsley
2 red *or* 4 green peppers	3 leaves basil
2 tbs olive oil	2 tbs breadcrumbs
salt, pepper	1 tbs capers
1 pinch thyme	

1. Cut the tomatoes into slices ¼ inch/½ cm thick.

2. Grill and peel the peppers as described in No. 45, remove their seeds, and cut lengthwise into strips.

3. Pour 1 tablespoon of olive oil into a short-handled enamelled cast-iron pan or earthenware dish (*pignata*), add a layer of tomatoes, a little salt and pepper, a small pinch of thyme, and a very little chopped parsley and basil. Follow with a layer of peppers cut into strips. Repeat the process (tomatoes, condiments, peppers), finishing with a layer of tomatoes.

4. Sprinkle with 1 tablespoon of olive oil, the breadcrumbs, and the capers. Preheat the oven to 475°F/240°C, gas mark 9.

5. Bake for 20 minutes.

6. Allow to cool, and refrigerate. Serve well chilled in the baking dish.

47 Aubergines with Garlic and Anchovies

Li Mérejaïna a l'Aïet é a l'Amploua
Les Aubergines à l'Ail et l'Anchois

For 6

2 very large *or* 4 small aubergines	3 cloves garlic, peeled
salt	4 anchovy fillets
1 tbs olive oil	1 large onion, peeled

1. Cut the aubergines into slices ¼ inch/1½ cm thick, salt them slightly, put them in a colander under a heavy weight, and leave for an hour at room temperature so they give up their juice.

2. Drain well and place in an oiled baking dish. Bake in a medium oven for 20 to 25 minutes.

3. Make a fine purée of the cooked aubergines, and put through a *chinois* (a fine conical strainer) to remove seeds and pieces of skin.

4. Leave the purée to cool. Chop the garlic and anchovies very finely, grate the onion, and mix with the aubergines.

5. Put in the refrigerator. This dish is served chilled.

● Do not use iron or aluminium utensils, as they will blacken the aubergines.

48 Pissaladière

La Pissaladiera / La Pissaladière

Pissaladière is a typically Niçois hors-d'oeuvre which got its name from *pissala*, a fish purée (No. 260): before being put in the oven, this onion tart was smeared with a piece of cloth that had been dipped in *pissala*.

Beware of the mass-produced versions of *pissaladière* that are sold on street stalls or in 'drugstores' in the south of France – the layer of onion is usually paper-thin. A proper *pissaladière* of the kind still found in Niçois food markets will boast a layer of onion at least half as thick as the base, if it is made of bread dough, and equally thick, if it is made of shortcrust pastry.

The dough

(Taken from *English Bread and Yeast Cookery* by Elizabeth David (Penguin, 1979), with kind permission of the author.)

For 10

1/2 oz/20 g yeast	2 tsp salt
4 tbs milk	2 eggs
1/2 lb/250 g plain white flour	4 tbs olive oil

'To make the dough: put the yeast into a cup with the milk. Mix it to a cream. Put the flour into a bowl with the salt, warm it for 4 or 5 minutes no longer – in a very low oven; add the yeast mixture, then the whole egg[s] and the olive oil. Mix all well together, then with your hands work the dough rapidly until it is smooth. Form it into a ball. Shake a little extra flour over it. Cover the bowl. Put it in a warm place and leave for 1 1/2 to 2 hours until the dough is well risen and very light.'

The filling

6 1/2 lb/3 kg onions, peeled	2 oz/50 g black olives
salt	10 anchovy fillets *or* 4 tsp *pissala*
2 cloves garlic, peeled	(No. 260)
bouquet garni	pepper
3 tbs olive oil	

1. Slice the onions finely, salt slightly, and put into a large thick-bottomed saucepan with the crushed garlic, *bouquet garni*, and 1 tablespoon of olive oil. Cover and simmer very gently until the onions are thoroughly cooked (they must not brown).

2. Put the risen dough into an oiled 10-inch/25-cm tart tin, press out until it fills the tin, and dry out in a medium-hot oven for 10 minutes.

3. After removing the *bouquet garni*, spread the cooked onions over the now dry dough. Make the layer as even as possible with a wooden spoon, dot with olives, and arrange the anchovy fillets in spokes (or, better, smear the whole surface of the onions with *pissala*). Sprinkle with 2 tablespoons of olive oil.

4. Bake in a very hot oven for about 15 minutes. Add pepper after removing the *pissaladière* from the oven. It can be eaten hot or warm, and will keep in a cool place for 4 or 5 days.

● The version of *pissaladière* found on the Italian side of the Alps has been influenced by the pizza, and in Liguria is often flavoured with 2 tablespoons of very concentrated tomato purée.

I and my friend Riri Cauvin, owner of the restaurant Le Gril Nautique, have invented our own version of *pissaladière*, which is quicker and more convenient to serve. Naturally, we call it *'le grillé nautique'*. What we have done really is to bring the pizza back over the frontier. Here is the recipe:

For 4

4 thick slices white bread	20 black olives
4 cloves garlic, peeled	8 anchovy fillets
2 slices ham	1 large pinch wild marjoram
8 slivers Gruyère *or* 8 tbs grated	(*origano*)
Parmesan	2 tbs olive oil
12 onion rings	pepper
16 slices tomato	

Toast the bread lightly and rub with garlic (1 clove per slice). Cover with successive layers of ham, cheese, onion, tomato, olives, anchovies, and wild marjoram. Sprinkle ½ tablespoon of olive oil on each piece of toast, add pepper, and brown under the grill for 3 minutes.

49 Socca

La Socca / La Socca

Even today, *socca* is the favourite mid-morning snack of manual workers. In the old days, *socca* vendors would go from one building site to another, transporting their precious wares on barrows. Perched on top of the vehicles there would be a large zinc construction housing a charcoal stove and the *socca* it was designed to keep warm. On hearing the cry: '*Socca, socca, caouda qué bullié!*' ('Piping hot socca for sale!'), the *bochou* (the boy on the site who had the job of running errands) would dart out and buy portions of *socca* for the workmen. Nowadays, *socca* vendors cater chiefly for market-gardeners and lightermen on market day, when they and their rivals selling *pissaladière* try to outdo each other in vaunting the merits of their wares.

Strictly speaking, you need a copper plate of the size suitable for a wood-fired oven in order to be able to make *socca*; but it can also be a success when cooked at home under the grill in a baking tin.

9 oz/250 g chickpea flour	**1 tsp salt**
2 tbs olive oil	

1. Put 18 fl oz/500 ml of cold water into a saucepan. With a whisk, incorporate the chickpea flour, the olive oil, and the salt. Beat well to ensure that there are no lumps.

2. Strain through a *chinois* (a fine conical strainer) into a bowl.

3. If you are lucky enough to have a wood-fired oven, pour the liquid on to two lightly oiled copper plates or griddles 20 inches/50 cm in diameter and 1 inch/2 cm deep, and bake in a very hot oven. If you want to try and make *socca* at home, pour the liquid into an oiled baking tin, making a layer of no more than ⅛ inch/2 to 3 mm, and put under a hot grill. Use a pointed knife to pierce any blisters which may form during cooking.

4. When the surface of the *socca* is well browned, even slightly burnt in parts, remove from the grill, cut into 2-inch/5-cm squares, and serve immediately with plenty of pepper.

● Naturally, the only really genuine *socca* is the one that has the inimitable flavour of a wood-fired oven . . .

50 Panisses

Li Panissa / Les Panisses

For 6

1 tsp olive oil	oil for deep frying
12 oz/300 g chickpea flour	salt, pepper

1. Lightly oil a dozen small saucers, and arrange them in a neat line.

2. Bring 2 pints/1 litre of water to the boil with a very little salt and the olive oil. Let the chickpea flour fall in a steady rain into the boiling water, while using the other hand to stir with a wooden spoon. Keep stirring indefatigably so as to prevent the mixture from burning. Wear kitchen gloves, or wrap tea-towels round your hands, otherwise you may get scalded by the bursting bubbles. After 5 to 10 minutes, the mixture will thicken: this means it is cooked.

3. Pour the mixture into the saucers, filling them completely and prodding down, if necessary, with the fingers (first dipping them in cold water). This step must be carried out very quickly (which is why the saucers have to be conveniently placed), as the chickpea paste sets in only a minute or two.

4. Once the *panisses* are in the saucers they can be kept for several hours in a cool place. But they are not yet completely cooked.

5. When you wish to carry out the final stage, remove them from the saucers and cut them into strips about 1 inch/2 cm wide. Heat the frying oil until it begins to smoke, and plunge the *panisses* into it.

6. When they are golden, remove with a fish slice, drain on kitchen tissue, and serve hot with pepper and salt to taste.

● *Panisses* can also be eaten cold with sugar (No. 245). This is why not too much salt should be added at the start of the recipe.

51 Basil Terrine

La Conca où Balico / La Terrine au Basilic

½ lb/250 g lean pork
½ lb/250 g veal
salt, pepper
½ lb/250 g calf's liver
4 fl oz/120 ml *grappa*

4 fl oz/120 ml olive oil
½ tsp thyme
20 large basil leaves
2 bay leaves

----

1. Put the pork and veal through the finest blade of the mincer. Mix together and season with salt and pepper.

2. Cut the liver into 1-inch/2-cm cubes and marinate for 2 hours in the *grappa*, olive oil, and thyme.

3. Put a 1-inch/2-cm thick layer of mince at the bottom of a terrine, a layer of basil leaves, a layer of liver, a layer of basil, a layer of mince, and repeat the process until the terrine is full, finishing with a layer of mince. Decorate with the bay leaves.

4. Put in a *bain-marie* in the oven, set at 400°F/200°C, gas mark 6, and cook for between 45 minutes and 1 hour. It is cooked when the pâté swims in fat, clear of the terrine.

5. Remove from the oven and leave under a board or dish the same shape as the terrine with a weight of about 2 lb/1 kg on top.

52 Young Rabbit with Fruit in Aspic

La Coumposta dé Counieù aï Frucha
La Compote de Lapereau aux Fruits

Ingredients for jelly

4 marrow bones
2 calf's feet
1 onion, peeled

2 stalks celery
4 carrots, peeled

Main ingredients

2 young rabbits weighing
2 lb/1 kg each
4 large onions, peeled
bouquet garni
2 cloves garlic, peeled
salt, pepper
4 tbs olive oil
¾ lb/300 g tomatoes
1 lb/500g of any *one* of the
following fruits (depending on
the time of year): peaches,

grapes, plums, pears, apples,
or figs
1 lemon
½ lb/250 g lean pork
¼ pint/150 ml of any *one* of the
following spirits (in
corresponding order to the
fruit used): cognac, *grappa,*
plum spirit, pear spirit,
calvados, or grappa

1. Bone the raw rabbits with a very sharp pointed knife. Put the meat in a casserole with the sliced onions, *bouquet garni*, chopped garlic, salt, and pepper. Brown over a very gentle heat in 2 tablespoons of olive oil, leaving the lid on.

2. Meanwhile put 2 tablespoons of olive oil in a frying pan and brown the rabbit bones over a fierce heat, then transfer to a large saucepan. Add the marrow bones, the calf's feet, 1 onion, the celery, the carrots, and 5 pints/3 litres of water. Bring to the boil and cook over a moderate heat for 3 hours.

3. When the rabbit meat has been gently sizzling for 15 minutes, remove from heat.

4. Peel, seed, and chop the tomatoes. Reduce in a small saucepan to a very concentrated purée.

5. Cut whichever fruit you are using into dice, except for the grapes, which should be peeled and stoned. Put them in a thick-bottomed casserole, add salt, and simmer with the juice of a lemon over a very gentle heat until virtually all the juice has evaporated.

6. Mince the pork and combine with the rabbit meat and tomato purée.

7. Remove the carrots from the calf's foot stock, slice finely, and add to the meat.

8. Moisten the mixture with about 1 pint/500 ml of stock.

9. Place a layer of the meat mixture at the bottom of a terrine, moisten with a few spoonfuls of spirit, add a layer of fruit, and season well with pepper. Repeat the process until the terrine is full, finishing with a layer of meat mixture. Top up with stock. Cover with aluminium foil.

10. Cook in a *bain-marie* for 40 minutes in an oven set at 475°F/240°C, gas mark 9.

11. Allow to cool. Serve thoroughly chilled. It should be eaten with a spoon, like a fruit compote.

● ● ●

53 Stuffed Vegetables
Lu Farçun / Les Farcis

The various versions of stuffed vegetables (Nos. 135, 157, 158, 185, 195, and 200), which can accompany hot meat and fish dishes, may also be served cold or chilled as an hors-d'oeuvre.

MEAT

54 Niçois Beef Stew
La Doba a la Nissarda / La Daube à la Niçoise

For 6

1½ oz/40 g dried cèpe mushrooms (weight before soaking)	4 cloves garlic, peeled
	1 stalk celery
2¾ lb/1,200 g stewing beef	*bouquet garni*
salt, pepper	6 large tomatoes
3 oz/80 g lard	7 fl oz/200 ml red wine
2 onions, peeled	3 tbs *grappa*
4 carrots, peeled	cayenne pepper (optional)

1. Soak the dried mushrooms in warm water.

2. Cut the meat into 1-inch/3-cm cubes. Season with salt and pepper.

3. Put 1½ oz/40 g of lard in a sauté pan and brown the quartered onions, sliced carrots, whole cloves of garlic, chopped celery, and *bouquet garni*.

4. Put 1½ oz/40 g of lard in another pan and brown the pieces of meat over a high heat. This will prevent the meat from disintegrating during cooking.

5. Once the pieces of meat are nicely browned, put them into a casserole and cook them over a moderate heat for 10 minutes or so.

6. Peel, seed, and chop the tomatoes, and add them to the meat along with the contents of the sauté pan, wine, *grappa*, and enough boiling water to cover the meat.

7. Bring to the boil, then turn down the heat and simmer very gently for 3 hours.

8. Add the soaked and drained cèpes. Correct seasoning and give it extra kick, if you so desire, with a pinch of cayenne pepper. Simmer gently for another hour.

9. Just before serving, degrease with a bulb baster – but leave one or two specks of fat floating on the gravy.

● Some people like to add lemon juice or grated Parmesan to their *daube*, so these should be available on the table. But on no account include them in the stew, otherwise, if any is left over, it will be unsuitable for making ravioli (No. 205).

55 Caillettes

La Couaïeta / Les Caillettes

This is the Niçois version of a very French dish. It probably entered our culinary tradition in 1793, when the Comté de Nice was incorporated into France for the first time.

Despite their apparent similarity to *alouettes sans tête* (veal olives or *paupiettes*), the Niçois *couaïeta* have their own very individual flavour. And whether eaten with carrots, peas, mashed potatoes, or sautéed potatoes they provide an excellent excuse for cracking a bottle or two of the excellent rosé wine produced in the hinterland of Nice, at Villars-sur-Var, for instance, or on the slopes of Patrimonio, in Corsica.

(Ed. note: Niçois *caillettes*, incidentally, bear no resemblance to the dish known by the same name elsewhere in France [flat sausages cooked in pig's caul].)

For 6

5 oz/150 g lean *petit salé* (see page xiii)	6 anchovy fillets
2 cloves garlic, peeled	2 hard-boiled eggs
4 sprigs parsley	2 tbs olive oil
1 pinch thyme	2 onions, peeled
12 very thin and very broad beef escalopes (preferably silverside)	1 stalk celery
	2 pints/1 litre stock
2 oz/50 g capers	

1. Chop up the *petit salé*, garlic, and parsley very finely, and mix well with a pinch of thyme.

2. Clear the largest working surface you can find, and spread the escalopes out on it. Along the edge of each piece of meat, lay one twelfth of the following: the mixture already made, the capers, the anchovy fillets, and the finely chopped hard-boiled eggs. Roll up the escalopes carefully, fold back the ends (to prevent any of the contents escaping during cooking), and tie firmly with strong thread all the way along.

3. Heat the olive oil in a casserole until just smoking, and brown the escalopes on all sides. Remove. Brown the finely sliced onions and celery in the casserole, then return the escalopes.

4. Add stock until it half-covers the *couaïeta*, and cook over a very gentle heat for 1½ hours, occasionally turning them over.

● *Caillettes* can also be made with veal instead of beef: though more tender, they are infinitely less tasty.

56 'Terror-Stricken' Beefsteak

Lou Bistec a l'Espaventada / Le Beefsteak 'Épouvanté'

This is an unpretentious little recipe invented, in two versions, by my maternal grandmother, for whom it was unthinkable to eat anything, even such a straightforward dish as steak, without giving it some tasty accompaniment.

It is the sort of simple recipe that is ideal for the single person, or the head of a family who has had to stay at home while his wife and children are on holiday.

For 1

First version

1 tbs olive oil	1 clove garlic, peeled
1 thin steak	salt, pepper

Heat the olive oil in a frying pan. Just as it is beginning to smoke, put in the steak, turning it over several times so that both sides are sealed. Crush the clove of garlic under the blade of a broad kitchen knife, and toss into the pan. When the steak is done, add salt and pepper to taste, and serve.

Second version

10 capers	2 tsp vinegar
3 gherkins	1/2 tsp flour
1 tbs olive oil	salt, pepper
1 thin steak	

1. Have ready the capers and gherkins, chopped.

2. Heat the olive oil in a frying pan. Just as it is beginning to smoke, cook the steak as in the first version.

3. Remove the steak to a warm plate. Put the gherkins, capers, vinegar, flour, salt, and pepper into the pan, and deglaze with a wooden spoon. If necessary, add a drop or two of water.

4. Return the steak to the pan, cover with sauce, and serve.

57 Niçois Tripe

Li Tripa a la Nissarda / Les Tripes à la Niçoise

For 10

5½ lb/2½ kg well-washed tripe	5 large stalks celery
2 lemons	6 cloves garlic, peeled
salt, pepper	10 tomatoes
1 lb/500 g veal shin, *or* 1 bullock's foot cut in half	*bouquet garni*
	1 pinch wild marjoram (*origano*)
4 large onions, peeled	4 tbs *grappa*
12 carrots, peeled	5 oz/150 g grated Parmesan

1. Blanch the tripe for 10 minutes in plenty of water. Remove and allow to cool.

2. Rub with lemon. Cut into strips 1 inch/2 cm wide and 2 inches/5 cm long, and season with salt and pepper.

3. Put a plate upside down at the bottom of a large pot (preferably earthenware). Add the veal shin or bullock's foot, tripe, sliced onions and carrots, celery cut into sections, garlic, peeled and seeded tomatoes, *bouquet garni*, and wild marjoram.

4. Pour in the *grappa* and add enough water to cover. Seal the lid of the pot with flour paste.

5. Cook in a very gentle oven for 8 to 10 hours.

6. Remove the contents of the pot gingerly (the lengthy cooking will have made them fragile), and arrange in a large, fairly deep baking dish. Remove the bones from the shin or foot, and spread the meat equally over the dish. Sprinkle with 3 oz/100 g of grated Parmesan. Brown under a hot grill.

7. Serve with a bowl of grated Parmesan on the side.

58 Kid

Lou Ménoun / Le Cabri

Kid is a seasonal meat and can be eaten only in late spring and early summer. Be careful that the animal you buy is not approaching adulthood, as it will not taste nearly so good.

For 12

20 red peppers	10 small onions, peeled
5½ lb/2½ kg very ripe tomatoes	10 large cloves garlic, peeled
6 tbs olive oil	½ bay leaf
1 kid weighing 11 lb/5 kg (cut up)	2 tsp thyme
2 pints/1 litre dry white wine	salt, pepper

1. Wash, seed, peel, and quarter the peppers as described in No. 45. Peel, seed, and chop the tomatoes. Set aside.

2. Put 3 tablespoons of olive oil into a very large frying pan and brown the pieces of kid well. As each piece is ready, transfer to a casserole (which should be kept warm – the browning process can take quite some time when you have to make do with the modern scaled-down versions of kitchen utensils and stoves!).

3. Deglaze the pan well with the white wine and pour over the kid.

4. Heat 3 tablespoons of olive oil in the same pan, and just as it is beginning to smoke put in the sliced onions, finely chopped garlic, bay leaf, and thyme. Brown well and pour into the casserole.

5. Add the peppers and tomatoes. Season with salt and pepper to taste.

6. Cover the casserole and cook over a moderate heat for 1 hour. Serve in the casserole.

59 Stuffed Breast of Veal

Lou Pietch / La Poche de Veau Farcie

For 12

1¼ lb/600 g Swiss chard tops
1 lb/500 g spinach
1 lb/500 g very small globe
  artichokes (if out of season,
  replace by courgettes and
  courgette flowers)
1 lb/500 g fresh peas, shelled (if
  out of season, frozen peas will do)
1 lb/500 g small broad beans,
  shelled
1 lb/500 g spring onions

10 large leaves basil
8 sprigs parsley
2 cloves garlic, peeled
2 oz/50 g rice
7 oz/200 g lean *petit salé*
  (see page xiii)
4 oz/100 g grated Parmesan
8 eggs
salt, pepper
1 boned breast of veal weighing
  about 2¾-3¼ lb/1¼-1½ kg

1. Put into a very large salad bowl: the Swiss chard tops and spinach, cut into thin strips, the sliced artichokes (without their spiny tips) or sliced courgettes and courgette flowers, the fresh or frozen peas, the broad beans, the sliced onions, and the basil, parsley, and garlic, all finely chopped.

2. Blanch the rice for 15 minutes and rinse well in cold water. Add to the stuffing along with the finely minced *petit salé* and grated Parmesan.

3. Beat the eggs well and incorporate, mixing well with a wooden spatula. Add salt and plenty of pepper.

4. Insert the stuffing into the breast of veal, which is pocket-shaped (*pietch* means 'pocket' in Niçois). Close the opening by sewing with string.

5. Lower into a large pot of bolling water and cook for 1½ hours over a moderate heat.

6. Remove and leave to cool. Put in refrigerator for 1 hour: this makes it possible to cut neat slices ½ inch/1 cm thick. Arrange the slices on a serving dish. Allow to get back to room temperature before seving with piquant sauce (No. 28).

● Some cooks like to add a decorative touch to the *pietch* by inserting a series of hard-boiled eggs in the centre of the stuffing. Others, again, leave the *pietch* to stand for an hour after removing it from the water, then brown it in a very hot oven. Neither of these devices, to my mind, increases the intrinsic quality of the dish.

60 Roast Veal with Peas and Artichokes

Lou Rouṡtit ∂é Vé∂éou aï Péou é aï Archicota
Le Rôti ∂e Veau aux Petits Poiṡ et aux Artichauts

For 8

3¹/4 lb/1¹/2 kg veal roast (boned rib
 end of loin if possible)
salt, pepper
2 tbs olive oil
30 pickling onions, peeled
2 cloves garlic, peeled
2 carrots, peeled
1 stalk celery

5 tomatoes
30 small globe artichokes
 (see page x)
¹/4 bay leaf
1 pinch thyme
3¹/4 lb/1¹/2 kg peas, shelled
2 tsp cornflour (optional)

1. Season the meat with salt and pepper.

2. Heat the olive oil in an oval casserole, and just as it is beginning to smoke put in the veal. Brown well on all sides.

3. Add the pickling onions, coarsely chopped garlic, whole carrots, celery, the peeled, seeded, and coarsely chopped tomatoes, artichokes (without their sharp tips), bay leaf, and thyme.

4. Cover the casserole, lower the heat, and cook gently, turning the veal over and basting it every 15 minutes.

5. After 1 hour, add the peas and simmer for another 30 minutes.

6. Transfer the contents of the casserole to another dish and keep warm. Deglaze the bottom of the casserole with a small glass of water, and boil for 5 minutes, stirring all the time with a wooden spoon. The sauce can be thickened, if desired, with cornflour previously diluted in 1 tablespoon of cold water.

7. Serve the veal on a long dish, surrounded by the artichokes. The peas should be served in another dish, and the gravy in a sauceboat.

61 Calf's Liver with Capers

Lou Fégé dé Védéou aï Tàpéri / Le Foie de Veau aux Câpres

For 20

1 whole calf's liver (about 8-9 lb/4 kg)	*bouquet garni*
6 thin strips pork fat	3 tbs olive oil
salt, pepper	6 tomatoes
2 onions, peeled	½ pint/250 ml rich stock
2 cloves garlic, peeled	½ lb/250 g capers

1. Lard the whole liver with a larding needle. Season with salt and pepper.

2. Put an oven-proof casserole (large enough to hold the liver) on the top of the stove, and over a high heat brown the sliced onions, finely chopped garlic, and *bouquet garni* in the olive oil.

3. When the onion has turned golden, place the liver in the casserole, cover, put in an oven set at 400°F/200°C, gas mark 6, and cook for 30 minutes. Then turn the liver over and cook for another 20 minutes.

4. While the liver is cooking, put the peeled, seeded, and coarsely chopped tomatoes in the stock and bring to the. boil. Leave to simmer very gently.

5. When the liver is done, take it out and place it on a carving board. Deglaze the casserole over a gentle heat with the tomato sauce, stirring all the time with a wooden spoon.

6. When the casserole has been deglazed, leave on a very low heat and carve the liver into neat slices ½ inch/1 cm thick. Arrange the slices on a long and fairly deep serving dish.

7. Correct the seasoning of the sauce, which should have plenty of kick, remove from the stove, and add the previously drained capers.

8. Pour the sauce over the slices of liver and serve.

● This dish can safely be kept warm for at least half an hour in a very low oven.

62 Calf's Tongue
La Lenga dé Védéou / La Langue de Veau

In Nice; tongue is served with piquant sauce (No. 28) or *saoussoun crut* (No. 21), whether it is pot roast (as here) or boiled. The following recipe for pot-roasting tongue can be used for other cuts of veal such as loin, chump end, kernel, or leg and for veal *fricandeau*. The length of cooking time varies, however, depending on the thickness of the meat.

For 4

1 whole calf's tongue	4 carrots, peeled
salt, pepper	1 tomato
1¹/₂ oz/40 g lard	4 sprigs parsley
20 pickling onions *or* 1 large onion, peeled	1 pinch thyme
	1 tbs cornflour
2 cloves garlic, peeled	3 tbs dry white wine or Madeira
1 stalk celery	(optional)

1. Season the tongue with salt and pepper, and brown it in very hot lard in an oval casserole.

2. When the tongue is well browned, turn it over and add the pickling onions or chopped large onion, crushed garlic, celery, carrots cut lengthwise into quarters, peeled and seeded tomato, chopped parsley, and thyme.

3. Cover and cook in a moderate oven for about 45 minutes or until done, turning over and basting the tongue every 10 minutes.

4. Pour off excess fat, deglaze over a high heat with very little water, and thicken with the cornflour, which should previously have been diluted in 3 tablespoons of cold water, white wine, or Madeira.

63 Porchetta

La Porchetta / La Porchetta

Originally a Piedmontese dish, *porchetta* is highly appreciated in Nice and the surrounding area. It can be eaten as a *mérenda* (mid-morning snack), hors-d'oeuvre, or main course.

For 20 to 25

1 suckling pig (gutted) with liver; heart, kidneys, tripe and sweetbreads	5 sprigs thyme
	1 bay leaf
3 tbs salt	1 oz/25 g black peppercorns
2 lb/1 kg fat-free loin of pork	5 oz/150 g lard
20 leaves sage (see page xii)	cayenne pepper

1. The pig supplied by the butcher should have a long opening along its belly. Turn the animal on its back and sprinkle 1 tablespoon of salt over the inside.

2. Put into a large mixing bowl:

(a) the liver, heart, kidneys, and sweetbreads, cut into ½-inch/1 cm dice;

(b) the tripe, well washed and blanched, cut into strips ½ inch/1 cm across;

(c) the loin, coarsely chopped with a knife;

(d) the sage leaves, finely chopped;

(e) the thyme leaves, removed from the stems, and the bay leaf broken into small pieces;

(f) the crushed peppercorns and 1¾ tablespoons of salt.

3. Wipe the inside of the pig with kitchen tissue. Mix all the ingredients well. Insert the stuffing and sew up carefully.

4. Rub the outside of the pig with a pommade of lard, cayenne pepper (a good pinch), and ¼ tablespoon of salt.

5. Place the pig on its belly in a deep roasting pan at least 18 inches/45 cm long. Roast in an oven set at 400°F/200°C, gas mark 6, for 2 hours, basting often. Remove from oven and leave for 30 minutes before serving. Carve into slices at least ½ inch/1 cm thick.

64 Roast Pork with Sage

Lou Pouarc Roustit a la Saùvia / Le Porc Rôti à la Sauge

Loin of pork is the best cut for this recipe, though a humble pork chop can be greatly improved by the insertion of a leaf or two of sage.

For 4

2 lb/1 kg loin of pork	pepper
10 leaves sage (see page xii)	salt
2 pinches thyme	

1. Bone the joint. Make small incisions in the fat and insert the sage leaves. Sprinkle with the thyme and some freshly ground pepper, then roll and tie the joint.

2. Salt the joint and put into a preheated oven set at 400°F/200°C, gas mark 6. After 10 minutes, turn down the heat to 325°F/160°C, gas mark 3, and roast for 1 to 1½ hours depending on the thickness of the joint.
It is cooked if the juice which seeps out of it when it is pricked is colourless, not pink.

3. Pour off as much excess fat as possible from the roasting pan and transfer the pork to a hot serving dish. Deglaze the roasting pan with a little warm water, pour over the pork, and serve.

● This dish goes well with unsweetened apple sauce.

65 Poor Man's Pork Chop with Artichokes

La Coustéléta où Paouré omé aï Archicota
La Côtelette du Pauvre Homme aux Artichauts

For 4

16 small globe artichokes	4 fl oz/120 ml white wine
(see page x)	3 oz/80 g *beurre manié* (butter
4 tbs olive oil	mixed with very little flour,
4 pork chops	i.e. ¾ oz/20 g)
salt	24 small gherkins

1. Cut up the artichokes as follows: remove the sharp tips of the leaves by cutting away from you as though sharpening a large pencil, then slice each vegetable very finely, starting from the stem end.

2. Brown the sliced artichokes in very hot olive oil for 3 minutes. Set aside and keep warm.

3. Salt the pork chops and fry.

4. When the chops are cooked, remove and keep warm; pour off fat from pan, deglaze with the white wine, and thicken with the *beurre manié.*

5. Add the thinly sliced gherkins to the sauce. Place the chops in a serving dish on a bed of sliced artichokes, and pour the sauce and gherkins over them.

● When small artichokes are not in season, you can still make this dish with the other ingredients.

66 Black Pudding
Lou Trulé / Le Boudin

I am giving this recipe, despite the problems even a dedicated cook will have in getting hold of the main ingredient (pig's blood), because it has been such a great favourite with the Niçois for more than 200 years.

For 8

1 lb/500 g onions, peeled	4 oz/100 g rice
2 oz/50 g lard	2½ pints/1½ litres pig's blood
small pig casing	2 oz/50 g demerara sugar
1 lemon	3 pinches thyme
9 oz/250 g pork fat	1 pinch powdered bay leaf
20 Swiss chard tops	salt, pepper

1. Slice the onions finely and fry in the lard until light golden. They must not go dark brown.

2. Wash the casing well in cold water and rub the inside with lemon.

3. Mince the pork fat.

4. Chop the Swiss chard tops finely.

5. Blanch the rice for 20 minutes in plenty of salted boiling water, and drain.

6. After making sure, with a fork, that there are no clots in the blood, mix it with the brown sugar, minced fat, onions, rice, Swiss chard tops, thyme, powdered bay leaf, salt, and pepper.

7. Fill the casing with the mixture through a funnel, having remembered of course to knot one end first. Twist the *boudin*, if ,you wish, into 10-inch/25-cm lengths, tying a piece of white string at each separation.

8. Lower into a large saucepan full of warm water. If possible, wind the *boudin* round an upturned chip basket during cooking.

9. Heat the water to just 210°F/99°C, and let it simmer (but never boil) almost imperceptibly for 45 minutes. Before removing the *boudin* from the water, make sure it is cooked: prick it carefully with a needle – if blood comes out, more cooking is needed.

● In Nice, *lou trulé* is eaten either sautéed in 4-inch/10-cm sections or poached (which makes for easier digestion).

67 Stewed Pork with Capers

Lou Poutité dé Pouarc aï Tàpéri

Le Ragoût de Porc aux Câpres

For 6

3¹/₄ lb/1¹/₂ kg hand of pork
salt, pepper
2 oz/50 g lard
bouquet garni consisting of: 1 stalk
   celery, 6 leaves sage (see page xii),
   1 sprig thyme, ¹/₄ bay leaf
   and 3 sprigs parsley

1 large onion, peeled
1 tsp flour
4 fl oz/120 ml dry white wine
2 tbs capers
2 gherkins
2 egg yolks

1. Cut the meat into 1-inch/2-cm cubes, removing all fat.

2. Season the pieces with salt and pepper. Heat the lard in a sauté pan and brown the meat slightly along with the *bouquet garni*.

3. Add the chopped onion, and before it has fully browned sprinkle with the flour. Season with more salt.

4. Cover and cook gently for 1¹/₂ hours.

5. Remove the pork with a slotted spatula and put it in another pan to keep warm. Take out the *bouquet garni*.

6. Put the white wine and an equal amount of water in the sauté pan, deglaze, and reduce by about a third.

7. Add the capers and gherkins, both finely chopped and mixed with the beaten egg yolks, away from the heat. Stir well until sauce has thickened very slightly to the consistency of thin custard (reheating the pan briefly if necessary).

8. Pour the sauce over the pork and serve.

68 Mutton Kebabs

La Rastélada dé Moutoun / Les Brochettes de Mouton

For 12 kebabs

3/4 lb/300 g boned shoulder of
  mutton
6 lamb's kidneys *or* 2 calf's kidneys
3/4 lb/300 g lamb's *or* calf's liver
3/4 lb/300 g lamb's sweetbreads
3/4 lb/300 g *petit salé* (see page xiii)
2 red peppers (*or* green in winter)

5 spring onions *or* 2 large onions,
  peeled
3 cloves garlic, peeled
pepper
2 tsp thyme
7 fl oz/200 ml olive oil
salt

1. Cut the shoulder, kidneys, liver, sweetbreads, and *petit salé* into
1-inch/2-cm cubes. Put each ingredient into a different dish, laid out in a line
along your working surface.

2. Cut the peppers and the onion layers into 1-inch/2-cm squares, or the
spring onions, including the green part, into sections. Put into two separate
dishes next to the five others.

3. Now arrange the dishes in the following order: *petit salé*, shoulder,
peppers, liver, kidney, onion, and sweetbreads. Skewer the ingredients in the
same order, repeating the process until each skewer is completely threaded.
The pieces should not be squeezed together too tightly; and the skewer should
always end with a piece of lean *petit salé*.

4. Crush the garlic in a long, deep dish, add plenty of freshly ground
pepper, and sprinkle with the thyme. Lay the kebabs on top and pour the olive
oil over them.

5. Marinate for at least 2 hours at a fairly low temperature, turning the
kebabs over every 30 minutes. Or, better, marinate for 12 hours in the
refrigerator, turning every 2 hours.

6. Salt slightly and lay the kebabs crosswise along a long, deep dish so they
do not touch the bottom. Grill or barbecue.

● The best accompaniment for these kebabs is rice.

69 Roast Leg of Mutton with Fresh Haricot Beans

La Gambéta dé Moutoun aï Faïoù Lagramua

Gigot de Mouton aux Haricots Blancs Frais

This is a perfect classical recipe for roast – or preferably spit-roast mutton, which is given extra flavour with thyme, garlic, and cayenne pepper.

For 8

3¼ lb/1½ kg very large fresh
   haricot beans
1 large onion, peeled
3 cloves garlic, peeled
2 pinches thyme

5 sprigs parsley
2 tbs olive oil
salt, pepper and cayenne pepper
1 leg of mutton

1. Put the beans, onion, garlic, thyme, parsley, and olive oil into a casserole or thick saucepan, just cover with water and bring to the boil. Simmer until cooked (the time needed will vary, depending on the age of the beans), adding water as necessary to keep covered. Season with salt, pepper, and cayenne pepper.

2. Roast the leg of mutton, on a spit if possible.

3. When the beans are cooked, deglaze the roasting pan with their remaining water.

4. Correct seasoning, and serve the meat with the juices from the roasting pan and with the beans.

70 Sheep's Testicles
Li Bala dé Moutoun / Les Bala de Mouton

This part of the sheep's anatomy is highly prized by the inhabitants of Nice, who are equally fond of calf's or bull's testicles. Those of the pig are thought to be inferior.

For 6

12 testicles	10 sprigs parsley
breadcrumbs	salt, pepper
1/4 pint/150 ml olive oil	1 lemon

1. Cut the testicles into slices 1/4 inch/1/2 cm thick and roll well in the breadcrumbs.

2. Heat the olive oil in a frying pan, and just as it is beginnig to smoke put in the sliced testicles. Brown well on both sides.

3. Remove with a fish slice and arrange on a serving dish. Fry the parsley in the same olive oil for 1 minute.

4. Decorate the dish with the parsley, add salt and pepper to taste, and squeeze the juice of a lemon over this most delicate of dishes.

71 Lamb's Fry

La Couradéta d'Agnéloun / La Fressure d'Agneau

For 18

6 lamb's kidneys
1 lamb's sweetbread
1 lamb's liver
1 lamb's heart
1 pig's lights
3 veal *onglets* (membranes
    between liver and lights)
2 veal kidneys
salt, pepper
6 medium onions, peeled

6 cloves garlic, peeled
7 fl oz/200 ml olive oil
6 tbs chopped parsley
1/2 bay leaf
5 pinches thyme
flour
1 lb/500 g cultivated mushrooms
    or 4 oz/100 g dried cèpes
1-1 1/2 bottles red wine

1. Cut up the meat into 1-inch/2-cm cubes, discarding all the tough, stringy, or gristly bits. Add salt and pepper, and set aside in the refrigerator while carrying out the next two stages.

2. Slice the onions finely and chop the garlic.

3. Heat 4 tablespoons of olive oil in a frying pan. Just as it is beginning to smoke, add the onion, garlic, parsley, bay leaf, and thyme. Cook until the onion and garlic are lightly browned, and transfer to a very large and thick-bottomed casserole.

4. Flour each piece of meat very lightly.

5. Heat 5 tablespoons of olive oil in a frying pan. Just as it is beginning to smoke, put in the meat and cook briskly. Turn the pieces from time to time with a wooden spoon so they stay well separated and are browned on all sides.

6. Transfer the meat to the casserole and mix all the ingredients together with a wooden spoon. Slice the mushrooms and add (if dried cèpes are used, they must first be soaked in lukewarm water for half an hour).

7. Pour in the red wine (which should be full-bodied if possible) until the ingredients are covered, and bring to the boil. Cook over a medium heat, uncovered, for 30 minutes.

● If you are not ready to serve, cover the casserole and leave on the lowest possible heat.

72 Mutton with Raisins and Pine-Nuts

Lou Moutoun aï Raïn é aï Pignoun

Le Mouton aux Raisins et aux Pignons

This recipe caught on in the Niçois area following the arrival of a large colony of Armenian expatriates in 1913. The easy-going and hardworking Armenians soon built up ties with even the most traditional milieux, and in no time the inhabitants of Nice had adopted this delicious combination of mutton, raisins, and pine-nuts. Ideally, a whole sheep (or lamb) should be cooked on a barbecue; but the recipe works equally well with just a leg spit-roasted in the oven.

---

1 sheep or lamb (*or* leg of either)
cayenne pepper, salt
1 oz/25 g butter
1 large onion, peeled
4 tbs olive oil   } for each 2 lb/1kg of meat
1 oz/25 g pine-nuts
1 oz/25 g raisins

---

1. Barbecue or spit-roast the meat, which should first be smeared with a mixture of salt, cayenne pepper, and butter.

2. Slice the onion and put in a thick-bottomed saucepan with 2 tablespoons of olive oil. Cook very gently until translucent.

3. Heat 2 tablespoons of olive oil in a frying pan and brown the pine-nuts slightly, stirring all the time.

4. Add the pine-nuts and the raisins, previously soaked in lukewarm water, to the onion. Add salt to taste.

5. This sauce is served separately, once the meat has been carved.

● The accompaniment to this dish is Persian-style rice (No. 224, Method 3).

73 Bundles of Lamb's Tripe
Lu Pelotoun d'Agnéloun / Les Pelotons d'Agneau

For 6

2 lb/1 kg lamb's intestines	2 pinches thyme
juice of 1 lemon	3 tbs olive oil
6 split-bamboo skewers	salt, pepper
6 leaves sage	

1. Wash the intestines well and boil for 30 minutes in salted water with the lemon juice.

2. Rinse well in cold water and leave to drain on a clean kitchen towel (or paper). Divide into six heaps.

3. Subdivide each heap by cutting the intestines into eight lengths. Wind each length round the index finger, slide off, and spike with a skewer. Repeat the process, induding a leaf of sage at one point, until each skewer carries eight such bundles.

4. Sprinkle with thyme, olive oil, salt, and pepper. Grill until crisp (over a barbecue if possible).

● This dish can be served with tomato sauce (No. 20), lemon juice, or mustard.

● ● ●

74 Chicken with Lemons
Lou Poulas où Limoun / Le Poulet au Citron

For 4

1 chicken of about 3 lb/1½ kg	½ bay leaf
3 tbs olive oil	7 fl oz/200 ml white wine
1 lb/500 g shin of veal	2 tomatoes
2 lb/1 kg veal bones	salt
2 carrots, peeled	1 tbs cornflour
1 large onion, peeled	3 tbs dry sherry
1 stalk celery	6 lemons
1 pinch thyme	1 tbs Grand-Marnier

1. Put the oil into a large sauté pan with the shin of veal, bones, carrots, onion, celery, thyme, and bay leaf. Brown very gently.

2. Pour off the fat. Add the white wine, reduce by half, and cover the ingredients with cold water. Bring to the boil, add the peeled, seeded, and coarsely chopped tomatoes, together with a very little salt. Simmer very gently for 4 hours.

3. Pour the liquid through a *chinois* (a fine conical strainer), degrease, and add the cornflour, which should first be dissolved in the sherry. Bring to the boil, allow to bubble for 2 minutes, and remove from heat.

4. Cut the rind of 4 lemons into a fine julienne, blanch for 10 minutes, strain, and add to the sauce along with their juice and the Grand-Marnier.

5. Serve the chicken, which should have been simply roasted in the usual way, on a round dish surrounded by cèpe remaining lemons, sliced. Cover with the sauce.

75 Sautéed Chicken with Tomatoes
Lou Poulas Soùtat aï Toùmati / Le Poulet Sauté aux Tomates

For 4

10 tbs olive oil	salt, pepper
6 medium onions, peeled	4 oz/100 g *petit salé* (see page xiii)
1 shallot, peeled	2 cloves garlic, peeled
1 pinch thyme	6 very ripe tomatoes
3 sprigs parsley	4 fl oz/120 ml white wine
1 chicken of about 3 lb/1½ kg, jointed	4 oz/100 g black olives
	juice of ½ lemon

1. Heat 5 tablespoons of olive oil in a frying pan. Just as it is beginning to smoke, add the quartered onions, shallot, thyme, and parsley. When the onion is lightly browned, set aside the contents of the pan.

2. Add another 5 tablespoons of olive oil, heat until just smoking, and sauté the chicken pieces, previously sprinkled with salt and pepper, and the chopped *petit salé* until well browned.

3. Add the cloves of garlic, the peeled, seeded, and coarsely chopped tomatoes, and the white wine. Turn the heat up full and cook, stirring often, until half the liquid has reduced.

4. Three minutes or so before serving, add the olives, lemon juice, and browned onion, shallot, and herbs.

● One variation of this recipe involves the addition, 10 minutes before serving, of a few cultivated mushrooms which have simmered in their own juice, or of previously soaked dried cèpe mushrooms.

76 Chicken Stuffed with Fresh Figs
Lou Poulas Farcit aï Belouna / Le Poulet Farci aux Figues

For 4

1/2 lb/250 g rice
3 oz/70 g butter
2 medium onions, peeled
10 fresh figs
1 chicken of between 2¾ lb and

3¼ lb/1,200 g and 1,500 g, with
its giblets
salt, pepper
1 tbs olive oil
cayenne pepper

1. Put the rice in a strainer, and wash in running warm water until the water runs clear. Drain well and set aside.

2. Melt 2 oz/50 g butter in a large, heavy saucepan and cook the sliced onions gently until they become translucent but not brown.

3. Peel the figs and cut them into 8 segments from top to bottom.

4. Chop the chicken giblets coarsely.

5. Add the figs and the giblets to the onions, and cook until the giblets are no longer pink. Add the rice, and mix well until each grain is well coated with butter.

6. Add 18 fl oz/500 ml water, season to taste with salt and pepper, and bring to the boil. Then turn down the heat and simmer gently for 25 to 30 minutes, or until all the liquid has been absorbed. Remove from heat, mix in the rest of the butter, and set aside.

7. Preheat the oven to 400°F/200°C, gas mark 6. Dry the inside of the chicken thoroughly with kitchen paper and insert about two thirds of the stuffing. Sew up the bird with white string.

8. Smear the chicken with the olive oil and sprinkle with salt and cayenne pepper. Place it breast down in a fairly deep roasting tin, and roast in mid-oven for 45 minutes. Pierce a leg of the bird with a thin skewer. If the juice that comes out is pale yellow, the chicken is cooked; if it is pink, roast for a further 5 to 10 minutes.

9. Leave the chicken for 5 minutes after removing from the oven – then it will be easier to carve. Reheat the remaining rice over a gentle heat, stirring from time to time, and serve separately.

77 Chicken with Raisins and Pine-Nuts

Lou Poulas aï Raïn é aï Pignoun
Le Poulet aux Raisins et aux Pignons

This recipe differs from the preceding one in only one respect: the fresh figs are replaced by 2 tablespoons of raisins, previously soaked in water, and 4 tablespoons of pine-nuts.

● ● ●

78 Jugged Rabbit

Lou Civié dé Couniéù / Le Civet de Lapin

For 6

1 tbs *grappa or* cognac	1 tomato
1 rabbit, jointed, and its blood and liver	1/2 bay leaf
	2 pinches thyme
3 tbs olive oil	11/2 tbs chopped parsley
2 oz/50 g *petit salé* (see page xiii)	salt, pepper
2 large onions, peeled	18 fl oz/500 ml red wine
1 clove garlic, peeled	2 tbs cornflour (optional)

1. Add the *grappa* or cognac to the rabbit's blood.

2. Brown the pieces of rabbit (reserving the liver) in a sauté pan with the olive oil.

3. Dice the *petit salé* and blanch for 5 minutes. Add to the rabbit along with the sliced onions, crushed garlic, the peeled, seeded, and coarsely chopped tomato, bay leaf, thyme, and parsley. Season with salt and pepper.

4. Pour the wine over the ingredients, bring to the boil, turn down the heat, and cook uncovered for 30 minutes.

5. Mash the rabbit's liver to a paste and mix with the blood. Pour into the sauté pan away from the heat, beating briskly in order to obtain a well amalgamated sauce.

6. Extra smoothness can be obtained by adding cornflour diluted in 5 tablespoons of cold red wine and simmering just below boiling point for 5 minutes.

● Before the use of starch to thicken sauces came in, the Niçois method was to add 1 or 2 walnuts, pounded to a fine paste in a mortar, to the cooking liquid: the result was an incomparably creamy sauce.

79 Rabbit with a Winter Savory Stuffing

Lou Couniêù Farcit où Pébré d'Aé
Le Lapin Farci à la Sarriette

For 6

6 Swiss chard tops
2 tbs olive oil
8 oz/250 g rice
18 fl oz/500 ml meat stock
1 rabbit, with liver and heart
4 oz/100 g *petit salé* (see page xiii)
2 onions, peeled

1 clove garlic, peeled
1 sprig thyme
1 large sprig winter savory *or* 1 tsp
    powdered winter savory
salt, pepper
2 oz/50 g lard
1/4 pint/150 ml white wine

1. Blanch the Swiss chard tops for 3 minutes and squeeze thoroughly until they contain no water at all.

2. Heat the olive oil in a thick-bottomed saucepan, add the rice, and stir well so that each grain is coated in oil. Pour in the stock and cook over a fairly high heat, stirring from time to time, until all the liquid is absorbed.

3. Chop the rabbit's liver and heart, Swiss chard tops, *petit salé*, onions, and garlic, and mix into the rice along with the thyme and winter savory leaves.

4. Insert this stuffing into the rabbit's belly, and sew up the abdominal wall with white string. Add a little salt and some pepper.

5. Smear the rabbit with lard, put it in a baking dish or, better, a roasting tin, and cook in a very gentle oven (325°F/160°C, gas mark 3) for 1 hour (or until cooked), basting frequently as it is liable to dry out.

6. Deglaze with the white wine and serve.

80 Sautéed Rabbit with Tomatoes

Lou Couniéù Soùtat aï Toùmati
Le Lapin Sauté aux Tomates

For 6

3 tbs olive oil
1 rabbit, jointed
6 medium onions, peeled
1 shallot, peeled
2 cloves garlic, peeled
4 oz/100 g *petit salé* (see page xiii)
2 pinches thyme

5 large leaves basil
3 sprigs parsley
6 very ripe tomatoes
1/4 pint/150 ml dry white wine
4 oz/100 g black olives
salt, pepper
juice of 1 lemon

1. Heat the olive oil in a large sauté pan, and just as it is beginning to smoke, brown the rabbit pieces thoroughly.

2. Chop the onions, shallot, and garlic finely. Cut the *petit salé* into strips measuring 1/2 by 1 inch/1 by 2cm.

3. Add the onions, shallot, garlic, *petit salé*, thyme, basil, parsley, and the peeled, seeded, and coarsely chopped tomatoes to the pan containing the rabbit pieces. Cook over a medium heat for 20 minutes, stirring occasionally to avoid any risk of burning.

4. Add the white wine and reduce the liquid by half.

5. Five minutes before serving, add the olives; and after removing from the heat, add salt and pepper to taste and sprinkle with the juice of a lemon.

81 Sautéed Rabbit as Eaten in the Niçois Suburb of Gairaut

Lou Couniéù Soùtat Gairautin
Le Lapin Sauté à la Mode de Gairaut

For 6

9 oz/250 g pickling onions, peeled
2 oz/50 g butter
9 oz/250 g button mushrooms
3 cloves garlic, peeled
1 large onion, peeled
4 fl oz/100 ml olive oil
1 rabbit, jointed
4 fl oz/100 ml red wine

½ pint/300 ml *saoussoun* (No. 20)
2 pinches thyme
3 sprigs parsley
1 pinch powdered winter savory
    or 1 small sprig winter savory
salt, pepper
croûtons

1. Cook the pickling onions very gently in a saucepan with the butter until transparent. Do not brown.

2. Put the button mushrooms in another saucepan with a tablespoonful of water, cover, and simmer over a very low heat until the water given off by the mushrooms has almost evaporated.

3. Crush the garlic and slice the onion. Heat the olive oil in a casserole. Just as it is beginning to smoke, add the garlic and onion, then the rabbit pieces.

4. When the rabbit pieces are well browned, pour off the oil and deglaze with the wine.

5. Turn down the heat and add the *saoussoun*, thyme, parsley, and winter savory. Correct seasoning.

6. Cover and cook over a medium heat. When the rabbit is cooked (the time needed will vary depending on its age), remove the pieces with tongs or a fish slice and put them in a saucepan with the pickling onions and the mushrooms.

7. Reduce the sauce in the casserole until slightly thickened, then pour over the rest of the ingredients. Reheat gently and keep warm until it is served (but not for more than half an hour).

8. Put the ingredients in a serving dish, and arrange the *croûtons* round the edge.

82 Thrushes with Olives

Lu Tòrdou Quina aï Oùliva / Les Grives aux Olives

(Ed. note: This and the following recipe have been included for the record, though for British readers they will be of academic interest only.)

For 6

6 thrushes	larding fat
12 juniper berries	3 tbs olive oil
32 black olives	salt, pepper
3 pinches thyme	sliced bread

1. Pluck, singe, and draw the thrushes. Put 2 juniper berries, 2 olives, and half a pinch of thyme inside each bird. Lard and truss.

2. Put the olive oil in a casserole and heat. Sauté the thrushes in the oil for 15 minutes. Season with pepper and a very little salt.

3. Add the rest of the olives and heat for 3 minutes. Serve on slices of bread fried in oil.

83 Spit-Roast Thrushes

Lu Tòrdou Quina a l'Asté / Les Grives à la Broche

(Ed. note: See preceding recipe.)

For 6

6 thrushes	3 cloves garlic, peeled
larding fat	3 pinches thyme
18 fl oz/500 ml dry white wine	1 pinch cayenne pepper
20 juniper berries	sliced bread
1 onion	2 tbs olive oil

1. Six hours before cooking is to begin, pluck, singe, lard, and truss the thrushes (they should not be drawn).

2. Put the birds into a deepish dish just big enough to hold them in one layer. Cover with the white wine, juniper berries, sliced onion, halved cloves of garlic, thyme, and cayenne pepper.

3. Leave to marinate for 6 hours at room temperature, turning the birds every hour.

4. Toast 6 slices of bread lightly and arrange in a dripping pan so they will catch the cooking juices of the thrushes.

5. Dab the thrushes dry with kitchen paper, smear with olive oil, put them on a skewer (or skewers), and grill or barbecue for 10 to 15 minutes, ideally in front of a blaze of vine branches.

6. Scoop out the insides of each bird and spread on the pieces of toast. Put the thrushes on top and serve.

84 Chamois

Lou Camous / Le Chamois

The various cuts of chamois are cooked in different ways. Cutlets, whether marinated or not, are good grilled with a simple seasoning of garlic, parsley, thyme and cayenne pepper.

Chamois fillet, which can also be marinated if desired, is excellent stewed (proceed as for the Niçois beef stew, No. 54) or even simply roasted, though in this case it must first be larded.

But the recipe I give here is for a haunch of chamois, a cut that deserves special treatment.

For 12

First operation: marinating the haunch

2 carrots, peeled	3 sprigs parsley
2 onions, peeled	4 fl oz/120 ml *grappa*
3 cloves garlic, peeled	1 pint/500 ml red wine
7-10 fl oz/200-300 ml olive oil	4 fl oz/120 ml vinegar
6 pinches thyme	1 haunch of chamois (*or* 1 haunch
1 bay leaf	of venison)
2 tsp black peppercorns	

1. Cook the sliced carrots, onions, and garlic in the olive oil gently in a covered saucepan for 5 minutes without browning them. Add all the other ingredients except the chamois, and simmer for 20 minutes.

2. Skin the haunch of chamois and place in a receptacle, into which it fits as tightly as possible. Cover with the completely cooled marinade. The meat must be entirely submerged. Leave in a cool place for 6 days, or in the refrigerator for anything up to a fortnight.

● The marinade should on no account be salted, as this would toughen the meat.

Second operation: making the *poivrade* sauce

the marinated haunch of chamois	the marinade liquid
larding fat	2 pints/1 litre veal stock (made as
2 oz/50 g lard	in steps 1 and 2 of No. 74)
2 onions, peeled	pepper
2 carrots, peeled	1 oz/25 g butter *or* 3 tbs double
1 clove garlic, peeled	cream
1/2 bay leaf	cranberry jelly (optional)
2 pinches thyme	

1. Using a short, pointed, and extremely sharp knife, bone the marinated haunch as follows: hold the joint upright, with the shin uppermost, insert the knife where the flesh starts, and work it gradually down the bone, releasing the meat all round. Don't do this too quickly, or else the meat will be disfigured. If you have difficulty in reaching the ball joint of the main leg bone, turn the haunch the other way up and proceed from the hip end.

2. With a larding-needle, insert 10 fat-strips crosswise into the haunch. Tie the meat into shape with strong white string.

3. Wipe dry the bones and the scraps and trimmings of marinated meat. Set aside.

4. Heat the lard in a thick-bottomed sauté pan, and cook the finely sliced onions, chopped carrots, crushed garlic, bay leaf, and thyme.

5. When the ingredients have turned golden brown, add the bones and meat trimmings. Brown them, then pour in about 1 pint/500 ml of the marinade.

6. Reduce by half over a medium heat. Dilute with the veal stock and simmer very gently for 2 hours. If the liquid seems to be getting too low, it may be necessary to add a few extra spoonfuls of stock. The salt in the stock should be enough to salt the sauce correctly.

7. Pour the sauce through a conical sieve (*chinois*). Add plenty of freshly ground black pepper. Just before serving, reheat, the sauce. When it is almost boiling, remove from heat and stir in the butter, cut into small cubes, with a wooden spoon. Amalgamate each cube of butter before adding the next. Do not attempt to reheat the sauce after this butter enrichment, as the butter may release itself from suspension and float on the surface. (The butter may be replaced by cream if desired.) Check seasoning.

8. The *poivrade* sauce can be turned into a venison sauce through the addition of 1 tablespoonful of cranberry jelly per litre of sauce.

Third operation: the roasting of the chamois

the larded haunch of chamois	salt
1 oz/30 g lard	marinade liquid

1. Preheat oven to 475°F/240°C, gas mark 9, about an hour before the sauce is going to be ready. Smear the larded haunch with lard, and sprinkle with salt.

2. Put the meat in the oven 40 to 45 minutes before serving.

3. The haunch of chamois should be cooked so that it remains slightly pink inside. The best way of telling whether it is cooked or not is to insert a meat thermometer into the cavity left by the bone: the meat should be just right when the thermometer reads 113°F/45°C.

4. Remove the meat from the oven. Deglaze the roasting pan with 3 tablespoons of strained marinade and add to the *poivrade* sauce. Serve with steamed new potatoes.

85 Haunch of Wild Boar

Lou Jamboun dé Senglié / Le Jambon de Sanglier

Wild boar, which is found in the immediate hinterland of Nice, naturally provides the same variety of cuts as the pig; and it is generally cooked in the same way as pork. Boar can also be used to make a delicious terrine (proceed as for No. 51, substituting tiny cubes of boar meat for the calf's liver, and not using any basil).

But as in the case of chamois, the cut that deserves special treatment is the haunch.

For 20

First operation: making the marinade

1 haunch wild boar	quantities to ensure the haunch
ingredients for the marinade in	is covered
No. 84, but increase the	

Proceed as in the first operation of No. 84. Marinate the haunch for at least 10 days, but no longer than 20 days, in a cool place.

Second operation: the roasting of the haunch

the marinated haunch of boar	2 tbs *béchamel* sauce
30 cloves	juice of 1/2 lemon
salt, pepper	1 oz/30 g butter
2 oz/50 g lard	cayenne pepper
1 pint/500 ml double cream	

1. Before roasting, stud both sides of the haunch with cloves. Add salt and pepper, and smear with lard. Put in an oven preheated to 475°F/240°C, gas mark 9. Turn the joint over after 15 minutes. After 30 minutes, turn the oven down to 425°/220°C, gas mark 7. Turn the joint over again after 45 minutes, and repeat the operation thereafter every 30 minutes until the boar is cooked. Test the joint after 2 hours of roasting with a larding or knitting needle. If the juice that runs out is colourless, the joint is ready.

2. Set the joint aside and pour the fat off the roasting pan. Deglaze with the cream and *béchamel* sauce over a gentle heat.

3. Strain the sauce through a fine conical sieve (*chinois*), and add, away from the heat, the lemon juice, the butter in small cubes (one by one), and cayenne pepper to taste. Check seasoning, and serve.

86 Snails

Lu Cantaréou / Les Escargots

In the *maquis* around Nice there lives a variety of small brown snail (*Helix aperta*) which spends the whole summer holed up in its shell, insulated from the heat by a film. The film dissolves with the first autumn showers, and the snail becomes active again. This is when the local population, both old and young, set off into the hills, well protected against the weather, carrying baskets which they hope to fill with their highly-prized quarry.

Per person

3 dozen small snails	3 sprigs parsley
2 handfuls of bran	1 pinch thyme
4 tbs coarse salt	1/2 bay leaf
vinegar	salt, pepper
1/2 onion, peeled	1/2 pint/300 ml olive oil
1 clove garlic, peeled	1/4 pint/150 ml *saoussoun* (No. 20)

1. Put the snails in a large bowl and cover with fine wire netting. Place in a cool room or on a shady balcony. Feed them on bran for a fortnight.

2. The day before you intend to cook the snails, cover them with coarse salt (1 oz/20 g salt per dozen snails), shake well, and leave them to froth. Pour off the slime (in order to be done thoroughly this will require four or five successive operations).

3. Next day, wash the snails well until the water runs clear. Then wash them again, this time in three successive lots of salted and very vinegary water.

4. Put the snails in a large saucepan, cover with water, and bring to the boil with the onion, garlic, parsley, thyme, bay leaf, salt, and pepper. Simmer gently for 3 hours.

5. Drain the snails well.

6. Heat the olive oil in a deep frying pan. Just as it is beginning to smoke, put in the snails (still in their shells), shake them, and wait for the oil to stop sizzling completely.

7. Remove from heat and take out the snails with a perforated ladle or scoop. Put them in a casserole, cover with hot *saoussoun*, and simmer for 30 minutes. The snails must be served piping hot.

SEAFOOD

87 Bogue
Li Buga / Les Bogues

The bogue, which is found in large quantities off the Nice coast, is a rather insipid fish. It can be eaten simply fried. But the best – and most typically Niçois – way of serving it is soused; this can be a main dish or an hors-d'oeuvre.

For 12

10 tbs olive oil	5 pinches wild marjoram (*origano*)
4 medium-sized onions, peeled	12 coriander seeds
4 cloves garlic, peeled	6 juniper berries
2 tbs chopped parsley	10 black peppercorns
24 bogues	salt
flour	1 lemon
1/2 pint/300 ml wine vinegar	

1. Heat the olive oil in a large frying pan. Just as it is beginning to smoke, put in the sliced onions, crushed garlic, and finely chopped parsley.

2. When the onions begin to turn golden, add the scaled, cleaned, and lightly floured bogues.

3. When the fish are well browned, remove from heat and add the vinegar, wild marjoram, coriander, juniper berries, and peppercorns.

4. Bring back to the boil, turn down the heat, and leave to simmer very gently (only just shaking) for 15 minutes.

5. Remove the fish individually and lay them in a single layer in a long, deep dish (two dishes may be necessary).

6. Salt the cooking liquid to taste and strain.

7. Pour the liquid over the fish and cover with a layer of thinly sliced lemon.

8. Put in the refrigerator and eat next day.

88 Forkbeard

La Moustéla / La Mostelle

Fished at depths of more than 650 feet/200 m, the forkbeard is rightly famous for its matchlessly delicate flesh, which does not require any special preparation. The fish is delicious poached, with melted butter and lemon juice.

The forkbeard is also cooked by some enthusiastic local chefs as though it were whiting (see recipes for whiting, Nos. 96, 97, and 98).

● ● ●

89 Grilled Sea Bass

Lou Loubas Rimat / Le Loup Grillé

The sea bass is one of the noblest of all Mediterranean fish, and remarkable for the sweetness of its flavour. It can be done in a number of classical French ways, such as *hollandaise*, *dugléré*, *meunière*, or cold, *à la russe*.

However, this delicious fish is best eaten, as it usually is in Nice, simply poached, with the addition of a drop or two of olive oil and a squeeze of lemon – none of its natural flavour is lost.

This is not to say, of course, that sea bass cannot be enjoyed in other ways which bring out its best qualities – grilled, for instance, or stuffed (No. 90).

For 6

2 sea bass of about 1¾ lb/800 g each	3 large sprigs wild fennel
salt, pepper	2 shallots, peeled
¼ pint/150 ml olive oil	3 tbs tomato pulp (No. 257)
juice of 1 lemon	1 small pinch cayenne pepper
6 pinches wild marjoram (*origano*)	

1. Score the cleaned fish at five points on each side, and rub with salt and pepper.

2. Mix together the following ingredients: the olive oil, lemon juice, wild marjoram and fennel, finely chopped shallots, tomato pulp and cayenne pepper.

3. Brush the bass on both sides with the mixture and grill or barbecue.

4. Turn the fish frequently while it is cooking, each time brushing on more of the olive oil mixture. Care should be taken, when cooking the bass *over* a fire, not to let any of the mixture fall on to the embers: it will burst into flame and oxidize the fish, giving it an unpleasant taste.

5. Pierce the bass with a skewer. When the liquid that oozes out is no longer pink, but completely transparent, the fish is cooked.

6. Serve the bass on its own, with, on the side, a small jug of olive oil or, if you have them, a selection of flavoured olive oils.

90 Stuffed Sea Bass
Lou Loubas Farcit / Le Loup Farci

For 8

1 sea bass of 3 lb/1½ kg
salt, pepper
1 tsp powdered fennel *or* a
   handful of dried fennel stems
½ lb/200 g ham or *petit salé*
   (see page xiii)
4 oz/100 g capers
¾ lb/300 g mushrooms

4 oz/100 g stoned black olives
1 large onion, peeled
2 cloves garlic, peeled
5 sprigs parsley
6 tbs olive oil
1 lb/500 g tomatoes
1¼ pints/750 ml dry white wine

1. Clean the fish and score its sides. Sprinkle with salt and pepper. Rub in the powdered fennel, both outside and inside. If dried fennel is available, pierce the skin of the fish with the slenderer stems, and put the thicker ones in its belly. Set aside.

2. Chop very finely the ham or *petit salé*, capers, mushrooms, olives, onion, garlic, and parsley, and mix well.

3. Heat the olive oil in a casserole. Just as it is beginning to smoke, put in the chopped ingredients and brown well.

4. Add the peeled, seeded, coarsely chopped, and drained tomatoes. Pour in the white wine and bring to the boil. Simmer until reduced by two thirds.

5. Bake the fish in an oiled dish for 30 minutes at 400°F/200°C, gas mark 6.

6. Remove the backbone of the bass, pour the sauce over one half of the fish, and cover with the other half to make it look as though it has been stuffed.

7. Serve very hot with new potatoes.

● ● ●

91 Dentex
Lou Denti / Le Denti

This very handsome fish is rarely seen on the fishmonger's slab, for the simple reason that it is snapped up by knowledgeable gourmets as soon as it is displayed.

It can be cooked in the same way as its close cousins, the pandora (No. 94) and the gilt-head bream (No. 95).

92 Grilled Red Mullet

L'Estrilha Rimada / Le Rouget Grillé

The red mullet is also known in France as *bécasse de mer* (sea woodcock), no doubt because it is highly prized by anglers, but also because red mullet, like woodcock, should not be gutted before cooking. Some purists claim that the fish should not even be scaled, either – which is surely going a bit far. After all, it is one thing to appreciate one's food, and quite another to enjoy fish scales getting stuck between one's teeth. Red mullet, and more particularly *rouget de roche* (*Mullus surmuletus*), a species easily distinguished by its darker colour and the stripes on its first dorsal fin, is a fish of incomparable flavour.

For 6

6 red mullet of about 6 oz/180 g each	3 sprigs parsley
salt, pepper	1 tbs capers
2 tbs olive oil	

1. Scale but do not gut the red mullet. Score them along the backbone. Rub well with salt and pepper, and smear with olive oil.

2. Grill or barbecue for 3 minutes each side.

3. Arrange the fish on a large dish and garnish with parsley and capers.

● Anchovy butter (No. 29), which goes particularly well with red mullet, should be served on the side.

93 Niçois Red Mullet

L'Estrilha a la Nissarda / Le Rouget à la Niçoise

For 6

12 red mullet of about 4 oz/100 g each	12 anchovy fillets
salt, pepper	36 black olives
flour	6 tbs capers
1 pint/500 ml olive oil	juice of 1 lemon
2 lb/1 kg tomatoes	3 tbs chopped parsley
3 lemons	2 oz/60 g butter

1. Scale but do not gut the red mullet. Score them lightly along their sides, season them with salt and pepper, and flour them.

2. Pour the olive oil into a smallish frying pan (the oil should be about 3/4 inch/2 cm deep), and heat. Just as it is beginning to smoke, put in some of the fish and fry them, basting often. When they are done on one side, turn them over. When they are cooked, transfer them with a fish slice to some kitchen paper to drain, and cook the next batch.

3. When all the red mullet are cooked, arrange them in a large gratin dish and cover with the peeled, seeded, coarsely chopped, and drained tomatoes. Place 2 thin slices of lemon, 1 anchovy fillet, 3 olives and ½ tablespoon of capers on each fish. Sprinkle with the juice of 1 lemon and finely chopped parsley.

4. Bake in the oven at 300°F/150°C, gas mark 2, for 20 minutes.

5. Just before serving, heat the butter in a saucepan until it is just beginning to turn golden brown, and pour over the fish.

94 Pandora

Lou Pagéou / Le Pageot

The pandora is, I think, one of the fish best suited to oven-cooking. Its flesh is not as dry as that of the gilt-head bream, and is firmer than that of sea bass, forkbeard, or whiting. If it weighs ¾ lb/300 g or more, the pandora can be braised.

For 6

2 oz/60 g butter	*bouquet garni*
1 onion, peeled	3 pandora of ¾ lb/300g each
2 carrots, peeled	salt
1 clove garlic, peeled	1 pint/500 ml dry white wine
6 black peppercorns	juice of 1 lemon
1 clove	

1. Melt the butter in a shallow oven-proof saucepan and cook the sliced onion, sliced carrots, whole clove of garlic, peppercorns, clove, and *bouquet garni*.

2. As the vegetables begin to brown, add the scaled and gutted fish, rubbed with salt. Continue to cook for a few minutes, without letting the vegetables get too brown.

3. Turn the fish over, pour in the white wine and lemon juice, and bake uncovered in the oven, at 400°F/200°C, gas mark 6.

4. Baste the fish frequently. After about 20 minutes, test whether the fish is cooked. The best way of doing this is to try to part the flesh above the gills from the backbone: if it comes away easily, the fish is cooked.

5. Arrange the fish on a serving dish, and add the strained cooking juices (it may be necessary to deglaze the pan with a little water).

95 Niçois Grilled Gilt-Head Bream

Lou Bésugou Rimat a la Nissarda

La Daurade Grillée à la Niçoise

Of all Mediterranean fish frequenting coastal waters, the gilt-head bream is usually placed very high on the list of excellence. Its flesh is flaky, easily digested, and extremely fine, though perhaps a little dry for my taste.

This dryness is only accentuated by the commonest method of cooking the fish, *à la meunière* (which, by the way, is not part of the Niçois culinary canon). Gilt-head bream is much tastier grilled, poached, or braised.

For 4

1 gilt-head bream of about 2 lb/1 kg
salt
6 tsp plain olive oil ⎫ mixed together (if you do not have
1 tsp olive oil with chillies ⎮ these in your store cupboard,
1 tsp olive oil with thyme ⎬ add a pinch of each flavouring
1 tsp olive oil with fennel ⎭ directly to 9 tsp plain olive oil)
juice of 1 lemon

1. Scale, gut, and score the fish. Salt lightly, and brush on a mixture of plain olive oil and olive oil flavoured with chillies, thyme, and fennel.

2. Grill or barbecue the fish.

3. Serve either with a mixture of flavoured olive oils and lemon juice, or one of the fish sauces described in the Sauces chapter.

● Gilt-head bream can also be cooked in the same way as sea bass (Nos. 89 and 90) or red mullet (Nos. 92 and 93).

96 Stuffed Blue Whiting

Lou Poutaſſoù Farcit / Le Merlan Farci

The blue whiting, known in Nice as the Parisian whiting, is certainly the most suitable for poaching of all Mediterranean fish. But it has other advantages: its subtly flavoured flesh makes it ideal for raw preparations; and the fish, being easily boned, is not difficult to stuff.

For 4

1 blue whiting of 2 lb/1 kg	2 spring onions
salt	1 small clove garlic, peeled
flour	1 stalk celery
1 egg	2 carrots, peeled
breadcrumbs	2 oz/60 g butter
1 tbs olive oil	meat glaze (optional)

1. Gut, scale, trim, and wash the fish. Make an incision all along the back, and remove the backbone.

2. Season the fish with salt, roll it first in flour, then in salted beaten egg, and lastly in breadcrumbs, and press in the breadcrumbs on both sides with a broad-bladed knife.

3. Heat the olive oil in a saucepan, add the finely chopped spring onions, garlic, celery, and carrots, cover, and stew gently.

4. When the vegetables are cooked, pour off their liquid and set aside. Mix the vegetables with a large pinch of breadcrumbs and stuff the fish through the slit in its back, but not too tightly.

5. Melt the butter in a baking dish, put in the blue whiting, and bake in the oven at 400°F/200°C, gas mark 6, basting often. When the fish is golden brown, add the liquid in which the vegetables were cooked (plus a little meat glaze if desired).

6. Serve in the baking dish.

97 Raw Blue Whiting
Lou Poutassoù Crut / Le Merlan Cru

Blue whiting can be eaten raw – or rather pickled in salt and lemon juice – as an hors-d'oeuvre or, especially in summer, as a main dish.

For 6

2 lb/1 kg blue whiting	1 bunch chives
coarse salt	2 tbs olive oil
6 lemons	½ pint/250 ml double cream
2 eggs	pepper
3 sprigs parsley	

1. With a very sharp, pointed knife, remove the flesh from the skin and bones of the fish in little flakes measuring about ½ inch by ¼ inch/1 cm by ½ cm. Put them in a bowl in a layer ½ inch/1 cm deep and sprinkle with coarse salt. Repeat the operation until every scrap of flesh has been removed from the fish. Place in the refrigerator for 3 hours.

2. Squeeze the juice of 6 lemons, and set aside. Boil the eggs for 10 minutes and peel.

3. After 3 hours, remove the fish from the refrigerator, put in a fine sieve, and leave under cold running water for at least 20 minutes. Taste to check that it has just the right degree of saltiness.

4. Drain the fish well and put it back in the bowl, along with the lemon juice. Mix well so that each piece is well coated in lemon juice, and return to the refrigerator for another 3 hours.

5. Chop finely the hard-boiled eggs, parsley, and chives. Mix them with the olive oil and double cream.

6. After 3 hours, drain the fish by pressing it firmly down in a sieve, but do not wash. Return yet again to the bowl along with the sauce. Grind plenty of black pepper over the ingredients and mix well. Taste, and add more salt if necessary.

98 Poached Blue Whiting

Lou Poutaʃʃoù Buit / Le Merlan Poché

For 4

2 large onions, peeled	2 cloves
5 sprigs parsley	salt, pepper
2 cloves garlic, peeled	1 blue whiting of 2 lb/1 kg
1 bay leaf	4 fl oz/100 ml olive oil
2 pinches thyme	juice of 1 lemon

1. Fill a fish-kettle or large saucepan three-quarters full with water. Add the sliced onions, parsley, garlic, bay leaf, thyme, and cloves. Bring to the boil, let it bubble for 20 minutes, then turn down the heat so that the water hardly moves at all. Add salt and pepper to taste.

2. Slip the scaled and gutted blue whiting into the liquid and poach for 35 to 40 minutes. Great care must be taken that the water does not begin to boil again.

3. Serve the fish with boiled potatoes and a few drops of olive oil and lemon juice.

99 Niçois Conger Eel

Lou Grounqué a la Niddarda / Le Congre à la Niçoise

As I have said earlier, the conger eel's chief claim to fame is as an essential ingredient of fish soup (No. 3). But the following recipe for the fish has plenty of character and flavour.

For 6

16 tbs olive oil	2 tbs chopped parsley
8 slices of conger eel of about	1 pinch thyme
5 oz/150 g each	1 small pinch saffron
4 fl oz/100 ml cognac	2 lb/1 kg tomatoes
3 onions, peeled	salt, pepper
2 cloves garlic, peeled	

1. Heat 10 tablespoons of olive oil in a large frying pan. Just as it is beginning to smoke, put in the slices of conger eel and brown well on both sides until the flesh draws away from the backbone. In view of the number of slices, this will probably require two or three successive operations.

2. Remove the conger with a fish slice. With a knife and fork, separate the flesh from the skin and backbone, and set aside.

3. Throw away the olive oil in the frying pan. Reheat the pan, put in the conger fillets, pour the cognac over them and set alight, shaking well until the flames have died down. Remove from heat.

4. Transfer the fish to a casserole with 2 tablespoons of olive oil, and keep warm over an extremely low heat.

5. Heat 4 tablespoons of olive oil in a frying pan and cook the sliced onions, chopped garlic, chopped parsley, thyme and saffron. Just as the onions are beginning to turn golden, add the peeled, seeded, coarsely chopped, and drained tomatoes. Season with salt and pepper.

6. Pour the tomato sauce over the conger eel, turn up the heat, and simmer for 10 minutes.

7. Serve with Persian rice (No. 224, Method 3).

100 Grilled Sardines
Li Sardina Rimat / Les Sardines Grillées

Along with the anchovy, the sardine is the fish that produces the biggest catches in the waters immediately off the coast of Nice and Saint-Jean-Cap-Ferrat. The variety of ways in which it is cooked locally is also greater than for any other fish.

On average, 5 oz/150 g of sardines will do for each person. But if by any chance you have invited a native of Nice, it is wiser to provide him or her with a ration of at least ½ lb/250 g.

For 6

18 sardines (*or* a total weight of 2 lb/900 g)	2 oz/60 g butter
4 fl oz/100 ml olive oil	1 small clove garlic, peeled
salt, pepper	4 sprigs parsley
	juice of lemon

1. Gut the sardines and rub them firmly with kitchen paper or a cloth: this will scale them quite adequately.

2. Brush them with olive oil and salt lightly.

3. Grill or barbecue the sardines for about 3 minutes on each side.

4. Place them on kitchen paper to drain, then arrange them on a serving dish.

5. Have ready some garlic butter – a mixture of butter, finely chopped garlic and parsley, lemon juice, salt, and pepper.

6. Put a knob of this butter on each sardine while they are still very hot, and serve.

● ● ●

101 Sardines Meunière
Li Sardina a la Mouliniera / Les Sardines Meunière

For 6

18 sardines (or a total weight of 2 lb/900 g)	flour
milk	½ pint/300 ml olive oil
	salt, pepper

1. Gut and scale the sardines. Moisten them with milk and roll them in flour.

2. Heat the olive oil in a large frying pan until it is almost smoking. Add the sardines.

3. As soon as the sardines are cooked (this should take about 3 minutes), remove and drain on kitchen paper. Season to taste and serve.

102 Niçois Stuffed Sardines

Li Sardina Farcit a la Nissarda
Les Sardines Farcies à la Niçoise

For 8

24 sardines (*or* a total weight of
2¾ lb/1,200 g)
10 Swiss chard tops
3 tbs olive oil
1 clove garlic, peeled
salt, pepper

1½ pints/1 litre mussels (discard any
that are not tightly shut)
1 stalk celery
2 eggs
breadcrumbs

1. Scale the sardines. Slit them along the belly and gut them. Open the fish, place on a board, skin-side upwards, and press firmly along the backbone. Turn over and remove the backbone and tail. Set aside in a cool place.

2. Cut the Swiss chard tops into thin strips and cook in a covered saucepan with 2 tablespoons of olive oil, the whole clove of garlic and a pinch of salt until the water given off by the leaves has evaporated.

3. Put the scrubbed and bearded mussels and the celery into a saucepan over a fierce heat, and cover. Shake vigorously from time to time. When the mussels have opened, remove them from their shells, discarding any that have refused to open, and set aside their cooking liquid.

4. Mix together the mussels, Swiss chard tops, and beaten eggs. Correct seasoning with pepper and a half of the mussels' cooking liquid (be careful not to let any sand be transferred with the liquid).

5. Stuff the sardines with the mixture. Some of it will be left over. This should be put on the bottom of an oiled gratin dish, and the sardines arranged side by side on top. Sprinkle with breadcrumbs and a little olive oil.

6. Gratiné the sardines in a very hot oven for 5 to 10 minutes.

103 Sardine Tian

Lou Tian dé Sardina / Le Tian de Sardines

The *tian* in its various forms is one of Nice's most individual and delicious specialities (see also Nos. 114, 162 and 198). But the sardine *tian* is of particular interest, both because of its highly subtle flavour, and because it shows how well an imaginative combination of ingredients can work.

For 6

1³/4 lb/800 g sardines	1¹/4 lb/600 g Swiss chard tops
2 lb/1 kg spinach	2 oz/50 g rice
4 tbs olive oil	4 eggs
2 cloves garlic, peeled	¹/2 lb/250 g grated Parmesan
salt, pepper	breadcrumbs

1. Gut, scale, and bone the sardines as described in No. 102 (in this recipe, each fish does not have to remain whole). Set aside in a cool place.

2. Cut the carefully washed spinach into thin strips and drain. Put it into a large saucepan with 2 tablespoons of olive oil and a whole clove of garlic. Cook until the liquid given off by the leaves has completely evaporated. Season with salt and pepper.

3. Put the Swiss chard tops through exactly the same process as the spinach.

4. Bring 3¹/2 pints/2 litres of water to the boil. Add the rice and cook for 15 minutes. Drain and rinse in cold water.

5. In a mixing bowl, beat the eggs well and add the rice, spinach, Swiss chard tops, 7 oz/200 g of grated Parmesan, and salt and pepper to taste. Mix thoroughly.

6. In a large, oiled gratin dish, spread a layer of mixture 1 inch/2.5 cm deep. Arrange the sardine fillets on top, and add another layer of mixture (about ¹/2 inch/1 cm deep). Sprinkle with olive oil, breadcrumbs, and the rest of the Parmesan.

7. Bake in a very hot oven for 20 minutes, then turn the heat up as far as it will go and brown for another 10 minutes or so.

104 Sautéed Sardines

Li Sardina Soùtat / Les Sardines Sautées

For 6

1³/₄ lb/750 g sardines	¹/₂ pint/300 ml olive oil
salt, pepper	2 tbs chopped parsley
flour	vinegar
2 cloves garlic, peeled	2 lb/1 kg tomatoes
1 pinch thyme	

1. Gut and scale the sardines. Season with salt and pepper, leave for 5 minutes, then flour.

2. Put the crushed cloves of garlic and the thyme in a frying pan with the olive oil, and heat. Just as the oil is beginning to smoke, put in the sardines and cook them until they are golden brown.

3. Remove the sardines with a fish slice and arrange them on a serving dish. Sprinkle with the chopped parsley and a few drops of vinegar. Keep warm.

4. Throw away most of the oil in the pan, but not the garlic or thyme. Add the peeled, seeded, coarsely chopped, and drained tomatoes, and place over a fierce heat.

5. When the tomatoes have given off most of their liquid, pour them immediately over the sardines. Sprinkle a few more drops of vinegar over the dish, and serve.

105 Deep-Fried Sardines

Li Sardina Frégit / Les Sardines Frites

For 6

3 eggs
salt
2 lemons
¾ lb/300 g flour
18 sardines (*or* a total weight of
  2 lb/900 g)

oil for deep frying
pepper
10 sprigs parsley

1. Beat the eggs well, salt them, and add the juice of half a lemon. Pour in the flour gradually, mixing well until a smooth batter is obtained.

2. Cut off the heads of the sardines. Gut and scale them, dip in batter so that they are completely coated, and transfer into a deep pan full of very hot, smoking oil.

3. When the sardines have turned golden brown, remove from the oil, sprinkle with pepper, and arrange on a serving dish with sprigs of deep-fried parsley and 6 lemon quarters.

106 Sardines with Peas

Li Sardina aï Péou / Les Sardines aux Petits Pois

For 6

1³⁄₄ lb/750 g sardines	³⁄₄ lb/300 g shelled peas
salt, pepper	1 clove garlic, peeled
¹⁄₄ pint/150 ml olive oil	*bouquet garni*
³⁄₄-1 oz/20-30 g flour	small pinch saffron
1 lettuce	³⁄₄ oz/20 g butter
3 spring onions	

1. Gut and scale the sardines, removing their heads. Season with salt and pepper, and leave for a few minutes.

2. Heat 3 fl oz/100 ml of olive oil in a frying pan. Flour the sardines and fry until brown.

3. Wash the lettuce and cut into strips. Slice the onions coarsely, including the stems.

4. Cook the onions gently in a saucepan in 2 fl oz/50 ml of olive oil for a few minutes, then add the peas, lettuce, crushed garlic and *bouquet garni*. Pour in about ¹⁄₂ pint/250 ml of water, season with salt, pepper, and saffron, and bring to the boil. Cook over a medium-high heat until the peas are done, then thicken with kneaded butter (the butter mixed well with ¹⁄₂ tablespoon of flour) as follows: add the kneaded butter away from the heat, return the saucepan to the stove over a heat diffuser, and keep just below simmering point for 5 minutes.

5. Put the sardines in a gratin dish, cover with the pea and lettuce mixture, and simmer for 7 to 8 minutes before serving.

● In some versions of this dish, new potatoes, half-cooked in a frying pan with olive oil, are put in to finish cooking with the pea and lettuce mixture.

107 Marinated Anchovies

Li Amploua Marinat / Les Anchois Marinés

As I have already mentioned, anchovies, together with sardines, are the most commonly caught fish in waters off the Niçois coast; equally, recipes Nos. 100 to 106 are excellent if the sardines indicated in the list of ingredients are replaced by fresh anchovies.

Most anchovies in Nice, of course, end up preserved in salt (No. 259). But there is one specific recipe for them which is particularly appreciated as an hors-d'oeuvre or as a cold main dish: marinated anchovies.

For 6

30 large fresh anchovies	4 tbs olive oil
4 onions, peeled	salt
1/2 lb/200 g carrots, peeled	30 black peppercorns
15 juniper berries	juice of 6 lemons
15 coriander seeds	6 cloves
6 tsp vinegar	2 bay leaves

1. Gut the anchovies and remove their heads, backbones, and tails.

2. Slice the onions and carrots finely.

3. Take a flat-bottomed earthenware dish about 4 inches/10 cm deep and of a capacity that will take three layers of filleted anchovies and their seasonings. On the bottom of the dish, place one third of the onions and carrots, 5 juniper berries, 5 coriander seeds, and 2 teaspoons of vinegar. Next, put in a layer of anchovy fillets, tightly packed, and cover with a tablespoon of olive oil, a large pinch of salt, and 10 peppercorns. Repeat the operation three times, and completely immerse the last layer of anchovies with the juice of the lemons.

4. Add a final tablespoon of olive oil, and arrange the cloves and bay leaves on top.

5. Leave for at least 24 hours. Serve chilled.

● Extra colour may be added by serving the anchovies with plenty of finely chopped parsley.

108 Mackerel with Tarragon

Lu Aurioun a l'Estragoun / Les Maquereaux à l'Estragon

For 6

6 large mackerel
1¹/₂ oz/40 g butter
juice of 1¹/₂ lemons
12 fl oz/350 ml dry white wine
1 clove garlic, peeled
pepper
4 egg yolks
¹/₄ pint/150 ml milk

¹/₄ pint/150 ml liquid in which
  mushrooms have been cooked
  (if available)
5 sprigs chervil
5 sprigs tarragon
5 sprigs parsley
4 leaves spinach
salt

1. Bake the gutted mackerel in the oven, set at 375°F/190°C, gas mark 5, with half the butter, the juice of half a lemon, 7 fl oz/200 ml of white wine, and the chopped garlic.

2. Put ¹/₄ pint/150 ml of white wine into a thick-bottomed saucepan with a generous amount of coarsely ground black pepper. Bring to the boil and reduce by half. Remove from heat and add the egg yolks. Stirring constantly with a wooden spoon, put back over a gentle heat and cook until the sauce is thick enough to adhere to the spoon.

3. Put through a very fine strainer, then return to the saucepan with the milk, the rest of the butter, the juice of a lemon and, if possible, the mushroom liquid. Mix well over a gentle heat. Set aside.

4. Chop the chervil, tarragon, parsley and spinach finely and blanch, uncovered, in ¹/₄ pint/150 ml of water for about 10 minutes. Pound herbs and remaining water (about 1 tablespoon) to a smooth paste, put through a fine sieve, and mix with the sauce. Season to taste.

5. When the mackerel have been baking for about 20 minutes, pour the sauce into their baking dish and cook for another 10 minutes. Serve on an oval dish and cover with sauce.

● ● ●

109 Mackerel with Peas

Lu Aurioun aï Péou / Les Maquereaux aux Petits Pois

Proceed as for sardines with peas (No. 106).

110 Niçois Octopus
Lou Pourpré a la Nissarda / La Poulpe à la Niçoise

The octopus, a species of mollusc armed with 8 tentacles which are lined with double rows of suckers, is, it must be admitted, a most unprepossessing creature, both to look at and to touch. But its flavour is in a league of its own – I have known tins of lobster meat often contain up to 50 per cent of octopus tentacles whose suckers have been removed by boiling.

The octopus can be prepared in a multitude of excellent ways. But I shall give only one recipe here for fresh octopus of the quality found at my old friend Marcelle Fède's stall in the Place Saint-François fish market in Nice.

Choose only young specimens, and ask your fishmonger to remove the octopus' ink. (If you wish to keep the ink, pierce the ink sac carefully over a saucepan.)

For 6

1 octopus of 2 lb/1 kg (*or* 2 of 1 lb/500 g each)	2 lb/1 kg tomatoes
3 tbs olive oil	*bouquet garni*
2 onions, peeled	4 fl oz/120 ml cognac
2 cloves garlic, peeled	salt, cayenne pepper

1. Put the octopus on a board and remove the beak and eyes. Empty the interior organs. Wash well in running water, making sure in particular that the suckers are absolutely clean.

2. Cut up the octopus into 1 inch/2 cm pieces. Put into a large, thick-bottomed sauté pan, cover, and place over a very gentle heat.

3. Heat the olive oil in a saucepan, and cook the sliced onion and chopped garlic. When they are golden brown, add the peeled, seeded, and coarsely chopped tomatoes, and the *bouquet garni*.

4. When the liquid that has seeped from the octopus pieces has evaporated, pour in 3 fl oz/90 ml of cognac and set alight. Shake well until all the flames have died down. Transfer to a casserole.

5. Deglaze the sauté pan with the rest of the cognac and pour into the casserole.

6. When the tomato sauce has reduced by about a third, add to the octopus and cook, covered, for 30 minutes. Season with salt (if necessary) and cayenne pepper.

● In Nice, octopus done in this way is usually served surrounded by boiled rice shaped by a ring mould.

● This recipe can be varied in a number of ways by the addition of further ingredients. A large pinch of saffron, or a tablespoon of curry powder, can for instance be added to the octopus at the same time as the tomato sauce.

If you have kept the octopus' ink, you can use it as follows: brown 2 cloves of garlic and 1 onion, chopped, in 1 tablespoon of very hot olive oil, add the ink, and pour over the octopus just before serving.

• • •

111 Deep-fried Cuttlefish or Squid

La Suoia o lou Taout Frégit / La Seiche ou l'Encornet Frits

The cuttlefish and its close relation the squid are much tenderer than octopus; but they have correspondingly less flavour. However, both cuttlefish and squid can be cooked in the same way as octopus (No. 110), and cuttlefish is particularly good in its own ink. But only cuttlefish or squid are suitable for deep-frying.

For 6

2 lb/1 kg cuttlefish *or* squid	7 oz/200 g flour
juice of 2 lemons	4 eggs
salt, pepper	oil for deep frying

1. Remove the eyes and beaks from the cuttlefish or squid, and wash well, particularly the suckers. Leave them to soak for a few minutes in the lemon juice.

2. Cut the cuttlefish or squid into strips ½ inch/1 cm wide, and season with salt and pepper.

3. Flour the pieces lightly, and wipe so that almost no traces of flour remain – the aim is above all to dry the fish.

4. Beat the eggs thoroughly and add 5 oz/150 g of flour until a fairly liquid batter is obtained.

5. Heat the oil until smoking. Dip the pieces of cuttlefish or squid into the batter and fry until golden. Drain on kitchen paper and serve.

112 Whitebait
Lou Mélet / La Petite Friture

Mélet – tiny sand-smelt about half the size of one's little finger – are the commonest form of whitebait along the coast of the Comté de Nice, though baby red mullet, grey mullet, and pandora are also used when in season.

In all cases, the cooking procedure is the same: flour the fish, fry in very hot olive oil; and sprinkle with lemon juice and coarsely ground black pepper.

• • •

113 Deep-Fried Nonats
Lu Nounat Frégit / Les Nonats Frits

Both *nonats* and *poutine* (Nos. 117 and 118; see also page ix) are fish in their larval state; the difference between them is one of consistency rather than of taste, and either can be used to make soup (No. 11). *Nonats* are tiny transparent gobies, while *poutine* are baby sardines or anchovies.

For 6

1¹/4 lb/600 g *nonats*	salt
¹/2 pint/250 ml milk	10 sprigs parsley
flour	1 lemon
oil for deep frying	

1. Put the *nonats* in the milk to soak. Separate them carefully.

2. Drain, flour, and place the fish on a coarse-grained sieve. Shake to remove excess flour.

3. Heat the oil. Just as it is beginning to smoke, strew with *nonats*.

4. Give a stir with a fork. When they are cooked, drain all the fish at once in a sieve, and salt.

5. Fry the parsley and put it on the *nonats*. Serve with lemon segments.

● The fish can also be seasoned with cayenne pepper, in which case the dish becomes *nounat a la diaou* or *nonats à la diable*. This term gave Auguste Escoffier (who was born in Villeneuve-Loubet and started his career as a chef in Nice) the idea for one of the many sauces he invented for royalty, *sauce diable*.

114 Tian de Nonats

Lou Tian dé Nounat / Le Tian de Nonats

For 6

15 Swiss chard tops	1 lb/500 g *nonats*
4 oz/100 g butter	salt, pepper
5 oz/150 g grated Parmesan	3 tbs olive oil
4 eggs	breadcrumbs

1. Wash the Swiss chard tops and chop finely.

2. Melt the butter in a saucepan. Before it turns brown, add the Swiss chard tops, cover, and cook until all the water given off by the leaves has evaporated.

3. Put 4 oz/100 g of the Parmesan, the beaten eggs, and the *nonats* in a mixing bowl. Add the Swiss chard tops, mix well, and season with salt and pepper to taste. At this point, 2 tablespoons of olive oil maybe added if desired.

4. Pour the mixture into a gratin dish big enough for the mixture to be 1 to 1½ inches/3 to 4 cm deep. Sprinkle with breadcrumbs, the rest of the Parmesan, and 1 tablespoon of olive oil. Put in the oven, set at 400°F/200°C, gas mark 6, for 20 minutes so that the top of the *tian* browns slightly.

● ● ●

115 Fritters of Nonats

Li Bignéta dé Nounat / Les Beignets de Nonats

For 6

3 eggs	13 sprigs parsley
salt	1 clove garlic, peeled
juice of ½ lemon	14 oz/400 g *nonats*
11 oz/300 g flour	oil for deep frying
pepper	2 tbs double cream (optional)

1. Beat the eggs well. Add salt and lemon juice. Stir in the flour, mixing well until a smooth, rather thick batter is obtained.

2. Add plenty of pepper, 3 sprigs of parsley, chopped, the chopped garlic, and the washed and well-separated *nonats*. Mix thoroughly.

3. Heat the oil until just smoking. Put the mixture into the oil, a tablespoon at a time. Cook the fritters for 5 minutes, turning them once. Drain and serve on paper napkins with 10 deep-fried sprigs of parsley.

● The fritters will have an even smoother consistency if double cream is added to the batter.

116 Salad of Nonats

Lu Nounat en Salada / Les Nonats en Salade

For 6

3 large onions, peeled
6 cloves garlic, peeled
bouquet garni
1 pinch wild marjoram (*origano*)
2³/4 lb/1,200 g *nonats*

salt, pepper
4 tbs olive oil
1 tbs chopped chives
¹/2 lemon or 1 tbs vinegar

1. Put the sliced onions and garlic, *bouquet garni*, and wild marjoram in 5 pints/3 litres of water, and bring to the boil. Keep boiling for 15 minutes.

2. Put the *nonats* in a very fine deep frying basket and lower them into the boiling water. Give them a stir with a wooden spoon.

3. As soon as the water comes back to the boil, remove the *nonats* and put them under cold running water for a second or two.

4. Drain and transfer to a salad bowl. Season with a light dressing of salt, pepper, olive oil, chopped chives, and vinegar or lemon juice.

• • •

117 Poutine or Nonat Omelette

La Méléta dé Poutina o dé Nounat
L'Omelette de Poutine ou de Nonats

For 6

12 eggs
salt
1¹/4 lb/600 g *poutine or nonats*

3 tbs chopped parsley
2 tsp olive oil

1. Break the eggs into a bowl, add a pinch of salt, and beat.

2. Pick any impurities out of the *poutine* or *nonats*, but do not wash. Stir into the beaten egg along with the finely chopped parsley.

3. Heat the olive oil in a frying pan, pour in the omelette mixture, and cook.

● The cooking of this omelette can be varied as follows: put 1 clove of garlic and a piece of red capsicum about 1 inch/2 cm long in the pan with the olive oil. When the oil is hot and ready for the omelette mixture, remove the garlic and capsicum, and cook the omelette.

118 Poutine with Chillies

La Poutina a la Pébréta / La Poutine au Piment

Poutine is so similar to *nonats* that recipes Nos. 112 to 117 work equally well for both fish. However, there is one specific recipe for *poutine* that would seem to have come from Spain and was unfortunately neglected for many years: *poutine* with chillies.

For 6

12 cloves garlic, peeled	1½ lb/600 g *poutine*
3 long, strong red chillies	2 tbs chopped parsley
12 tbs olive oil	salt

1. Take twelve small earthenware ramekins which can be heated directly on an electric hot plate or on a heat diffuser over a gas ring. In each ramekin, put a clove of garlic, quartered, a ring of chilli, and 1 tablespoon of olive oil.

2. Wash the *poutine* and divide it into twelve little heaps of 2 oz/50 g each.

3. Heat the ramekins. When the oil begins to smoke, remove them from the heat and immediately put a portion of *poutine* in each of them. Sprinkle with parsley and salt. Shake each ramekin vigorously so that the fish fry well separated from each other.

4. Serve, if possible, with chopsticks or wooden forks – a metal fork can burn the lips.

119 Estocaficada

This pungent stew, made with stockfish (wind-dried cod – see page ix), is without any doubt the most popular in the whole canon of typically Niçois dishes. It has always quickened the tastebuds of gourmets and, indeed, inspired poets of every description, from local bards writing in Niçois, to Paul Valéry, whose favourite dish it was, and Jules Romains, who made a point of eating it during each of his many stays in Nice.

A great local favourite, *estocaficada* is also much appreciated by tourists intelligent enough not to be put off by its powerful smell. Its bark is worse than its bite, and I have known several people who, after long trusting the less than enthusiastic reactions of their noses, have later wished they had become acquainted earlier with the delights of this superb stew.

For 6

2 lb/11 kg stockfish	thyme, bay leaf, winter savory,
4 oz/100 g stockfish guts	fennel, and marjoram
5 large onions, peeled	4 lb/2 kg very ripe tomatoes
5 cloves garlic, peeled	4 yellow, red, or green peppers
1 bay leaf	salt, pepper
1/2 pint/250 ml olive oil	2 lb/1 kg new potatoes
1/4 pint/150 ml *grappa*	12 oz/300 g black olives
bouquet garni consisting of parsley,	

1. Saw the stockfish into sections 1 to 1 1/2 inches/3 to 4 cm thick, and put into a large pan of water along with the stockfish guts. Leave under dripping cold water tap, so that the water is constantly being changed, for 8 days.

2. The day the dish is to be made – and a good 6 hours before the mealtime – remove the stockfish from the pan in which it has been soaking. Pick the flesh away from the skin and bones, and set aside. Put the skin, bones, and mucous membranes from the stomach wall into 3 1/2 pints/2 litres of water with 2 onions, 1 clove garlic, and 1 bay leaf, bring to the boil, and simmer gently.

3. Shred the flesh of the stockfish in a bowl, and drain. Heat the olive oil in a sauté pan. When it is hot, put in the stockfish and stir continuously with a wooden spoon.

4. When the shredded fish turns golden brown, add the *grappa*, the rest of the onions and garlic, finely chopped, and the *bouquet garni*. Mix well and transfer to a large and thick-bottomed casserole. Deglaze the sauté pan with the peeled, seeded, and coarsely chopped tomatoes, and add to the mixture in the casserole, along with the stockfish guts, cut into strips 1/4 inch/5 mm wide, and the sliced peppers. Add plenty of pepper, and some salt (allowing for the olives which are added later). Cook over a low and regular heat, tightly covered, for at least 2 hours.

5. Quarter the new potatoes and steam them. Half an hour before the stockfish is done, add the olives and the potatoes to the casserole. Add salt to taste just before seving.

● When served, the *estocaficada* should be quite a liquid stew, with plenty of juice for the potatoes to mop up. So if in the course of the cooking the liquid seems to be reducing too much, add a ladleful or two of the broth in which the stockfish trimmings have simmered.

● There should be one or more little jugs of olive oil on the table when the dish is served, as it is traditional in Nice to sprinkle a few drops of olive oil over one's *estocaficada*.

● There is another, less orthodox, way of eating stockfish, described to me by my father, who spent his childhood on the quayside of Saint-Jean-Cap-Ferrat harbour, and corroborated by my friend, Honoré Toscan, native of Saint-Jean and octopus-fisher extraordinary, who was twenty-five years my father's junior.

According to their story, there used to be an old fisherman known as Barba Chiquin (*barba* means 'uncle', and *chiquin* 'someone who likes his drink'), who would summon the child population of Saint-Jean-Cap-Ferrat to witness his performance of the following recipe:

1. Take 4 oz/100 g of unsoaked stockfish, place it against a rock, and beat it to a coarse powder with a hammer.

2. Put the stockfish into a mortar and pound to a paste with 4 cloves of garlic.

3. Heat some olive oil in a frying pan till it smokes, and brown 2 chillies in it.

4. When the oil begins to smoke again, add the mixture of stockfish and garlic.

5. As soon as it has turned golden, spread the mixture and the chillies on a hunk of brown bread – and tuck in!

120 Salt Cod with Leeks

La Merlussa aï Pouaré / La Morue aux Poireaux

For 6

1¾ lb/800 g salt cod (see page ix)
2 large onions, peeled
2 cloves garlic, peeled
bouquet garni
flour

¼ pint/150 ml olive oil
12 large leeks
1 pint/500 ml meat stock
pepper

1. Soak the cod (which should be as light-coloured as possible) for at least 48 hours. Cut it into 2-inch/5-cm pieces and put into 3½ pints/2 litres of water with the onions and garlic, sliced, and the *bouquet garni*. Bring to the boil and simmer for 15 minutes.

2. Dab the pieces of cod dry, flour lightly and fry in very hot olive oil till golden brown. Transfer to the bottom of a gratin dish with a fish slice.

3. Slice the leeks (the white part only) and brown slightly in the same pan. Put them on top of the cod, add the stock and plenty of pepper, and put in a hot oven for about 20 minutes.

4. Serve with mashed or boiled potatoes.

● Salt cod can also be eaten with *aïoli* (No. 26).

● ● ●

121 Grilled Spiny Lobster

La Lingousta Rimada / La Langouste Grillée

There was a time when locally fished lobsters were to be found in relative abundance in the fish markets of Nice. Nowadays, though, only if you are on particularly good terms with a fisherman will he consent to sell you a lobster on the side from time to time.

However, modern communications are such that lobsters from all over the world are now on sale in any French market. Whether one prefers the Tunisian spiny lobster to its rivals from Mauritania, the Caribbean, and even Brazil is a matter of taste. But the lobster remains a delicious – and expensive – shellfish which deserves to be cooked with great care.

The best way of preserving the lobster's superb flavour is to grill it, as fishermen used to do when they got back to land.

For 2

First version

The oldest method consists of wrapping the live lobster in wire netting and placing it 8 inches/20 cm above red-hot embers which are covered with a thin layer of white ash. The lobster must be turned frequently, otherwise the shell will burn before the flesh inside is completely cooked.

After about 20 minutes, a 1³/4 lb/800 g lobster will turn brown. At this point, remove it from the wire netting, place it on a large wooden board and split it lengthwise with a cleaver.

The trouble with this recipe is that the steam coming from the lobster as it cooks can escape only at the point where the legs are joined to the body – and this results in their falling off.

It is, on the other hand, the best way of preserving the full flavour of the spiny lobster, which should be served simply with melted butter and freshly ground pepper.

For 4

Second version

1. Choose 2³/4-lb/800-g live hen lobsters (they can be distinguished from cock lobsters by the larger swimmerets under their tail and by the final pair of legs on their body, which end with pincers instead of a hook as in the case of cock lobsters).

2. Cut each live lobster in half as follows: place it flat on a board, hold a cleaver lengthwise against its back, and give it a crisp, hard blow with a heavy mallet.

3. When you have finished cutting the lobsters in two, place the halves flesh-side up, scoop out the brownish soft matter (tomalley) and the orange-red roe, and put in a saucepan.

4. Prepare a barbecue. Put the half-lobsters, shell downwards, on the barbecue, if possible in a double metal rack. Cook gently. If the shells begin to burn, turn down the heat (or raise the lobsters farther away from the source of heat).

5. When the flesh begins to contract away from the shell, turn the lobsters over and brown the other side gently. The whole process should not take longer than about 15 minutes, and care must be taken not to let the lobster meat get too dry. If the lobster is to be kept warm make sure the shell side is facing the source of heat.

6. Serve with lobster sauce (No. 31) and boiled rice.

122 Niçois Sole
La Sola a la Nissarda / La Sole à la Niçoise

For 6

3 large sole of about ¾ lb/300 g
  each *or* 6 small sole of about
  5-7 oz/150-200 g each
salt, pepper
2 shallots, peeled
2 tbs olive oil
juice of 2 lemons
2 tbs dry white wine

¼ lb/150 g button mushrooms
¾ lb/400 g tomatoes
1 lettuce
1 stalk celery
1 clove garlic, peeled
½ bay leaf
2 tbs each chopped parsley and
  chives

1. Remove the skin from the darker side of the fish; trim, gut, and clean carefully. Score the middle of the back and season with salt and pepper.

2. In an enamelled cast-iron gratin dish, brown the chopped shallots lightly in 1½ tablespoons of olive oil, then add the juice of 1 lemon and the white wine.

3. Clean and trim the mushrooms, heat in a saucepan with ½ tablespoon of olive oil, and set aside when they have given off their liquid.

4. Put the sole in the gratin dish, pour in the mushroom liquid, and cover with the peeled, seeded, coarsely chopped, and drained tomatoes.

5. Cut the lettuce into thin strips and blanch for 5 minutes with the chopped celery and garlic.

6. Lay the mushrooms, lettuce, celery, garlic, and bay leaf (broken into little pieces) over the fish, and salt lightly. Bake in an oven set at 375°F/190°C, gas mark 5, for 20 to 25 minutes, basting frequently so that the sauce is considerably reduced.

7. Serve with a sprinkling of lemon juice, and chopped chives and parsley.

● ● ●

123 Grey Mullet
Lou Mujou / Le Mulet

The grey mullet is a very common fish along the Mediterranean coast. It is closely related to the sea bass, and although not so delicately flavoured naturally costs much less. It can be cooked in the same way as sea bass (see Nos. 89 and 90).

124 Trout Sainte-Claire

La Truta a la Santa Clara / La Truite Sainte-Claire

The only freshwater fish eaten in Nice, apart from eel, is trout, which is very common in the mountain streams behind the city. It is cooked in a variety of classical ways that are encountered all over France. But in Vieux-Nice, the old quarter of the city, the trout is given characteristically local treatment.

For 6

6 trout
6 small sprigs fennel (wild fennel if possible)
salt, pepper
4 tbs olive oil
1 lb/500 g lean *petit salé* (see page xiii)

1 lb/500 g button mushrooms
4 oz/100 g capers
1 large onion, peeled
4 cloves garlic, peeled
5 sprigs parsley
1¹/4 pints/750 ml dry white wine

1. Gut and wipe clean the trout. Put a sprig of fennel in each stomach cavity, season with salt and pepper, and set aside.

2. Heat 3 tablespoons of olive oil in a deep saucepan. Just as it is beginning to smoke, put in the *petit salé* diced finely, and brown. Add the mushrooms, very finely chopped, and the capers. Cook over a gentle heat for 30 minutes.

3. Add the onion, garlic, and parsley, all finely chopped, and the white wine. Continue to cook until the liquid has reduced by half.

4. Arrange the trout in an oiled gratin dish, and cover with the sauce. Bake in the oven at 425°F/220°C, gas mark 7, for 20 minutes.

• • •

125 Eel as served at Chez le Bicou

L'Anguila doù Bicou / L'Anguille du Bicou

When Napoleon III built a dyke along the left bank of the River Var, to celebrate France's annexation of the Comté de Nice in 1860, the Var plain became, from the mountains in the north right down to the sea, an enormous expanse of pasture land crisscrossed by *beal* (little canals), which diverted water from the river to irrigate the fields. The *beal* were full of eels, and local restaurants such as Chez le Bicou (which has now disappeared to make way for Nice airport) and Chez Cougnet, at Saint-Isidore, always had a plentiful supply of the creatures. We used to make special trips out there just to taste the eels, which because they came from running water had no trace of the muddy flavour that sometimes mars the fish. It is worth making the effort to procure equally clean-tasting eels when tackling the following recipe from Chez le Bicou.

For 6

4 lb/1,800 g eels	1 pint/500 ml dry white wine
salt, pepper	2 lb/1 kg tomatoes
flour	2 cloves garlic, peeled
12 tbs olive oil	2 tbs chopped parsley
2 onions, peeled	6 slices bread

1. Skin the eels and chop into 2-inch/5-cm pieces. Put in a saucepan, cover with water, bring to the boil for a minute or two, drain, and dry with kitchen paper. Season with salt and pepper, and roll in flour.

2. Put 6 tablespoons of olive oil in a sauté pan and heat until just smoking. Brown the chopped onions in it, then add the eel pieces. Cook for 10 minutes, turning frequently.

3. Pour in the white wine, and bring to the boil. Reduce by half. Add the peeled, seeded, coarsely chopped, and drained tomatoes, season to taste, and sprinkle with the chopped garlic and parsley. Cover and cook gently for 30 minutes.

4. Fry the bread in the remaining olive oil, arrange on a serving dish, pour the cooking liquid over it and place the eel pieces on top.

● ● ●

126 Sea-Urchin Omelette
La Méléta d'Alissoun / L'Omelette d'Oursins

The sea-urchin is now, of course, a familiar feature of French restaurant menus. It is eaten with a spoon, usually just accompanied by rye bread, but sometimes by a few drops of lemon juice as well. Our ancestors, however, tackled the sea-urchin in a less reverential way: they cut it open, swilled out the dark granular inside with sea-water, scooped out the coral flesh with a small piece of bread, and savoured it while opening the next sea-urchin.

One truly local speciality has remained with us: sea-urchin omelette.

For 6

12 eggs	12 sea-urchins
pepper	2 tsp olive oil
juice of 1 lemon	

1. Break the eggs into a bowl and beat, but not too vigorously. Add a very little pepper and the juice of half the lemon. Mix thoroughly.

2. Remove the coral from the sea-urchins with a spoon, run briefly under cold water, and incorporate into the eggs.

3. Heat the olive oil in a frying pan, pour in the omelette mixture, and cook, according to taste, until either creamy or firm. Serve with a sprinkling of lemon juice.

• • •

127 Limpet Omelette
La Méléta d'Alapia / L'Omelette d'Arapèdeſ

Everyone is familiar with these rough-shelled little cones and their proverbial ability to cling to rocks (to foil them, give them a quick, firm, sideways tap). The flesh of the limpet is very tough and, to be honest, not memorably good. However, its not very marked taste appeals to those who enjoy seafood for its freshness and its aftertaste of the sea.

Limpets are caught chiefly in spring. They are either eaten, like sea-urchins, on their own with a little bread, or put into an omelette: proceed as in No. 126, replacing sea-urchins by 2 oz/60 g of limpets per person.

• • •

128 Violet
Lou Vioulet / Le Violet

This creature, unlike the limpet, is very strong-tasting; and even people who are very fond of violets cannot usually consume more than a dozen. The *violet* (*Microcosmus sulcatus*) has a leathery skin and is shaped rather like a bagpipe. It is cut in half lengthwise, and the edible yellow part inside is scooped out with a spoon or the thumb. It can be eaten on its own, or with bread.

Particularly delicious small *violets* are found on fairly deep rocks between Nice and Menton.

129 Sea Anemones

Lu Rastuguet / Les Orties de Mer

In winter, fishermen catch the sea anemone (or, more precisely, the snake-locks anemone) as follows: they tie to the end of a bamboo stick a fork whose prongs have been shortened by half, bent to an angle of 90 degrees, and sharpened on a grindstone. They lean out of the boat and, using a bucket whose bottom has been replaced by glass, scan the rocks for anemones. When they find one, they cut it off the rock with a sharp, neat stroke of the fork and lift it up into the boat, being careful not to touch it. The creature thoroughly deserves its French name of *ortie de mer* (sea nettle), as it can cause very nasty burns on the face or on the inner sides of the arms and thighs. I mention this because in summer people fish for it by diving into the water with a mask, carrying the sharpened fork.

Sea anemones are extremely rich in phosphorus and may cause sleeplessness in children or highly-strung individuals. They also go bad very easily, and should on no account be consumed more than 12 hours after being fished. It is a good idea to bring them home in a large bucket of sea water and put them in a cool place. Never leave sea anemones in the refrigerator or in sunlight.

At night, the anemones glow slightly, like the luminous figures of an alarm-clock. Their iodine and phosphorus content is such that the water in which you are keeping them (briefly) is heated to a temperature of at least 95°F/35°C.

Sea anemones are usually eaten with aperitifs or as an hors-d'oeuvre, and are extremely filling.

For 4

5 tbs vinegar	polenta flour *or* semolina
24 sea anemones	7 fl oz/200 ml olive oil

1. Put 4½ quarts/5 litres of water and the vinegar in a bowl and rinse the anemones well. This can be done with the bare hands, as the anemones lose their power to sting as soon as they come into contact with vinegary water. With the fingers, remove all the grit inside the anemones, and transfer them to another bowl. Rinse thoroughly once, then drain. Do not leave them for any length of time in the colander, as their taste can be affected by contact with metal.

2. Dry the anemones in kitchen paper and roll them in polenta flour or semolina.

3. Heat the olive oil in a frying pan. Just as it is beginning to smoke, put in the anemones and fry for 2 minutes, turning often.

4. Serve piping hot on a layer of paper napkins.

VEGETABLES

130 Artichokes with Thyme
Li Archicota a la Férigoula / Les Artichauts au Thym

This dish is also known in French as *artichauts à la barigoule*. *Barigoule* is a deformation of the Provençal word *farigoule*, which, like the Niçois *férigoula*, means 'thyme'.

For 6

18 young globe artichokes (see page x)	2 cloves garlic, peeled
5 tbs olive oil	2 pinches thyme
1 onion, peeled	salt, pepper
	2 oz/50 g *petit salé* (see page xiii)

1. Trim the artichokes as follows: remove two rows of leaves and cut off the dark-green tips of the others. Peel the stem.

2. Into a round casserole put 4 tablespoons of olive oil, the sliced onion, quartered cloves of garlic, and thyme. Pack the artichokes tightly into the casserole, leaves uppermost, season with salt and pepper, sprinkle with 1 tablespoon of olive oil, and strew with diced *petit salé*. Cover and cook over a low heat. As the artichokes may take more than an hour to cook, keep some water simmering in a saucepan so that they can be moistened from time to time. The cooking time will range from 45 to 90 minutes, depending on the size of the artichokes.

● Artichokes with thyme can easily be kept warm (covered) for more than an hour.

131 Stuffed Artichoke Bottoms
Li Archicota Farcit / Les Fonds d'Artichauts Farcis

Large artichokes, such as those of the Breton variety (see page x), are best eaten stuffed.

For 6

6 large globe artichokes	a piece of white bread the size of an
5 oz/150 g *petit salé* (see page xiii)	egg
2 onions, peeled	2 tbs chopped parsley
1 clove garlic, peeled	2 egg yolks
2 tbs olive oil	salt, pepper
3 tbs stock	

1. Blanch the artichokes for about 15 minutes in boiling water. Remove from heat and leave to cool.

2. When they are cool, scrape the edible part off the base of each leaf and put in a bowl.

3. Remove the chokes and set aside the bottoms.

4. Chop the *petit salé*, onions, and garlic, and put in a pan over a high heat with the olive oil.

5. When the onions begin to turn golden, add the white bread, previously soaked in stock and mashed, the flesh from the artichoke leaves, the chopped parsley, and the egg yolks. Remove immediately from heat and mix thoroughly. Season with salt and pepper.

6. Fill each artichoke bottom with the mixture, arrange in a gratin dish, and put to brown in a hot oven for 20 minutes. Serve hot.

132 Marinated Artichokes

Li Archicota en Samoira / Les Artichauts en Marinade

For 6

24 small globe artichokes (see page x)	5 sprigs parsley
	1 stalk fennel (if possible, wild fennel)
1/4 pint/150 ml dry white wine	
6 tbs olive oil	2 pinches thyme
juice of 2 lemons	1/2 bay leaf
salt, pepper	1 clove garlic, peeled
1 stalk celery	12 pickling onions, peeled

1. Trim the artichokes as follows: remove one row of leaves and cut off the dark-green tips of the others.

2. Into a large sauté pan put 1/2 pint/250 ml of water, the white wine, olive oil, lemon juice, a large pinch of salt, and 1 tablespoon of very coarsely ground pepper.

3. Bring to the boil, and add the artichokes, celery, parsley, fennel, thyme, bay leaf, garlic, and onions.

4. When the liquid has come back to the boil, cover and continue to cook over a medium heat until the marinade has reduced by three-quarters. Leave to cool.

5. Artichokes done in this way are usually served cold as an hors-d'oeuvre.

● ● ●

133 Barbecued Artichokes

Li Archicota où Fugaïroun / Les Artichauts au Barbecue

For 6

12 medium-sized globe artichokes (of the so-called 'Roman' variety, if possible – see page x)	2 lemons
	salt, pepper
	6 tbs olive oil

1. Three hours before the meal is due to start, remove the artichokes' tougher outside leaves and slice in half down the middle. Rub each half with lemon juice, season with salt and pepper, and brush with olive oil. Put the artichoke halves, cut-side up, in a cool place.

2. Prepare a barbecue and arrange the artichokes on the grill. Cook on both sides until they are tender when pierced with a skewer.

● The Roman variety has a stem that is edible for much of its length.

134 Marinated Wild Asparagus

Lu Espargou en Samoira

Les Asperges Sauvages en Marinade

Asparagus are usually eaten in Nice with vinaigrette, as they are elsewhere, so I shall give only the Niçois recipe for wild asparagus, which in April, under olive trees, stick out of the ground like little pencils. They have a quite inimitable flavour.

For 6

¼ pint/150 ml dry white wine	3 pinches thyme
6 tbs olive oil	2 cloves garlic, peeled
juice of 2 lemons	6 spring onions
salt	50 wild asparagus tips
1 tbs peppercorns	

1. Into a sauté pan put ½ pint/250 ml of water, the white wine, olive oil, lemon juice, a large pinch of salt, the slightly crushed peppercorns, the thyme, the crushed garlic, and the onions cut up in ½-inch/1-cm lengths, including the green stalks. Cover, bring to the boil, and cook for 20 minutes.

2. Add the asparagus tips, stir, cover, and cook for another 20 minutes over a very gentle heat. Leave to cool.

● Asparagus done this way are eaten cold either as an hors-d'oeuvre or in the place of a salad.

135 Stuffed Aubergines

Li Mérenjaïna Farcit / Les Aubergines Farcies

For 12

6 aubergines
1 clove garlic, peeled
1 large onion, peeled
2 anchovy fillets
1 tbs breadcrumbs
2 oz/50 g *petit salé* (see page xiii)

4 oz/100 g grated parmesan
2 eggs
salt, pepper
2 tbs olive oil
1/2 pint/250 ml *saoussoun* (No. 20)

1. Remove the stems and prickly ends of the aubergines. Wash the aubergines, dry, and blanch for 15 minutes with the garlic and the quartered onion.

2. Cut the aubergines in half lengthwise. Scoop out the flesh and set aside.

3. Wash the salt off the anchovy fillets, mash, and put in a mixing bowl with the breadcrumbs, diced *petit salé*, Parmesan, beaten eggs, and aubergine flesh. Check seasoning and add salt and pepper if necessary.

4. Fill the aubergine shells with the mixture and lay in an oiled gratin dish. With a small spoon, spread a thin layer of *saoussoun* over each aubergine; sprinkle with olive oil and bake in a medium oven for 1 hour.

136 Aubergine Gratin

Li Mérenjaïna Broustoulit / Les Aubergines au Gratin

For 6

6 large aubergines	1 pinch wild marjoram (*origano*)
10 tbs olive oil	4 leaves basil
4 cloves garlic, peeled	salt, pepper
1 lb/500 g very ripe tomatoes	flour

1. Peel the aubergines and cut lengthwise into thin slices. Sprinkle with salt and pile the slices on top of each other in a deep round dish. Cover with a plate and a heavy weight.

2. Heat 4 tablespoons of olive oil. Just as it is beginning to smoke, put in the chopped garlic. When it is golden brown, add the peeled, seeded, coarsely chopped, and drained tomatoes, the wild marjoram, and the chopped basil. Season with salt and pepper.

3. Drain the aubergine slices and dry with kitchen paper. In another pan heat 6 tablespoons of olive oil until just smoking. Fry the lightly floured slices in it briefly on both sides. Remove them and drain on kitchen paper.

4. Lay a row of aubergine slices in a well-oiled gratin dish, and cover with a layer of tomato sauce. Repeat the operation until the ingredients are used up, ending with a layer of tomato sauce.

5. Bake in a medium oven for 30 minutes.

● ● ●

137 Aubergines with Eggs

Li Mérenjaïna a l'Où / Les Aubergines à l'Oeuf

For 6

6 medium-sized aubergines	pepper
salt	4 egg yolks
1 onion, peeled	2 oz/50 g *petit salé* (see page xiii)
1 pint/500 ml *béchamel* sauce	1 tbs olive oil
2 oz/50 g grated Parmesan	

1. Remove the stems and prickly ends of the aubergines. Blanch the aubergines for 20 minutes in salt water with the quartered onion.

2. Leave the aubergines to cool, then cut them in half lengthwise. Scoop out the flesh with a teaspoon and set aside in a mixing bowl.

3. Make a fairly thick *béchamel* sauce, and add the Parmesan to it. Add pepper to taste.

4. Mash the aubergine flesh in the bowl with a fork, and gradually mix in the egg yolks, the *béchamel* sauce, and the diced *petit salé*. Fill the aubergine shells with the mixture, lay them in an oiled gratin dish, and brown in a hot oven for 15 minutes.

• • •

138 Aubergine Fritters

Li Mérenjaïna en Bignéta / Les Beignets d'Aubergines

For 6

4 medium-sized aubergines	salt
5 oz/150 g flour	½ pint/250 ml milk
2 eggs, separated	pepper
1 tsp olive oil	oil for deep frying

1. Peel the aubergines and cut them into roundels ½ inch/1 cm thick. Salt them and lay on the bottom of a deep round dish. Cover with a plate and a weight of about 2 lb/1 kg.

2. Put the flour into a mixing bowl. Make a well in the middle. Put in 2 egg yolks, a teaspoon of olive oil, and a pinch of salt. With a whisk, gradually incorporate the cold milk. At the last moment, beat the 2 egg whites until stiff and fold into the batter.

3. Dry the aubergine slices with kitchen paper, grind a little pepper on them, and drop them into the batter.

4. Heat the deep-frying oil till smoking, then quickly spoon in the aubergine slices, which should be completely covered in batter. Fry until golden, then drain on kitchen paper.

139 Aubergines with Onions and Tomatoes

Li Mérenjaïna aï Céba é aï Toùmati
Les Aubergines à l'Oignon et à la Tomate

For 6

3 large aubergines (if possible, long and thin)	6 tomatoes
	3 tbs olive oil
salt	6 cloves garlic, peeled
6 large onions, peeled	2 tbs chopped parsley

1. Clean the aubergines, remove their stems and prickly ends, peel, and cut in half lengthwise. Make two or three incisions along the thickest part of the aubergines, on the cut side. Sprinkle salt on them, place them in several layers in a bowl, and cover with water. Put a plate on top of them with a weight of about 1 lb/500 g, and leave for 30 minutes at normal room temperature.

2. Slice the onions into rings and put them in a large sieve standing on a hollow dish. Sprinkle them with 3 tablespoons of salt and toss well so that it is evenly distributed. Leave for 30 minutes. Then wash the onions very thoroughly under running warm water, squeezing them so that they lose every trace of salt.

3. Put the onions into a bowl with the peeled, seeded, chopped and drained tomatoes, and mix.

4. Put 2 tablespoons of olive oil in an enamelled iron gratin dish large enough to take all the aubergines in a single layer.

5. Drain the aubergines, rinse them in cold water, pat them dry with kitchen paper, and arrange them in the dish, cut side up.

6. Cover with the tomato and onion mixture. Put a clove of garlic on each aubergine half and sprinkle with 1 tablespoon of olive oil. Pour ½ pint/ 250 ml of water into the bottom of the dish and bring to the boil over a high heat.

7. Put into a slow oven and leave for 1¼ hours, so the aubergines are tender.

8. The aubergines should be served at room temperature, with a spoonful or two of the cooking juices and some chopped parsley.

140 Boiled Swiss Chard Tops
La Bléa Buida / La Blette Bouillie

Swiss chard tops go into a very large number of Niçois dishes, but are almost never eaten on their own except boiled, much in the same way as spinach.

For 6

25 Swiss chard tops	vinaigrette *or* olive oil
salt	

1. Bring 4½ quarts/5 litres of water to the boil.

2. Wash the Swiss chard tops thoroughly, dry carefully, and put into the boiling water with a pinch of salt.

3. Vegetables should never be overcooked, as they are, unfortunately, all too often. Each variety retains its own characteristic flavour when lightly cooked, whereas the lengthy boiling to which vegetables are usually subjected results in them all tasting like hay. So after 10 minutes, remove the chard from the boiling water and leave to drain in a colander for at least 2 hours.

4. Swiss chard tops cooked in this way are eaten cold, either with vinaigrette or simply with a little olive oil.

● ● ●

141 Swiss Chard Stalks
Li Couasta dé Bléa / Les Côtes de Blette

For 6

3 cloves garlic, peeled	1 lb/500 g Swiss chard stalks
1 onion, peeled	1 anchovy fillet
9 sprigs parsley	1 tbs flour
½ bay leaf	1 tbs olive oil
3 pinches thyme	salt, pepper
piece of chilli ½ inch/1 cm long	

1. Put 1 clove of garlic, the onion, 6 sprigs of parsley, the bay leaf, thyme, and chilli in a large saucepan with 4 pints/2 litres of water. Bring to the boil and simmer for 1 hour.

2. Cut the Swiss chard stalks into 1½-inch/4-cm lengths and blanch in the *court-bouillon* for 10 minutes.

3. Pound the anchovy fillet and 2 cloves of garlic to a paste in a mortar.

4. Put the flour and olive oil into a small thick-bottomed saucepan, mix well, and cook gently until a *roux* is obtained. Add the anchovy and garlic paste and the rest of the parsley, chopped. Mix thoroughly, then dilute with about ½ pint/300 ml of the *court-bouillon*. Simmer very gently until the sauce has thickened slightly. Adjust seasoning.

5. Put the Swiss chard pieces into a gratin dish, cover with the sauce, and brown lightly under a grill.

● ● ●

142 Trouchia
La Trouchia / La Trouchia

Trouchia, a kind of omelette made with Swiss chard tops, is a tasty and substantial dish. Because it is good when eaten cold, and is firm and easily transported, it forms the basis of picnic fare in the Nice area.

For 6

4½ lb/2 kg Swiss chard tops	2 tbs chopped parsley
8 eggs	salt, pepper
7 oz/200 g grated Parmesan	4 tbs olive oil
3 tbs chopped chervil	

1. Wash the Swiss chard tops thoroughly and cut into strips ⅛ inch/3 mm wide.

2. Beat the eggs in a large bowl and add the Parmesan, Swiss chard tops, and finely chopped chervil and parsley. Season with salt and plenty of pepper.

3. Put 3 tablespoons of the olive oil into a large non-stick frying pan (plenty of oil is needed as the *trouchia* absorbs a lot), add the omelette mixture, and place over a medium heat, prodding vigorously with a wooden spoon until the Swiss chard strips sink to the level of the edge of the pan. Cover with a dish of exactly the same size as the frying pan at its circumference, and cook over a moderate heat for 20 minutes.

4. Make sure the *trouchia* has not stuck to the pan (hence the importance of using a non-stick pan), and, with a strong, confident movement, turn the pan and the plate upside down so the *trouchia* sits on the plate. Return the pan to the stove, add 1 tablespoon of olive oil, and slide the *trouchia* back into the pan to cook on the other side. Put the plate back on the pan and cook over a moderate heat for a further 30 minutes.

● This is quite a tricky recipe, as the Swiss chard tops must be given time to cook properly without burning (which makes them turn bitter).

● A few basil leaves may also be used to flavour *trouchia*.

143 Marinated Broccoli
Lu Brocoli en Samoira / Les Brocoli en Marinade

For 6

2¾ lb/1,200 g broccoli	salt
¼ pint/150 ml dry white wine	2 tbs very coarsely ground pepper
4 tbs olive oil	2 pinches thyme
juice of 2 lemons	2 cloves garlic, peeled
5 sprigs parsley	6 spring onions

1. Blanch the broccoli for 10 minutes in plenty of slightly salted, gently boiling water.

2. Put into a sauté pan ½ pint/250 ml of water, the white wine, olive oil, lemon juice, parsley, pepper, a pinch of salt, thyme, garlic, and the spring onions cut up into 1-inch/3-cm lengths, including the green stalk.

3. Bring to the boil, cover, and cook over a medium heat for 30 minutes.

4. Cut the drained broccoli into walnut-sized pieces and add to the sauté pan. Bring back to the boil and cook, uncovered, for another 10 minutes.

5. Like all vegetables cooked in this way, the broccoli should be eaten at room temperature.

• • •

144 Niçois Cardoons
Lou Cardou Nissart / Le Cardon Niçois

This somewhat rare vegetable used to be grown specifically for Christmas: it formed the *plat de résistance* of the Christmas dinner. But the people of Nice came to like it so much that they now eat it throughout the winter.

Cardoon juice stains the fingers almost indelibly, so it is advisable to use kitchen gloves when preparing them for cooking.

For 6

3 lb/1½ kg cardoons	½ chilli
5 cloves garlic, peeled	1 tbs flour
2 large onions, peeled	1 tbs olive oil
8 sprigs parsley	4 anchovy fillets
1 bay leaf	salt, pepper
2 sprigs thyme	

1. Trim the cardoons, keeping only the central portion of each stalk. Cut up into 1-inch/3-cm lengths, removing all pieces of stringy fibre. Put each piece into cold water as it is ready, so as to avoid blackening.

2. Put 5 pints/3 litres of water into a large saucepan with 2 cloves of garlic, the quartered onions, 5 sprigs parsley, the bay leaf, thyme, and chilli. Bring to the boil.

3. Blanch the cardoon pieces in the *court-bouillon* for 20 minutes. Then drain and set aside in a thick-bottomed casserole.

4. Put the flour and olive oil into a small thick-bottomed saucepan, mix well, and cook gently until a *roux* is obtained.

5. Wash all the salt off the anchovy fillets, and remove bones if necessary. Put in a mortar with 3 cloves of garlic and pound to a paste. Chop the remaining parsley and add. Mix well, add to the *roux*, and cook for a few minutes stirring continuously with a wooden spoon.

6. Dilute the *roux* with ½ to ¾ pint/300 to 400 ml of the *court-bouillon*. Simmer very gently until the sauce has thickened slightly. Adjust seasoning.

7. Pour the sauce over the cardoons and warm gently until ready to serve.

● ● ●

145 Braised Celery
Lu Api Broustoulit / Le Céleri Braisé

For 6

6 medium-sized celery heads	1 clove garlic, peeled
2 tbs olive oil	¼ bay leaf
2 oz/50 g *petit salé* (see page xiii)	½ pint/250 ml stock
1 carrot, peeled	salt, pepper
1 onion, peeled	

1. Cut off the celery tops to make each head 6 inches/15 cm long. Wash and brush thoroughly, running water between the stalks to remove all traces of grit.

2. Blanch the celery heads in boiling water for 5 minutes.

3. Put the olive oil in a casserole and gently brown the diced *petit salé*, the chopped carrot, onion, and garlic, and the bay leaf. Dilute with the stock, and add the celery. Adjust seasoning.

4. Cover and bake in a low oven for 40 minutes.

5. Take out the celery and cut in half lengthwise. Arrange on a dish and cover with the cooking liquid.

146 Marinated Celery
Lu Api en Samoira / Le Céleri en Marinade

For 6

6 medium-sized celery heads	salt
6 tbs olive oil	1 tsp very coarsely ground pepper
1/4 pint/150 ml dry white wine	2 tbs chopped parsley
juice of 2 lemons	6 shallots, peeled
2 sprigs thyme	

1. Remove from the celery heads any stalks that are too stringy or any leaves that are too green. Then wash thoroughly, running water between the stalks to remove all traces of grit. Quarter the celery heads lengthwise, and cut up each piece into 1-inch/3-cm lengths.

2. Heat the olive oil in a frying pan. Just as it is beginning to smoke, put in the celery pieces and brown for 3 minutes. Set aside.

3. Into a sauté pan put 1/2 pint/250 ml of water, the white wine, the lemon juice, the thyme, a pinch of salt, the pepper, the chopped parsley, and the finely sliced shallots. Bring to the boil, cover, and cook for 15 minutes. Add the celery pieces and the oil in which they have cooked. Bring back to the boil and cook, uncovered, over a medium heat for another 15 minutes.

4. Celery cooked in this way can be eaten either at room temperature instead of salad or as a cold hors-d'oeuvre.

• • •

147 Niçois Cèpes
Lu Boulet a la Nissarda / Les Cèpes à la Niçoise

For 6

31/4-4 lb/11/2-13/4 kg cèpe mushrooms	salt, pepper
4 tbs olive oil	3 cloves garlic, peeled
juice of 1 lemon	5 sprigs parsley
	2 tbs chopped chives

1. Wash the cèpes thoroughly in several changes of water.

2. Separate the stems from the caps, and put them both in a saucepan with 1 inch/2 cm of water, a pinch of salt, 1 tablespoon of olive oil, and the lemon juice. Bring to the boil, cook for 2 minutes, and drain.

3. Heat 2 tablespoons of olive oil in a frying pan. Just as it is beginning to smoke, put in the caps of the mushrooms and cook until well browned. Season with salt and pepper, and arrange upside down in an oiled gratin dish.

4. Chop the cèpe stems, garlic, and parsley, and brown in the frying pan over a fierce heat. Fill the upturned caps with the mixture, strew with finely chopped chives, and put into a very hot oven for 5 minutes.

● ● ●

148 Marinated Cultivated Mushrooms

Lu Boulétet en Samoira
Les Champignons de Couche, dits 'de Paris', en Marinade

Cultivated mushrooms are often known as *champignons de Paris* in French – which does not stop them being grown in vast quantities in the Comté de Nice, where they are cooked in most of the ways familiar from classical French cuisine. The following recipe is a typically Niçois invention.

For 6

1¹/4 lb/600 g cultivated mushrooms	2 sprigs thyme
5 tbs olive oil	3 leaves rosemary
¹/4 pint/150 ml dry white wine	1 clove garlic, peeled
juice of 3 lemons	³/4 lb/300 g pickling onions, peeled
salt	4 oz/100 g sultanas
1 tsp very coarsely ground pepper	

1. Wash and brush the mushrooms thoroughly. Put them in a saucepan with 1 tablespoon of olive oil, cover, and put over a gentle heat. The mushrooms will give off their liquid. Continue cooking until it has completely evaporated, making sure to remove the saucepan from the heat just as soon as the mushrooms are almost dry.

2. Into a sauté pan put ¹/2 pint/250 ml of water, the white wine, the juice of 2 lemons, 4 tablespoons of olive oil, a large pinch of salt, the pepper, thyme, and rosemary, the halved clove of garlic, the pickling onions, and the sultanas (which should have already soaked for 1 hour in lukewarm water). Bring to the boil, add the mushrooms, and cook, covered, over a fairly high heat until the volume of liquid has reduced by three-quarters.

3. Leave to cool and add the juice of 1 lemon before serving.

● Two tablespoonfuls of *saoussoun* (No. 20) can also be added before serving if so desired.

149 Lactarius sanguifluus or Lactarius deliciosus
Lu Boulet Sanguin / Les Sanguins

For 6

4 lb/2 kg *Lactarius sanguifluus or
  L. deliciosus* (see page xi)
6 tbs olive oil
1 clove garlic, peeled
2 pinches thyme

1/4 pint/150 ml dry white wine
1/2 bay leaf
juice of 2 lemons
salt
1 tsp peppercorns

1. Wash and brush the mushrooms thoroughly. Cut both caps and stalks into slices 1/4 inch/5 mm thick.

2. Heat the olive oil in a sauté pan. Just as it is beginning to smoke, put in the sliced mushrooms, the garlic, and the thyme. When they are well browned, add the white wine, bay leaf, lemon juice, a good pinch of salt, the peppercorns, and enough water to cover.

3. Bring to the boil, cover, and cook until the volume of liquid has reduced by three-quarters.

4. *Lactarius sanguifluus* cooked in this way is usually served hot, either to accompany a meat dish or as a course on its own. However, it is equally good cold.

● ● ●

150 Marinated Chayote
La Chaïota en Samoira / La Chayote en Marinade

For 6

3 chayotes
4 tbs olive oil
2 cloves garlic, peeled
6 spring onions
7 fl oz/200 ml dry white wine
juice of 2 lemons

salt
1 tsp coarsely ground pepper
2 small stalks celery
2 tbs chopped parsley
2 sprigs thyme
1/4 bay leaf

1. Peel the chayotes, cut them in half, and discard their single seeds; these are enclosed in husks, which should also be removed with the point of a knife. Cut up the flesh into 1-inch/3-cm cubes.

2. Heat the olive oil in a sauté pan, then add the garlic, the spring onions cut into 1-inch/3-cm sections (including the green part of the stalk), and the chayote pieces. Brown well for about 10 minutes, then add the white wine, 1/2 pint/250 ml water, the lemon juice, a large pinch of salt, the pepper, finely sliced celery, chopped parsley, thyme, and bay leaf.

3. Bring to the boil, cover, and reduce over a medium heat for 40 minutes.

● ● ●

151 Stewed Scarole

La Chicoria Broustoulit / La Chicorée Braisée

For 6

the green leaves of 4 scaroles	2 sprigs parsley
1 tbs flour	1 clove garlic, peeled
1 tbs olive oil	6 tbs juice from a roast (failing that,
1 onion, peeled	stock will do), *or* 3 tbs cream
1 carrot, peeled	salt, pepper
1 pinch thyme	

1. Cut the scaroles in half, discard any bruised or discoloured parts, and keep the white leaves for a salad.

2. Blanch the green leaves for 5 minutes in salted boiling water.

3. Strain, rinse in cold water, squeeze out as much liquid as possible, and chop finely.

4. Make a *roux* with the flour and olive oil, then add the onion and the carrot (both whole), the thyme, and the chopped parsley and garlic. Incorporate the scarole, mix well, and add two thirds of the meat juice or cream. Season with salt and pepper.

5. Put the mixture into a casserole, cover, and put in a medium oven for 1 1/2 hours. When the time is up, remove the onion and carrot, dilute if necessary with the rest of the meat juice or cream, and serve.

152 Stuffed Cabbages

Lu Capoun / Les Choux Farcis

For 6

6 small, well-rounded green cabbages	3 eggs
2 oz/50 g rice	3 tbs olive oil
5 oz/150 g *petit salé* (see page xiii)	salt, pepper
4 oz/100 g grated Parmesan	1¼ pints/750 ml vegetable stock

1. Remove all the leaves of the cabbages, putting the large and small leaves into separate piles.

2. Wash the large leaves, plunge for a minute or two into boiling water, and lay out on a clean tea-towel. Flatten their midribs with a broad knife or rolling-pin.

3. Wash and blanch the small leaves from the cabbage hearts, then chop very finely.

4. Boil the rice for 10 minutes. Cut the *petit salé* into very small pieces.

5. Put the chopped cabbage leaves, strained rice, *petit salé*, Parmesan, and beaten eggs into a large bowl and mix well. Add 2 tablespoons of olive oil and a good teaspoon of ground pepper, and salt if required, and mix again. Now stuff the large cabbage leaves with the mixture: use one, two, or three (but no more) leaves to make each ball, making sure that the stuffing is completely enveloped, and truss with white thread.

6. Arrange the stuffed cabbage leaves tightly in a casserole, and cover completely with stock. Cover and cook in a medium oven for 1½ hours.

7. Take the stuffed cabbage leaves out of the casserole, remove the thread, put them in an oiled gratin dish and dry in a hot oven for 15 minutes. Another method is to brown them in a frying pan: this makes them tastier but less digestible.

● See also No. 2.

153 Cauliflower Gratin
Lou Caoulé-Flou Broustoulit / Le Gratin de Chou-Fleur

Raw cauliflower is one of the basic vegetables served with *bagna caouda* (No. 23); but, once blanched, it can also be eaten with a simple vinaigrette dressing or in fritters (according to the procedure used for aubergines in No. 138). There can be no doubt, however, that the commonest method of preparing cauliflower in the Nice area is in a gratin.

For 6

1 large cauliflower	breadcrumbs
salt	pepper
5 tbs olive oil	4 oz/100 g grated Parmesan

1. Blanch the cauliflower in plenty of salted water for 15 minutes.

2. Strain, leave to cool, and cut into chunks about 2 inches/5 cm long. Pack tightly into a gratin dish, sprinkle evenly with the olive oil, breadcrumbs, pepper and Parmesan, and brown in a hot oven.

● ● ●

154 Savoy Cabbage with Rice
Lou Caoulé Rissa où Ris / Le Chou Frisé au Riz

For 6

1 large Savoy cabbage	2 pinches thyme
12 slices smoked streaky bacon	salt, pepper
2 carrots, peeled	2 oz/50 g rice
1 large onion, peeled	6 thin slices ham

1. Excise the stem of the cabbage. Blanch the cabbage in salted water for 5 minutes.

2. Line the inside of a round casserole with the bacon, and place the cabbage in the middle.

3. Ease the leaves of the cabbage open, and put the sliced carrots and onion in the middle with a sprinkling of thyme, salt, and pepper. Cover the casserole and put in a low oven for 20 minutes.

4. Remove the casserole from the oven, ease the leaves of the cabbage open again and drop in the rice. If the cabbage looks likely to dry up, add a little boiling water. Cover and bake for another 45 minutes.

5. Just before serving, lay the slices of ham over the top of the cabbage and cover. When they have had time to heat up, serve.

155 Brussels Sprouts
Lu Caoulé Belga / Les Choux de Bruxelles

For 6

2 lb/1 kg Brussels sprouts	2 cloves garlic, peeled
6 tbs olive oil	salt, pepper

1. Trim and wash the sprouts. Put them in salted boiling water and simmer for 15 minutes (boiling damages the compactness of the leaves).

2. Plunge in cold water and drain. Heat the olive oil in a frying pan until it is just beginning to smoke, then add the sprouts. Fry gently until cooked.

3. Chop the garlic finely and sprinkle over the sprouts. Add salt and pepper to taste.

● Brussels sprouts can also be served as a purée: simply purée them after the final stage and decorate with fried *croûtons*.

● ● ●

156 Courgette Salad
Li Cougourdéta en Salada / Les Courgettes en Salade

For 6

12 very small courgettes	1 tbs vinegar or ½ tbs lemon juice
4 tbs olive oil	salt, pepper

1. Wash the courgettes and blanch in salted boiling water for 20 minutes. Drain.

2. Make a salad dressing with the other ingredients, pour it over the courgettes when they are lukewarm, and serve.

157 Stuffed Courgettes

Li Cougourdéta Farcit / Les Courgettes Farcies

For 12

12 small courgettes (round, if possible – see page x)	5 leaves basil
1 large onion	4 oz/100 g grated Parmesan
2 oz/50 g rice	2 eggs
1 clove garlic, peeled	salt, pepper
2 oz/50 g *petit salé* (see page xiii)	breadcrumbs
	1 tbs olive oil

1. Wash the courgettes and blanch them in unsalted water for 15 minutes along with the onion, peeled and quartered.

2. Cook the rice in plenty of water for 20 minutes, then drain.

3. Cut the courgettes in half and place them, cut-side up, on a table. Scoop out the flesh of each half-courgette with a small spoon, taking care not to pierce the skin.

4. Chop the courgette flesh, the onion, garlic, *petit salé*, and basil.

5. Mix well in a large bowl with the Parmesan, rice and beaten eggs. Add salt and pepper to taste.

6. Fill the courgettes with this mixture, sprinkle with a few breadcrumbs, and arrange in a previously oiled gratin dish. Cook in a medium oven for 45 minutes.

158 Stuffed Courgette Flowers

Li Flou dé Cougourdéta Farcit
Les Fleurs de Courgettes Farcies

For 6

18 courgette flowers	2 eggs
2 small courgettes	2 oz/50 g grated Parmesan
1 onion, peeled	salt, pepper
1 oz/25 g rice	1 tbs olive oil
1 oz/25 g *petit salé* (see page xiii)	1 clove garlic, peeled

1. Remove the pistil from each courgette flower.

2. Blanch the courgettes and the onion for 15 minutes, then drain.

3. Boil the rice for 20 minutes, then drain.

4. Chop the onion, mash the courgettes with a fork, cut 6 courgette flowers into strips, chop the *petit salé* and beat the eggs. Put in a large bowl with the rice and Parmesan, and mix well. Season to taste and add the garlic, finely chopped.

5. Open out the remaining courgette flowers and press gently flat on a board. Fill the centre of each flower with the stuffing, using a small spoon and taking great care not to pierce the petals. Wrap the petals one by one over the stuffing so that it is completely covered.

6. Arrange the stuffed flowers, lengthwise and head to tail, in a previously oiled gratin dish into which they fit neatly, and cook in a medium oven for 30 minutes.

● In one variation of this dish, *saoussoun* (No. 20) is spread thinly over the stuffed flowers after 20 minutes' cooking time. They are then returned to the oven for a further 15 minutes.

159 Courgette Flower Fritters
Li Bignéta dé Flou dé Cougourdéta
Les Beignets de Fleurs de Courgette

For 6

36 courgette flowers	1 tsp olive oil
5 oz/150 g flour	1/2 pint/250 ml milk
2 eggs	3 tbs chopped parsley
salt, pepper	oil for deep frying

1. Wash the courgette flowers. Remove their stems and the rather tough pistils inside the petals. Set aside.

2. Put the flour in a mixing bowl. Make a well in the middle and put into it 2 egg yolks, a pinch of salt, and the olive oil. Beat with a whisk, and, still beating, gradually add the milk. Whip the egg whites until stiff and fold into the mixture.

3. Chop the parsley and incorporate into the batter. Season with salt and pepper.

4. Dip the flowers one after the other into the batter and drop into very hot deep-frying oil. Transfer when golden to a serving dish lined with paper napkins.

● Courgette flower fritters are served warm, but not sizzling, either with a *saoussoun* (No. 20) or with a *saoussoun crut* (No. 21).

● ● ●

160 Courgette Gratin
Li Cougourdéta Broustoulit / Les Courgettes au Gratin

For 6

3 cloves garlic, peeled	salt, pepper
12 small courgettes	breadcrumbs
1 tbs olive oil	2 oz/50 gg grated Parmesan

1. Put the garlic into a large saucepan with 4 pints/2 litres of water and bring to the boil. After 30 minutes' boiling, add the courgettes. Blanch for 15 minutes, then drain.

2. Leave the courgettes to cool, cut into slices, and arrange in an oiled gratin dish.

3. Sprinkle with salt, pepper, breadcrumbs and Parmesan, and cook in a medium oven until brown on top. Serve piping hot.

161 Courgette Purée

La Puréa dé Cougourdéta / La Purée de Courgettes

For 6

12 small courgettes	3 tbs olive oil
1 onion, peeled	2 leaves basil
3 cloves garlic, peeled	salt, pepper

1. Blanch the courgettes for 20 minutes in salted boiling water. Strain, allow to cool, break into pieces with the fingers, and leave to drain in a colander for at least an hour.

2. Slice the onion and garlic, and brown in a frying pan with the olive oil. Add the courgettes and chopped basil, mix well, and purée. Season with salt and pepper. Put the purée into a thick-bottomed saucepan over a gentle heat, and simmer until a thicker purée consistency is obtained.

● Courgette purée may be served either with *croûtons* fried in olive oil or with fried eggs on top (1 per person).

● ● ●

162 Courgette Tian

Lou Tian dé Cougourdéta / Le Tian de Courgettes

For 6

2 lb/1 kg courgettes	3 eggs
10 Swiss chard tops	6 leaves basil *or*, if unavailable, 2 tbs
10 courgette flowers	chopped parsley
3 tbs olive oil	2 oz/50 g lean *petit salé* (see page xiii)
2 onions, peeled	2 oz/50 g grated Parmesan
1 clove garlic, peeled	salt, pepper
2 oz/50 g rice	

1. Blanch the courgettes in plenty of boiling water. When they can be easily pierced with a pointed knife, cut into 2-inch/5-cm lengths and leave to drain for an hour.

2. Purée (but not too smoothly) the courgettes and mix with the chopped Swiss chard tops and sliced courgette flowers.

3. Heat 2 tablespoons of the olive oil in a frying pan and brown the finely chopped onions and garlic. Stir into the puréed courgette mixture.

4. Blanch the rice in plenty of water for 10 minutes, then rinse in warm water until it has lost all its starch and the water runs clear. Drain and mix with the other ingredients.

5. Beat the eggs, add the finely chopped basil or parsley, the *petit salé* cut into small dice, the Parmesan, salt, and pepper, and mix with the other ingredients.

6. Pour all the ingredients into an oiled gratin or soufflé dish and cook in a medium oven for 45 minutes. Then turn up the heat and brown the top for a further 10 minutes. Serve immediately.

• • •

163 Courgette Pie
La Tourta dé Cougourdéta / La Tourte de Courgette

This recipe is a particular favourite with the people who live in the upper part of the Comté de Nice, around the villages of Sospel, Moulinet, and Breil: they find it a very practical picnic dish when they make outings on the mountains that overlook the valley of the River Bévéra.

For 6

1 lb/500 g courgettes (*or* pumpkin – see page x)	2¹/₂ oz/70 g grated Parmesan
¹/₂ oz/15 g rice	salt, pepper
1 onion, peeled	5 oz/150 g flour
1 egg	2 tbs olive oil

1. Wash the courgettes, wipe dry, and cut into ¹/₂-inch/1-cm dice. Put them in a bowl, sprinkle with salt, shake well, and leave them to give up their liquid for an hour. Then transfer them to a colander and rinse in plenty of cold water.

2. Pat the courgette pieces dry and put in a mixing bowl with the rice, chopped onion, egg, and Parmesan. Add pepper and a little salt, mix well, and set aside.

3. Make a well in the flour and put into it 1 pinch of salt, 1 tablespoon of olive oil, and 4 tablespoons of water. Knead vigorously and form into a smooth ball. Cut the ball in half and leave for an hour.

4. Roll out half the pastry and line an oiled medium-sized (12 inch/30 cm) tart tin (the pastry should be no more than ¹/₁₀ inch/2 mm thick). Fill with the courgette mixture to a depth of no more than ¹/₂ inch/1¹/₂ cm. Moisten the pastry rim with water or beaten egg.

5. Roll out the rest of the pastry and lay on the mixture to form a lid. Knock up the edges. Prick the lid with a fork, and brush lightly with olive oil.

6. Put into a hot oven for 40 minutes, then under a grill (if possible while still in the oven) for 5 minutes.

7. Take the pie out of the oven, cover with a clean teacloth, and leave at room temperature for 15 minutes, so the pastry does not crumble when cut. Serve hot or cold.

● (Ed. note: The quantity of pastry for this pie may seem impossibly small; but, when rolled very thin as indicated in the recipe, it produces a firm, dry yet unbrittle crust that is indeed ideal for picnics.)

● ● ●

164 Creamed Spinach
Lu Spinouos a la Créma / Les Épinards à la Crème

For 6

7¹/₂ lb/3¹/₂ kg spinach	¹/₂ pint/250 ml double cream
4 tbs olive oil	salt, pepper
1 small clove garlic, peeled	1 pinch sugar

1. Wash the spinach carefully in several changes of water. Plunge into a large saucepan of boiling salted water and cook for about 10 minutes. The spinach will be cooked when a leaf can be crushed between the fingers. Avoid overcooking, which renders the vegetable tasteless.

2. Strain the spinach in a colander and rinse in cold water. Remove to a chopping board, squeezing each handful well between the fingers to remove as much moisture as possible. Chop finely and leave to drain in a fine sieve.

3. Heat the olive oil in a thick-bottomed saucepan and add the finely chopped garlic. Just as it is beginning to turn golden, put in the spinach and cook for 5 minutes, stirring often with a wooden spoon.

4. Add the cream and continue cooking gently until a smooth purée is obtained.

5. Season with salt, pepper, and the sugar, and serve.

165 Spinach in Meat Juice
Lu Spinouos où Jus / Les Épinards au Jus

For 6

7½ lb/3½ kg spinach
4 tbs olive oil
1 small clove garlic, peeled
salt, pepper

1 pinch sugar
4 fl oz/120 ml meat juice (from a roast
  or stew)

1. Cook the spinach as in No. 164, steps 1 to 3.

2. Season with salt, pepper, and the sugar. Mix in two thirds of the meat juice and simmer for 2 minutes.

3. Transfer to a serving dish, sprinkle with the rest of the juice, and serve immediately.

● ● ●

166 Niçois Spinach
Lu Spinouos a la Nissarda / Les Épinards à la Niçoise

For 6

7½ lb/3½ kg spinach
5 tbs olive oil
2 cloves garlic, peeled

salt, pepper
6 eggs

1. Wash the spinach carefully in several changes of water. Drain, then cut into strips ¼ inch/½ cm thick.

2. Heat 4 tablespoons of olive oil in a thick-bottomed saucepan and add the finely chopped garlic. Just as it is beginning to turn golden, put in the spinach, season with salt and pepper, and, stirring constantly with a wooden spoon, cook until all the liquid has evaporated.

3. Beat the eggs and mix with the spinach. Transfer to a gratin dish, sprinkle with 1 tablespoon of olive oil, and put in a very hot oven for 10 minutes.

● This dish can either be served with meat or fish, or else constitute a main course, in which case 1 or 2 eggs per person should be broken over the spinach before it is put in the oven.

167 Spinach with Currants and Pine-Nuts

Lu Spinouos aï Raïn e aï Pignoun

Les Épinards aux Raisins et aux Pignons

For 6

7¹/₂ lb/3¹/₂ kg spinach
5 oz/150 g small currants
4 tbs olive oil

7 oz/200 g pine-nuts
salt, pepper

1. Wash the spinach carefully in several changes of water. Plunge into a large saucepan of boiling salted water and cook for about 10 minutes. The spinach is cooked when a leaf can be crushed between the fingers. Avoid overcooking, which renders the vegetable tasteless.

2. Strain the spinach in a colander, press down well, and leave to drain for an hour.

3. Soak the currants in lukewarm water for at least half an hour.

4. Heat the olive oil in a thick-bottomed saucepan and add the pine-nuts. Just as they are beginning to turn brown, add the currants and mix well with a wooden spoon. As soon as the oil heats up again, incorporate the spinach.

5. Season with salt and pepper, and serve.

● ● ●

168 Niçois Braised Florentine Fennel

Lou Fénouï Dous Broustoulit a la Nissarda

Le Fenouli Braisé à la Niçoise

For 6

³/₄ lb/300 g tomatoes
6 Florentine fennel heads

2 tbs olive oil
salt, pepper

1. Peel, seed, coarsely chop, and drain the tomatoes.

2. Slice off the base of the fennel heads and remove all the tougher stalks.

3. Drop the fennel into plenty of boiling salted water and blanch for 5 minutes. Strain and rinse with cold water.

4. Heat the olive oil in a casserole. Cut the fennel heads in half lengthwise and lay them face down in the casserole. Cover and simmer over a low heat for 30 minutes.

5. Add the tomatoes, season with salt and pepper, cover again, and simmer for a further 20 minutes. If there seems to be too much liquid, remove the lid and cook uncovered until the sauce has almost completely evaporated.

• • •

169 Marinated Florentine Fennel
Lou Fénouï Dous en Samoira / Le Fenouil en Marinade

For 6

6 Florentine fennel heads	2 sprigs thyme
6 tbs olive oil	½ bay leaf
1 tsp crushed black peppercorns	3 sprigs parsley
salt	2 cloves garlic, peeled
2 oz/50 g small currants	¼ pint/150 ml dry white wine
1 small stalk celery	juice of 2 lemons

1. Slice off the base of the fennel heads and remove all the tougher stalks. Cut the fennel into strips about ½ inch/1cm thick.

2. Put the olive oil, the crushed peppercorns, and a large pinch of salt into a sauté pan, and heat. Add the currants, which should have been previously soaked for about 30 minutes in lukewarm water, a *bouquet garni* consisting of celery, thyme, bay leaf, and parsley, and the garlic, whole. When these ingredients are beginning to brown in the oil, add the fennel, making sure it touches the bottom of the pan. Stir for 5 to 6 minutes.

3. Pour in the white wine, lemon juice, and ¼ pint/150 ml of water. Bring to the boil, cover, and cook over a moderate heat until the marinade has reduced by two thirds. Allow to cool to room temperature, then serve.

170 Broad Beans with Lettuce

Li Fava a la Lachouga / Les Fèves à la Laitue

For 6

3¹/₄ lb/1¹/₂ kg broad beans, shelled *or*	1 sprig *or* 1 pinch winter savory
1³/₄ lb/800 g dried broad beans	salt, pepper
6 spring onions	1 oz/30 g butter
2 lettuces	1 oz/30 g flour

1. Whether fresh or dried, fully-grown broad beans must have their outer skin removed (in the case of dried beans, this is done after they have been soaked).

2. Put the beans in a thick-bottomed saucepan with the onions cut into 1-inch/3-cm lengths (including the green stem), the lettuce, cut into strips ¹/₁₀ inch/2¹/₂ mm wide, the winter savory, and salt and pepper to taste. Almost cover with boiling water.

3. Bring to the boil and cook over a gentle heat for 30 minutes, or until almost all the liquid has evaporated.

4. Check the seasoning. Make a *beurre manié* with the butter and flour, and, over a very low heat, beat the paste into the remaining broad bean liquid until a proper sauce consistency is obtained.

• • •

171 Salad of Young Broad Beans

Li Favéta en Salada / Les Févettes en Salade

For 8

3¹/₄ lb/1¹/₂ kg young broad beans, shelled	3 carrots, peeled
	4 tbs olive oil
6 spring onions	1 tbs vinegar *or* ¹/₂ tbs lemon juice
2 lettuces	salt, pepper

1. Remove the small, bitter stem by which the broad beans are attached to their pods.

2. Bring plenty of salted water to the boil. Drop in the broad beans, onions, lettuces (whole), and carrots. Cook over a moderate heat for 45 minutes, then drain well.

3. Serve at room temperature with a dressing made with oil, vinegar or lemon juice, salt, and pepper.

172 Sautéed Young Broad Beans

Li Favéta Soùtat / Les Févettes Sautées

For 6

3¹/₄ lb/1¹/₂ kg young broad beans, shelled
¹/₂ lb/250 g *petit salé* (see page xiii)
6 tbs olive oil
6 spring onions

1 pinch winter savory
1 clove garlic, peeled
5 sprigs parsley
salt, pepper

---

1. Remove the small, bitter stem by which the broad beans are attached to their pods.

2. Chop the *petit salé* into very small pieces.

3. Heat the olive oil in a casserole and put in the *petit salé*. Just as it is beginning to colour, add the broad beans, the onions cut into ¹/₂-inch/1-cm lengths (including the green stem), the winter savory, and the garlic and parsley, both finely chopped.

4. Cook over a moderate heat, stirring constantly with a wooden spoon. The broad beans are ready when they have all changed colour from green to grey-green – at this point, when they are neither completely raw nor completely cooked, their flavour is at its peak. Season to taste with salt and pepper.

173 Young Broad Beans with Garlic
Li Favéta a l'Aïet / Les Févettes à l'Ail

For 6

3¹/₄ lb/1¹/₂ kg young broad beans, shelled
6 tbs olive oil

6 cloves garlic, peeled
¹/₂ lb/250 g breadcrumbs
salt, pepper

1. Remove the small, bitter stem by which the broad beans are attached to their pods.

2. Heat the olive oil in a flying pan. Just as it is beginning to smoke, drop in the cloves of garlic, previously crushed under a broad-bladed knife. Stir vigorously. When the garlic begins to colour, add the broad beans and cook over a fierce heat, stirring all the time.

3. When almost all the broad beans have turned grey-green, add the breadcrumbs and stir briskly to prevent them from either sticking to the pan or burning. Season with salt and pepper. Continue to cook for a minute or two, then transfer the contents of the pan to warmed serving dish.

● ● ●

174 French Beans with Garlic
Lu Faïoù fin a l'Aïet / Les Haricots Verts à l'Ail

For 6

1¹/₄ lb/600 g French beans
6 tbs olive oil
6 cloves garlic, peeled

7 oz/200 g breadcrumbs
salt, pepper

1. Top and tail the French beans, wash, and cut into 1-inch/3-cm lengths.

2. Heat the olive oil in a flying pan. Just as it is beginning to smoke, drop in the cloves of garlic, previously crushed under a broad-bladed knife.

3. When the garlic begins to colour, add the French beans and stir with a wooden spoon.

4. Cook over a fierce heat. When the French beans turn dark-green, add the breadcrumbs and stir briskly to prevent them from either sticking to the pan or burning.

5. Continue to cook for a moment or two, transfer to a warm dish, and add salt and pepper to taste.

175 Niçois Ragout of Haricot Beans

Lou Poutité dé Faïòù Grana a la Nissarda

Le Ragoût de Haricots Blancs à la Niçoise

For 6

2 lb/1 kg fresh haricot beans, shelled, or 1 lb/500 g dried

2 onions, peeled

12 sprigs parsley

7 oz/200 g lean pork

1 lb/500 g stewing mutton

7 oz/200 g *petit salé* (see page xiii)

6 tbs olive oil

2 cloves garlic, peeled

2 lb/1 kg tomatoes

½ bay leaf

1 small pinch thyme

½ pint/250 ml beef stock

salt, pepper

1. Put the beans in a large saucepan with 1 onion and 4 sprigs of parsley, cover with plenty of water, and bring to the boil (if dried haricot beans are used, they should first be soaked for 2 to 3 hours).

2. Cut the pork and mutton into chunks about 1 inch/3 cm square, and the *petit salé* into ½-inch/1-cm dice. Heat the oil in a sauté pan, and put in the meat.

3. When the meat has browned, add 1 chopped onion, the garlic crushed under a broad-bladed knife, the peeled, seeded, coarsely chopped, and drained tomatoes, 4 sprigs of parsley, the bay leaf, and the thyme. Cook over a brisk heat until the onion and garlic begin to colour, then add the beef stock, cover, and leave over a very low heat.

4. When the haricot beans are nearly cooked, add them to the meat, mix well, cover, and simmer very gently for at least an hour.

5. Before serving, season with salt and pepper and sprinkle with 4 chopped sprigs of parsley.

176 Haricot Bean Salad
Lu Faïoù Grana en Salada / Les Haricots Blancs en Salade

For 6

1¼ lb/600 g fresh haricot beans, shelled, *or* ¾ lb/300 g dried
1 large onion
1 clove garlic

½ bay leaf
3 sprigs parsley
3 tbs olive oil
salt, pepper

1. Put the beans in a large saucepan with the peeled onion and garlic, bay leaf, and parsley, cover with plenty of water, and bring to the boil (if dried haricot beans are used, they should first be soaked for 2 to 3 hours).

2. When the beans are cooked, drain well, then transfer to a salad bowl while still warm. Sprinkle with the olive oil, season with salt and pepper to taste, and serve immediately.

● ● ●

177 Braised Lettuce
Li Lachouga Broustoulit / Les Laitues Braisées

For 6

12 young lettuces
salt, pepper
1 pinch grated nutmeg
6 thin slices *petit salé* (see page xiii)
7 tbs olive oil

1 onion, peeled
2 carrots, peeled
1 pinch thyme
1 bay leaf
1 pint/500 ml veal stock

1. Remove any wilted leaves and trim the stems of the lettuces, which should be very small. Wash in several changes of water. Blanch for 5 minutes in a large saucepan of boiling salted water.

2. Drain, rinse in cold running water, squeeze out excess moisture, and place on a large chopping board.

3. Season the lettuces with salt, pepper, and nutmeg. Take 4 lettuces, lay them together lengthwise on the board, press down slightly to flatten them, roll 2 slices of *petit salé* round them, and tie together with strong thread into a sausage-shaped bundle. Repeat the operation with the rest of the lettuces.

4. Heat 6 tablespoons of olive oil in a casserole and, over a brisk heat, brown the chopped onion, sliced carrots, thyme, and bay leaf. Add the lettuce bundles, pour in ½ pint/250 ml of the veal stock, cover, and cook gently for 35 to 40 minutes.

5. Remove the lettuces, untie the bundles, set aside the *petit salé* and cut each lettuce in half lengthwise.

6. Fold each half lettuce over and arrange tightly in an oiled heat-proof serving dish. Heat the rest of the veal stock and pour over the lettuce. Boil uncovered for a few minutes, then serve with the diced *petit salé* on top.

● ● ●

178 Lentil Salad
Li Lentilha en Salada / Les Lentilles en Salade

For 6

11 oz/300 g brown lentils	*bouquet garni*
1 large onion, peeled	salt
6 carrots, peeled	4 tbs olive oil
2 cloves garlic	pepper

1. Put the lentils in warm water and soak for at least 6 hours in a large saucepan. Add the whole onion, carrots, peeled garlic, and *bouquet garni*, cover with more water if necessary, and bring to the boil.

2. In the early stages of boiling, skim the lentils. Then add salt, cover, and cook gently for an hour, or until the liquid reduces to form a thickish sauce.

3. Transfer to a salad bowl, sprinkle with olive oil and pepper, and serve warm.

● ● ●

179 Boiled Corn on the Cob
Lou Gran Turc Buit / Le Maïs Bouilli

For 6

6 cobs	pepper
2 pints/1 litre milk	6 tbs olive oil *or* 4 oz/100 g butter
salt	

1. Cut off the maize stalks 1 inch/3 cm below the cob. Remove the beards and larger leaves.

2. Put 2 quarts/2 litres of water and the milk into a high, narrow saucepan, add a large pinch of salt, and bring to the boil. Drop in the cobs, stalk end up, and cover with a folded, clean teacloth to keep the cobs in place. Simmer for 40 minutes.

3. Drain and serve in a folded napkin. The cobs are eaten with freshly ground pepper and melted butter or warm olive oil.

180 Grilled Corn on the Cob
Lou Gran Turc Rimat / Le Maïs Grillé

For 6

salt	pepper
6 cobs	6 tbs olive oil *or* 4 oz/100 g butter

1. Put 3 large pinches of salt into 11 pints/6 litres of cold water. Add the cobs, with their leaves and beards, and soak for 3 hours.

2. Remove the cobs from the water 2 hours before you intend to cook them, and strip off their beards, though not their leaves. Leave to drain.

3. Put the cobs, still wrapped in their leaves, on or under a grill and turn from time to time until the leaves have practically burnt away.

4. At this point (after about 40 minutes' cooking), rub off the burnt leaves with heat-proof gloves. The cobs are now ready: they can be eaten either on the cob, or shelled, in a salad bowl. In either case, they are served with freshly ground pepper and melted butter or warm olive oil.

● ● ●

181 Marinated Sweet Corn
Lou Gran Turc en Samoira / Le Maïs en Marinade

For 6

6 tbs olive oil	juice of 2 lemons
10 spring onions	2 oz/50 g sultanas, previously
1 clove garlic, peeled	soaked
1/2 bay leaf	1/4 pint/150 ml dry white wine
1 pinch thyme	11/4 lb/600 g fresh sweetcorn
salt	grains (*or* 11/4 lb/600 g
1 tsp crushed black peppercorns	well-drained tinned sweet corn)

1. Heat the olive oil in a sauté pan. Just as it is beginning to smoke, put in the onions cut into 1-inch/3-cm lengths (including the green stem), the garlic, bay leaf, thyme, salt, peppercorns, lemon juice, sultanas, white wine, and 1/2 pint/250 ml of water.

2. Bring to the boil, add the corn grains, cover, and reduce over a fairly high heat until most of the liquid has evaporated.

3. Leave to cool, and serve as an hors-d'oeuvre.

182 Mesclun Salad*
Lou Mesclun / Le Mesclun

For 6

4 oz/100 g rocket leaves	4 tbs olive oil
4 oz/100 g young dandelion leaves	1 tbs vinegar *or* ½ tbs lemon juice
2 young lettuces	salt, pepper

1. Discard wilted leaves and wash rocket, dandelion, and lettuce leaves very carefully in several changes of water. Dry thoroughly.

2. Serve with a vinaigrette dressing made of olive oil, vinegar or lemon juice, salt and pepper.

● A few leaves of watercress and/or chervil may be added to the salad.

* See page x.

• • •

183 Turnip Gratin
Lu Navéou Broustoulit / Les Navets au Gratin

For 6

2¾ lb/1,200 g very young, tender turnips	2 tbs olive oil
1 onion, peeled	salt, pepper
1 clove garlic, peeled	5 oz/150 g grated Parmesan

1. Wash and peel the turnips, trimming them all to the size of a small new potato.

2. Put the sliced onion, finely chopped garlic, and olive oil into a gratin dish, and arrange the turnips neatly on top. Season with salt and pepper.

3. Cook in a medium oven for 20 minutes. Remove, and prick the turnips with a pointed knife: if they are still rather firm, add ¼ pint/150 ml of water and cook for a further 10 minutes. Repeat the operation if necessary, until the knife pierces the vegetables easily.

4. Sprinkle the gratin with grated Parmesan, and brown in a hot oven.

184 Marinated Onions

Li Céba en Samoira / Les Oignons en Marinade

For 6

6 tbs olive oil	1 tsp coriander seeds
2 lb/1 kg pickling onions, spring onions, *or* onions, peeled	1 tsp black peppercorns
	2 tsp sugar
5 sprigs parsley	juice of 2 lemons
2 cloves garlic, peeled	1/4 pint/150 ml dry white wine
5 oz/150 g Malaga raisins	2 tbs vinegar
4 pinches thyme	salt
1/2 bay leaf	

1. Heat the olive oil in a sauté pan. Just as it is beginning to smoke, add the onions (quartered in the case of ordinary-sized onions). When they turn golden, add the parsley, garlic, raisins, thyme, bay leaf, coriander seeds, peppercorns, sugar, lemon juice, white wine, vinegar, and salt to taste.

2. Bring to the boil, cover, and cook over a fierce heat.

3. Keep a sharp eye on operations, and when the liquid has reduced by half, remove the lid and continue to reduce over a gentle heat until a syrupy sauce is obtained. Serve cold.

185 Stuffed Onions
Li Céba Farcit / Les Oignons Farcis

For 12

6 very large onions	2 eggs
2 oz/50 g rice	salt, pepper
2 oz/50 g lean *petit salé* (see page xiii)	breadcrumbs
5 leaves basil	2 tbs olive oil
4 oz/100 g grated Parmesan	

1. Peel the onions, cut in half crosswise, and blanch in simmering water for 10 minutes.

2. Drain well, and scoop out the centre of each half onion, leaving only the two outer layers of flesh. Set aside.

3. Cook the rice in plenty of water for 20 minutes, strain, and put into a mixing bowl. Add the chopped onion centres, the finely chopped *petit salé* and basil, the Parmesan, and the beaten eggs. Season to taste with salt and pepper, and mix well.

4. Fill the onion shells with this mixture, arrange them in an oiled gratin dish, and sprinkle generously with breadcrumbs.

5. Pour a few drops of olive oil over each onion half and bake in a medium oven for 30 minutes.

6. Stuffed onions can be eaten hot; but in summer they are better served cold, along with other stuffed vegetables.

● ● ●

186 Panisses with Leeks
Li Panissa aï Pouaré / Les Panisses aux Poireaux

For 6

3 lb/1½ kg *panisses* (No. 50)	1 lb/500 g leeks
3 tbs olive oil	½ pint/250 ml meat stock
salt, pepper	

1. Cut the *panisses* into strips ½ inch/1 cm thick and arrange in an oiled gratin dish. Sprinkle with plenty of pepper.

2. Slice the leeks finely, put in a saucepan with 2 tablespoons of olive oil, cover, and cook very gently until transparent. Season with salt and pepper.

3. Spread the leeks over the *panisses*, add the stock, and brown in a very hot oven for 10 minutes.

187 Marinated Leeks

Lu Pouaré en Samoira / Les Poireaux en Marinade

For 6

3 tbs olive oil
18 very tender, small leeks
3 sprigs parsley
1 pinch thyme
1 pinch winter savory

1 clove garlic, peeled
salt, pepper
juice of 2 lemons
1/2 pint/250 ml dry white wine

1. Heat the olive oil in a sauté pan. Cut the leeks into 1-inch/3-cm lengths and add to the pan along with the parsley, thyme, winter savory, garlic, and pepper.

2. When all the ingredients have browned, add a pinch of salt, the lemon juice, the white wine, and 1/4 pint/150 ml of water. Bring to the boil, cover, and cook over a moderate heat until only a quarter of the liquid remains. Leave to cool and serve.

• • •

188 Leeks with Saffron

Lu Pouaré où Safran / Les Poireaux au Safran

For 6

2 tbs olive oil
6 spring onions
2 cloves garlic, peeled
6 tomatoes
1 3/4 lb/800 g leeks
1 small pinch saffron (this may be

replaced by a larger pinch of curry powder *or* paprika)
salt, pepper
1 lb/500 g potatoes (new if possible), peeled

1. Heat the olive oil in a casserole, and brown the finely chopped spring onions in it. Crush the garlic under a broad-bladed knife and add along with the peeled, seeded, coarsely chopped, and drained tomatoes.

2. When these ingredients begin to boil, add the leeks and saffron, just cover with water, and bring back to the boil. Season with salt and pepper. Cook briskly for 25 minutes.

3. Add the potatoes and continue to cook over a high heat for a further 20 minutes.

189 Chickpea Stew
La Cuecha dé Cèé / La Potée de Pois Chiches

For 6

¾ lb/300 g dried chickpeas	1 onion, peeled
salt	1 clove
¾ oz/20 g flour	3 lettuces
1 clove garlic, peeled	3 tbs olive oil

1. Soak the chickpeas in a bowl of water for 24 hours with a good pinch of salt and the flour.

2. Put the chickpeas in an enamelled iron casserole (the use of metal utensils should be avoided, because of the way they react to chickpeas), along with the garlic and the onion with a clove stuck in it. Cover with water and bring to the boil.

3. Just as the water is beginning to boil, lower the heat, add the 3 well-washed lettuces and the olive oil, and continue to simmer very gently for 2 hours.

● Chickpeas cooked as described may be eaten in a variety of ways: (a) with their cooking liquid, as a soup; (b) cold, as a salad, with part or none of their cooking liquid (which will have turned into a jelly similar to a meat jelly) and a vinaigrette dressing; or (c) puréed, served hot with a little olive oil.

190 Marinated Chickpeas

Lu Cèé en Samoira / Les Pois Chiches en Marinade

For 6

¾ lb/300 g dried chickpeas	6 tbs olive oil
salt	1 tsp black peppercorns
¾ oz/20 g flour	1 sprig thyme
2 cloves garlic, peeled	6 pickling onions, peeled
1 onion, peeled	¼ pint/150 ml dry white wine
1 clove	juice of 2 lemons
3 lettuces	

1. Cook the chickpeas as described in the previous recipe (No. 189), using 1 of the cloves of garlic and 3 tablespoons of the olive oil. Drain well.

2. Heat the remaining 3 tablespoons of olive oil in a sauté pan. Just as it is beginning to smoke, put in the cooked chickpeas and stir well with a wooden spoon.

3. When the oil stops sizzling, add the peppercorns, thyme, the remaining clove of garlic, and the pickling onions. Cook for 2 minutes, then pour in the white wine, ¼ pint/150 ml of water, and the lemon juice. Bring to the boil, cover, and, over a moderate heat, reduce the cooking liquid by two-thirds.

4. Leave to cool, and serve at room temperature.

191 Mange-Tout Peas Peasant-Style

Lu Goulut a la Païsana / Les Mange-Tout à la Paysanne

For 6

3 lb/1½ kg mange-tout peas	4 spring onions
7 oz/200 g *petit salé* (see page xiii)	pepper
6 tbs olive oil	1 pinch sugar

1. Top and tail the peas, making sure all string is removed. Wash and drain.

2. Cut the *petit salé* into thin slices and blanch in boiling water for 5 minutes. Then cut up into small dice.

3. Heat the olive oil in a sauté pan. Just as it is beginning to smoke, put in the *petit salé*, the spring onions cut into ¾-inch/2-cm lengths (including the green stem), some freshly ground pepper, and the sugar.

4. Add the mange-tout peas, cover, and simmer over a very low heat for 40 minutes. By the time the peas are ready for serving, they should be very slightly browned.

• • •

192 Marinated Mange-Tout Peas

Lu Goulut en Samoira / Les Mange-Tout en Marinade

For 6

3 tbs olive oil	1 sprig thyme, 1 sprig fennel, and
1 clove garlic, peeled	¼ bay leaf
6 spring onions	1 tsp crushed black peppercorns
3 lb/1½ kg mange-tout peas	juice of 2 lemons
bouquet garni, consisting of	¼ pint/150 ml dry white wine
3 sprigs parsley, 1 stalk celery,	salt

1. Heat the olive oil in a sauté pan. Just as it is beginning to smoke, put in the garlic and the spring onions cut into 1-inch/3-cm lengths (including the green stem). Brown slightly.

2. Top and tail the mange-tout peas, making sure all string is removed. Cut each pod into two or three pieces and add to the pan along with the *bouquet garni*, peppercorns, lemon juice, white wine, ¼ pint/150 ml of water, and salt.

3. Bring to the boil, cover, and cook over a moderate heat until only a quarter of the liquid remains. Leave to cool and serve.

193 Peas with Artichokes

Lu Péou aï Archicota / Les Petits Pois aux Artichauts

For 6

2 lettuces	2 spring onions
1 lb/500 g peas, shelled	5 oz/150 g lean *petit salé* (see page xiii)
1 lump sugar	6 small globe artichokes
salt	(see page x)
3 tbs olive oil	pepper

1. Shred the lettuces, put them in a saucepan with the peas, add the sugar and a large pinch of salt, and just cover with boiling water.

2. Boil fiercely for 20 minutes, and test the peas to see if they are done.

3. Heat the olive oil in a sauté pan, and brown the spring onions cut into 3/4-inch/2-cm lengths (induding the green stem), the diced *petit salé* and the sliced artichoke hearts.

4. Drain the peas, mix with the contents of the sauté pan, add pepper, and serve.

● ● ●

194 Red Pepper Gratin

Lu Pébroun Broustoulit / Les Poivrons au Gratin

For 6

12 red peppers	3 tbs olive oil
6 anchovy fillets	11 oz/300 g breadcrumbs
6 cloves garlic, peeled	pepper

1. Remove the stems of the peppers. Slit the vegetables lengthwise along one side and remove all the seeds.

2. Pound the anchovy fillets and garlic to a fine paste in a mortar, then incorporate 2 tablespoons of the olive oil and the breadcrumbs.

3. Lay the peppers in a large oiled gratin dish and, using a teaspoon, spread the mixture in the mortar as evenly as possible over the peppers. Sprinkle with pepper. Brown well in a medium oven.

195 Stuffed Peppers
Lu Pébroun Farcit / Les Poivrons Farcis

For 12

18 large red or yellow peppers	2 cloves garlic, peeled
5 tbs olive oil	11 oz/300 g rice
7 oz/200 g *petit salé* (see page xiii)	4 oz/100 g grated Parmesan
3 large onions, peeled	4 eggs
6 leaves basil	salt, pepper

1. Wash and dry the peppers carefully. Cut round the stems of 12 peppers, pull out, and carefully remove all the seeds inside each pepper. Cut the remaining peppers in half and remove seeds.

2. Heat 4 tablespoons of the olive oil in a thick-bottomed saucepan, and add the finely diced *petit salé*, the sliced onion, the finely chopped basil and garlic, the halved peppers cut into thin strips, and the rice. Brown slightly, then add 1¼ pints/750 ml of boiling water. Cook uncovered for 20 minutes, making sure the liquid does not dry up completely.

3. Leave the stuffing to cool. Add the Parmesan and beaten eggs, season with salt and pepper to taste, and mix well.

4. Fill the peppers with the stuffing and arrange on a large oiled gratin dish. Cook in a medium oven for 15 minutes, then turn the peppers over and cook for a further 15 minutes.

196 Potato Gratin
Li Tantifla Broustoulit / Les Pommes de Terre au Gratin

For 6

3 lb/1½ kg firm, juicy potatoes	1 small onion, peeled
4 tbs olive oil	salt, pepper
11 oz/300 g grated Parmesan	1 pint/500 ml chicken *or* beef stock

1. Peel the potatoes and cut into extremely thin slices (between ½ and 1 mm thick).

2. Heat the olive oil in a large enamelled iron gratin dish on top of the stove, and just as it is beginning to smoke cover with a layer of potatoes. Remove from stove and sprinkle with half the Parmesan.

3. Slice the onion and spread evenly over the gratin. Add a little salt and plenty of pepper. Cover with the rest of the potatoes, and pour in the heated stock.

4. Bake in a medium oven for 25 minutes.

5. Remove from the oven, sprinkle with the rest of the Parmesan, and continue to cook in a very hot oven until the cheese has browned.

● ● ●

197 Niçois Ratatouille
La Rataouïa Nissarda / La Ratatouille Niçoise

Ratatouille is, needless to say, one of the best-known and most highly appreciated of Niçois dishes. Indeed, it has now firmly established itself on the menus of many French restaurants, both in France and abroad. But this does not mean that the version commonly encountered outside the Comté de Nice bears any relation to the genuine traditional product. Common faults include undercooking or overcooking of one or more of its ingredients, a consistency that is either too smooth or not homogeneous enough, and incorrect proportions of the various vegetables. The reason for this is, no doubt, that *ratatouille*, contrary to popular belief, is a particularly long and tricky dish to prepare.

I have given proportions for a large amount of *ratatouille* rather than for a specific number of servings, as it is an especially useful dish to have plenty of. It can be eaten cold or slightly warm as an hors-d'oeuvre, or hot as a main course; it accompanies all meat dishes admirably; and it can easily be kept in a refrigerator for several days.

2 lb/1 kg aubergines	18 tbs olive oil
2 lb/1 kg courgettes	10 small cloves garlic, peeled
¾ oz/20 g flour	5 pinches thyme
2 lb/1 kg green peppers	5 sprigs parsley
2 lb/1 kg onions, peeled	20 leaves basil
3 lb/1½ kg tomatoes	salt, pepper

1. Cut the aubergines and courgettes crosswise into slices ½ inch/1 cm thick and put in separate bowls. Sprinkle evenly with the flour.

2. Remove the stems and seeds of the peppers, and cut into thin slices. Set aside.

3. Slice the onions and set aside.

4. Peel, seed, coarsely chop, and drain the tomatoes. Set aside.

5. Heat 6 tablespoons of the olive oil in a frying pan and brown the aubergine slices. Put 3 tablespoons of oil in a second frying pan and brown the courgette slices. Repeat the operation in a third and a fourth frying pan with the peppers and the onions, though over a more gentle heat (if you do not possess four frying pans, the operations can be carried out successively in the same pan or pans).

6. Put 3 tablespoons of olive oil in a thick-bottomed saucepan, add the finely chopped garlic, thyme, parsley, basil, and the tomatoes, and simmer gently until a sauce-like consistency is obtained.

7. Place a very large casserole over the lowest possible heat, and transfer the aubergines, courgettes, peppers, and onions, one after the other, from their pans to the casserole the moment they are cooked (overcooking is fatal, so test frequently with a pointed knife). The time needed for each vegetable will, of course, vary.

8. When the tomato sauce is ready, add to the vegetables and stir gently. After a minute or two, remove any excess olive oil with a bulb baster, season with salt and pepper to taste, and serve.

198 Spring Tian

Lou Tian dé Prima / Le Tian de Printemps

The most characteristically Niçois, tastiest, and, alas, most ephemeral of all the *tians* (see page xiv) is this version, which, if it is to be made to perfection, must combine young broad beans, fresh peas, small artichokes, and spring onions.

For 6

9 eggs	12 small globe artichokes
4 oz/100 g grated Parmesan	(see page x)
salt, pepper	6 spring onions
³⁄4 lb/300 g young broad beans,	10 Swiss chard tops
shelled	1 tbs olive oil
³⁄4 lb/300 g peas, shelled	

1. Break the eggs into a bowl and beat with the Parmesan, salt, and pepper.

2. Add the young broad beans (if unobtainable, use mature broad beans with their tough outer skin removed), the peas, the artichokes cut into thin slices after their outer leaves have been removed, the spring onions cut into ³⁄4-inch/2-cm lengths, and the Swiss chard tops cut into thin strips. Mix all the ingredients thoroughly.

3. Pour the mixture into an oiled gratin dish and cook in a medium oven for 45 minutes. It is also possible, though more difficult, to cook the ingredients in the same way as *trouchia* (No. 142).

● ● ●

199 Tomato Gratin

Li Toùmati Broustoulit / Les Tomates au Gratin

For 6

6 large ripe tomatoes	3 tbs chopped parsley
salt	7 oz/200 g breadcrumbs
1 clove garlic, peeled	2 tbs olive oil
1 anchovy fillet	pepper

1. Cut the unpeeled tomatoes in half crosswise. Squeeze the seeds and juice out of each half, then sprinkle the insides with a little salt to extract more moisture. Wait 10 minutes. Turn the tomato halves face down on a sieve or colander so the liquid runs out.

2. Pound the garlic and anchovy fillet to a paste in a mortar, add the very finely chopped parsley, and mix well.

3. Arrange the tomato halves face up on an oiled gratin dish, distribute the garlic, anchovy, and parsley paste evenly on each half, sprinkle with the breadcrumbs, a few drops of olive oil, and pepper, and cook in a very hot oven for 20 minutes.

• • •

200 Stuffed Tomatoes
Lu Toùmati Farcit / Les Tomates Farcies

For 12

8 tomatoes	2 oz/50 g *petit salé* (see page xiii)
salt	2 oz/50 g beef
4 tbs olive oil	4 oz/100 g pork
2 onions, peeled	2 eggs
2 cloves garlic, peeled	4 oz/100 g grated Parmesan
6 Swiss chard tops	pepper

1. Cut 6 unpeeled tomatoes in half crosswise. Squeeze the seeds and juice out of each half, then sprinkle the inside with a little salt to extract more moisture. Leave for 10 minutes, then turn the tomato halves face down on a sieve or colander so the liquid runs out.

2. Meanwhile, put into a casserole 2 tablespoons of the olive oil, the chopped onions, 2 peeled, seeded, and coarsely chopped tomatoes, the chopped garlic and shredded Swiss chard tops, and the finely chopped *petit salé*, beef, and pork. Mix thoroughly.

3. Cook this mixture over a moderate heat for about 15 minutes, then leave to cool.

4. Add the beaten eggs and Parmesan to the filling, stir well, and correct seasoning.

5. Fill the tomato halves with the mixture and arrange them face up in a large oiled gratin dish. Sprinkle with a little olive oil and cook in a medium oven for 30 minutes.

THE ITALIAN
CONNECTION

Pasta, Gnocchi, Polenta and Rice

A Note on Cooking Pasta

Opinions vary as to what constitutes a normal portion of *pasta* for someone
with a healthy appetite. I know *pasta* freaks who do not baulk at a 1-lb/500-g
helping. But most Niçois restaurateurs allow for 7 oz/200 g of cooked pasta
per person, and this seems to me a reasonable amount. So in the following
recipes I have given quantities of between 2¼ oz/65 g and 3 oz/85 g of dried
pasta per person (dried *pasta* swells to between two and three times its weight
during cooking, depending on the variety).

Cooking *pasta* is not as straightforward as it might seem, and has an
enormous bearing on the quality of the final dish. When I was a child, I knew a
charming lady from Alsace who kept on lamenting the fact that she could not
cook *pasta* successfully: she thought it was because she did not soak it long
enough! Dried *pasta* should, of course, go straight from the packet into
boiling water.

Here are some general rules for cooking *pasta*:

1. One of the first essentials is plenty of boiling salted water – at least 2½
pints/1½ litres for every 4 oz/100 g of *pasta*. Use less water and your *pasta* will
suffer in quality.

2. Pour in the *pasta* and stir carefully with a wooden spoon to stop it
sticking to the bottom of the saucepan or forming knots.

3. As soon as the *pasta* is very slightly resistant (*al dente*, in Italian) when
tasted, remove from heat and strain immediately into a large sieve or colander.
Douse with just enough cold water to stop the cooking process, but not so
much that the *pasta* gets cold. Shake well and transfer immediately either
back to the saucepan it was cooked in or to a warmed bowl. The cooking time
of *pasta* will, of course, vary depending on the type and on whether it is dried
or freshly made. Spaghetti takes from between 10 to 15 minutes, large
macaroni anything up to 20 minutes. Only 3 or 4 minutes are needed for
freshly made *pasta*.

201 Fresh Pasta

Li Nouïa o li Pasta Fresca / Les Nouilles ou les Pâtes Fraîches

In Nice, there are two basic types of fresh *pasta*, one slightly richer than the other. They resemble tagliatelle, and both can be eaten either fresh or dried. If the *pasta* is paper-thin, as it should be, and if the proper care is taken during both the making and the cooking to stop it sticking together, it is quite irresistibly delicious.

Fresh *pasta* can be eaten on its own with oil or butter and/or a little grated Parmesan. It can also replace macaroni in Nos. 208 to 213, and forms an ideal basis for Nos. 203 to 205.

For 6

First version

1¼ lb/600 g flour	4 oz/100 g fine semolina *or* polenta
4 eggs	flour
1 oz/25 g salt	

1. Pour the flour on to a very large wooden board or, better, a marble-topped table. Make a well in the middle and pour in the beaten eggs, 1 tablespoon of water, and the salt. Gradually incorporate the flour into the eggs and water with your hands until the paste can be made into a ball.

2. Knead vigorously for 10 minutes, flouring the hands and working surface when necessary. When the ball has the right smooth and elastic consistency, put it in a bowl, cover with a tea-cloth, and leave for 1 hour.

3. Divide the ball into 5 or 6 pieces. On a well-floured surface, roll each piece out until paper-thin (i.e. when you can see the wood or marble through it). Sprinkle with semolina or polenta flour and leave for 30 minutes.

4. Cut the pieces up into regular rectangles (about 6 by 10 inches/15 by 25 cm), fold over twice, and slice into strips ¼ inch/5 mm wide. The *pasta* is now ready for cooking.

5. If the *pasta* is not to be eaten immediately, pick it up in handfuls and drop it from a height of 1 foot/30 cm on to a clean cloth. Store in a cool, dry place.

Second version

1¼ lb/600 g flour	1 oz/25 g salt
6 whole eggs and 4 egg whites	4 oz/100 g fine semolina *or* polenta
4 tbs olive oil	flour

Proceed as in the first version, replacing the 4 eggs by 6 eggs and 4 egg whites, and the water by 4 tablespoons of olive oil.

202 Green Fresh Pasta
Li Pasta Fresca Verdi / Les Pâtes Fraîches Vertes

For 6

3/4 lb/300 g Swiss chard tops	6 eggs
1 1/4 lb/600 g flour	1 oz/25 g salt

1. Blanch the Swiss chard tops for 10 minutes in boiling water. Cut into strips and squeeze out as much moisture as possible. Purée till very smooth.

2. To make the *pasta*, proceed as in No. 201 (first version), adding the Swiss chard purée to the flour along with the beaten eggs, the salt, and 1 tablespoon of water.

• • •

203 Fresh Pasta with Cream and Parmesan
Li Pasta Fresca a la Créma é où Froumaï
Les Nouilles à la Crème et au Fromage

For 8

7 oz/200 g butter	2 3/4 lb/1,200 kg fresh *pasta* (No. 201,
1/2 pint/250 ml double cream	second version)
7 oz/200 g grated Parmesan	salt, pepper

1. Beat 6 oz/180 g of softened butter with a wooden spoon until creamed. Gradually incorporate the cream and grated Parmesan. Allow to reach room temperature 15 minutes before use.

2. Cook the *pasta* as indicated at the beginning of this chapter, remembering that fresh *pasta* needs only 3 or 4 minutes' boiling. Drain well.

3. Heat 3/4 oz/20 g of butter in a thick-bottomed saucepan. When it has stopped foaming, add plenty of pepper and several spoonfuls of the butter and Parmesan mixture. When this has melted, put in the *pasta* and cover with the rest of the sauce. Mix well until all the ingredients are hot. Check that there is enough salt. Serve in a warmed dish.

204 Cannelloni

Lu Cannelloni / Les Cannelloni

For 6

12 pieces of *pasta* (No. 201, first
   version), each measuring 5 by
   3 inches/12.5 by 7.5 cm (i.e. one
   quarter of the rectangle in step 4),
   or 12 pieces of bought *cannelloni*
12 oz/400 g Swiss chard tops
12 oz/400 g beef stew (No. 54)

3 oz/75 g *petit salé* (see page xiii)
1/2 lb/250 g grated Parmesan
3 eggs
salt, pepper
3/4 oz/20 g butter
7 fl oz/200 ml beef stew sauce

1. Cook the *pasta* pieces as indicated at the beginning of this chapter.
Drain, allow to cool, and lay out on a marble-topped table or, better, a clean
cloth.

2. Blanch the Swiss chard tops for 10 minutes in salted boiling water, drain,
squeeze out as much moisture as possible, and chop finely. Chop the beef and
petit salé, and mix well with the Swiss chard tops, 7 oz/200 g of the Parmesan,
and the beaten eggs. Add salt and pepper to taste.

3. Spread 7 or 8 teaspoons of stuffing lengthwise on each piece of *pasta*, roll
up to form a cylinder, and arrange on a buttered gratin dish.

4. Pour the beef sauce over the *cannelloni*, sprinkle with the rest of the
Parmesan, and brown slightly in the oven.

● Cooked veal or chicken can replace the beef in this recipe. In this case, the
cooking juices of the veal or chicken are poured over the *cannelloni* before
browning.

● The meat in the stuffing can also be replaced by cooked fish, shrimps, and
mushrooms.

205 Niçois Ravioli
Li Raïola a la Nissarda / Les Ravioli à la Niçoise

For 8

The Paste

1 lb 9 oz/700 g flour	1 oz/25 g salt
5 eggs	

The Filling

2 lb/1 kg Swiss chard tops	1 pinch nutmeg
1 lb/500 g beef stew (No. 54)	1 clove garlic, peeled
2 eggs	1 small onion, peeled
7 oz/200 g grated Parmesan	salt, pepper
1 pinch thyme	7 fl oz/200 ml beef stew sauce

1. Make a paste according to No. 201 (first version) and roll out into two paper-thin sheets.

2. Blanch the Swiss chard tops for 10 minutes in salted boiling water, drain, squeeze out as much moisture as possible, and chop finely. Mix well with the chopped beef, beaten eggs, half of the Parmesan, thyme, nutmeg, chopped garlic and onion, salt and pepper. If the filling seems a little dry, add some beef sauce.

3. Take one sheet of paste and dot with little mounds of the stuffing (a good teaspoon at a time) 1 inch/2 cm apart. Pinch each mound to a peak and cover loosely with the second sheet of paste.

4. Press gently between the mounds of stuffing so the two sheets of paste stick together.

5. Divide the ravioli with a roller-cutter, making sure all the edges are well closed. Well floured, they will keep for a few hours in a cloth; but if left for too long before being cooked they tend to ferment.

6. Slide the ravioli gently into boiling water and cook until they rise to the surface. Remove with a perforated spoon and drain on a cloth. Transfer to a warmed serving dish and cover with beef sauce and the rest of the Parmesan.

● In Nice, where ravioli are a great favourite, the basic ingredients of the stuffing are usually beef and Swiss chard. But sometimes veal, chicken, or pork are included, or even used on their own. Other versions of ravioli have a stuffing made of fish or cream cheese (as in Russia).

206 Oncle-Jean

Lu Barba-Jouan / Les 'Oncle-Jean'

For 8

The Paste

1 lb 5 oz/600 g flour	1 tbs olive oil
1 egg	1 large pinch salt

The Filling

6¹/₂ lb/3 kg pumpkin (see page x)	¹/₂ lb/250 g rice
2 oz/50 g onion, peeled	¹/₄ lb/100 g grated Parmesan
1 clove garlic, peeled	2 eggs
2 tbs olive oil	salt, pepper

1. The day before you intend to cook the *Oncle-Jean*, peel the pumpkin, cut it into 2-inch/5-cm dice, and boil for 20 minutes in salted water.

2. Drain in a colander, cover with a heavy plate, and leave to give up its moisture for 24 hours.

3. Make a paste according to No. 201 (first version) and roll out into a paper-thin sheet.

4. Chop the onion and garlic finely and brown in 1 tablespoon of the olive oil. Boil the rice for 10 minutes and drain. Purée the pumpkin.

5. Put the Parmesan, beaten eggs, rice, garlic, onion, and pumpkin purée into a bowl and mix thoroughly. Add salt and pepper to taste.

6. Cut the paste into discs with a round pastry-cutter about 3 inches/7 cm in diameter, and put 1 tablespoon of filling on each disc. Draw up the sides, moisten the edges slightly, and pinch together to form little purses.

7. Put the *Oncle-Jean* on to a lightly oiled gratin dish and cook in a hot oven until they are slightly browned on top.

● In another version, pumpkin is replaced by 4¹/₂ lb/2 kg of spinach, and the dish is then known as *boussotou*.

207 Quicou
Li Quicou / Les Quicou

For 6

10 Swiss chard tops	salt, pepper
3 eggs	1 lb 5 oz/600 g flour
3 tbs olive oil	7 oz/200 g grated Parmesan

1. Cut the Swiss chard tops into very fine strips and wash in several changes of water until it runs almost clear (instead of green). Drain thoroughly and dry with a clean cloth.

2. Put the beaten eggs, olive oil, pepper, a pinch of salt, and the Swiss chard tops into a bowl and mix well. Gradually incorporate the flour, adding a few drops of water from time to time, until a thick, smooth paste is obtained.

3. Roll out the paste until it is $1/10$ inch/2 mm thick. Cut up into strips 2 by 1 inches/5 by 2 cm with a roller cutter, and put them on to a well-floured cloth.

4. Cook in boiling water for about 10 minutes, drain and serve with plenty of grated Parmesan.

• • •

208 Macaroni Cheese
Lu Macaroni Broustoulit / Les Macaronis au Gratin

For 6

14 oz/400 g macaroni	9 oz/250 g grated Parmesan
salt	1 oz/25 g flour
9 oz/250 g butter	1 pint/500 ml milk

1. Cook the macaroni in boiling salted water as indicated at the beginning of this chapter, making sure it is decidedly *al dente*.

2. Stir in 5 oz/150 g of the butter and 5 oz/150 g of the Parmesan.

3. Make a *béchamel* sauce with 2 oz/50 g of the butter, the flour, and the milk. Stir into the macaroni.

4. Put the macaroni into a buttered gratin dish and push down so there are no air pockets left. Sprinkle with the rest of the Parmesan, dot with the remaining 2 oz/50 g of butter, cut into pea-sized pieces, and brown in the oven.

209 Macaroni in Meat Juice

Lu Macaroni où Jus / Les Macaronis au Jus

For 6

1 lb/500 g very ripe tomatoes	1 oz/30 g dried cèpe mushrooms
3 tbs olive oil	14 oz/400 g macaroni
1/2 pint/250 ml beef *or* veal juice	salt, pepper
(from a roast *or* stew)	1 oz/30 g butter

1. Peel, seed, and coarsely chop the tomatoes. Cook in the olive oil in a sauté pan for 10 minutes, add the meat juice and the dried mushrooms (previously soaked in warm water for 1 hour), and reduce until the consistency of a liquid sauce is obtained.

2. Cook the macaroni in boiling salted water, as indicated at the beginning of this chapter. Season with pepper and the butter.

3. Pour the sauce over the macaroni.

• • •

210 Macaroni with Garlic

Lu Macaroni a l'Aïet / Les Macaronis à l'Ail

For 6

14 oz/400 g macaroni	1 tbs meat juice (from a roast *or*
2 tbs olive oil	stew)
2 cloves garlic, peeled	2 oz/50 g butter
1/2 lb/250 g very ripe tomatoes	salt, pepper
1 lump sugar	

1. Cook the macaroni as indicated at the beginning of this chapter.

2. Heat the olive oil in a frying pan. Just as it is beginning to smoke, put in the whole cloves of garlic and brown. Add the peeled, seeded, coarsely chopped, and drained tomatoes and the sugar. Cook over a very high heat until the acidity of the tomatoes has disappeared.

3. Remove from heat and stir in the meat juice and butter. Check seasoning and pour over the macaroni.

211 Macaroni with Anchovies
Lu Macaroni a l'Amploua / Les Macaronis à l'Anchois

For 6

14 oz/400 g macaroni
6 anchovy fillets
3 tbs olive oil
3 very ripe tomatoes

1 clove garlic, peeled
1 pinch thyme
3 tbs chopped parsley
pepper

1. Cook the macaroni as indicated at the beginning of this chapter.

2. Desalt the anchovies for as long as necessary, remove any bones, and pound to a coarse paste.

3. Heat the olive oil in a frying pan, and just as it is beginning to smoke put in the peeled, seeded, coarsely chopped, and drained tomatoes, crushed garlic, anchovies, thyme, and chopped parsley. Stir well and reduce. Add pepper to taste.

4. Pour the anchovy sauce over the macaroni and serve.

● ● ●

212 Niçois Macaroni
Lu Macaroni a la Nissarda / Les Macaronis à la Niçoise

For 6

14 oz/400 g macaroni
2 tbs olive oil
2 onions, peeled
2 cloves garlic, peeled

1 lb/500 g very ripe tomatoes
2 oz/50 g grated Parmesan
salt, pepper

1. Cook the macaroni as indicated at the beginning of this chapter.

2. Heat the olive oil in a frying pan. Just as it is beginning to smoke, put in the chopped onions and brown. Add the crushed cloves of garlic and the peeled, seeded, coarsely chopped, and drained tomatoes, and cook for 10 minutes.

3. Pour the sauce over the macaroni, sprinkle with the Parmesan, add salt and pepper to taste, mix well, and serve.

213 Macaroni with Chicken Breasts, Ham, and Mushrooms

Lu Macaroni Jetée-Promenade
Les Macaronis Jetée-Promenade

For 6

14 oz/400 g macaroni	1/2 lb/250 g mushrooms
3 oz/85 g butter	1/2 lb/250 g cooked ham
2 oz/50 g grated Parmesan	1 small black truffle
1/2 oz/15 g flour	salt, pepper
1/2 pint/300 ml milk	breadcrumbs
7 fl oz/200 ml double cream	1/4 pint/150 ml veal juice (from a
boned breasts of 1 chicken	roast *or* stew)

1. Cook the macaroni as indicated at the beginning of this chapter.

2. When it is cooked and drained, add 2 oz/50 g of the butter, the Parmesan, and 18 fl oz/500 ml of cream sauce (a *béchamel* made with 1/2 oz/15 g of the butter, 1/2 oz/15 g of flour and 1/2 pint/300 ml of milk, into which 7 fl oz/ 200 ml of cream has been beaten by spoonfuls over a gentle heat). If the truffle you are using comes from a tin, flavour the cream sauce with its juice. Add the cooked chicken breasts, cut into small dice, and the mushrooms, ham, and truffle, all sliced. Season with salt and pepper and mix thoroughly.

3. Butter a charlotte mould heavily and roll plenty of breadcrumbs round the inside so that the surface is completely covered.

4. Fill the mould with the macaroni mixture, press well down, and cook in a very hot oven for 15 to 20 minutes.

5. The breadcrumbs should have formed a brown crust. At this point, unmould the preparation on to a round serving dish, and serve with hot veal juice.

214 Spaghetti with Eggs

Lu Spaghetti a l'Où / Les Spaghetti aux Oeufs

For 6

4 oz/100 g butter	5 oz/150 g *petit salé* (see page xiii)
3 whole eggs and 3 egg yolks	1 pinch cayenne pepper
7 oz/200 g grated Parmesan	1/2 pint/300 ml cream
1 lb 2 oz/500 g spaghetti	salt, pepper
1 tbs olive oil	

1. Cream the butter with an electric beater or a fork until light and mousse-like.

2. In another receptacle, beat the eggs and egg yolks well and mix in half the Parmesan.

3. Cook the spaghetti as indicated at the beginning of this chapter.

4. Heat the olive oil in a frying pan and brown the *petit salé* cut into 1/4-inch/1/2-cm dice, until crisp. Pour off half the fat in the pan, and add the cayenne pepper and cream. Stir, remove from heat, and keep warm.

5. Put the cooked spaghetti with the creamed butter in a heated large serving dish. Mix thoroughly with two forks so that all the spaghetti is coated with butter.

6. Immediately incorporate the mixtures of *petit salé* and cream, and of egg and Parmesan, check seasoning with salt and pepper, and serve quickly with the rest of the Parmesan on the side.

• • •

215 Spaghetti with Pistou

Lu Spaghetti où Pistou / Les Spaghetti au Pistou

For 6

3 large cloves garlic, peeled	7 oz/200 g pine-nuts
10 large leaves basil	1 lb 2 oz/500 g spaghetti
7 oz/200 g grated Parmesan	salt, pepper
3 tbs olive oil	2 oz/50 g butter (optional)

1. Prepare a *pistou* sauce (No. 7) with the garlic, basil, half the Parmesan, and the olive oil. Pound the pine-nuts coarsely and mix into the *pistou*.

2. Cook the spaghetti as indicated at the beginning of this chapter, add salt and pepper to taste, and mix thoroughly with the *pistou*. If the spaghetti looks too dry for your taste, add the butter and mix again. Sprinkle with the rest of the Parmesan and serve immediately.

216 Spaghetti with Shellfish

Lu Spaghetti aï Couquilha / Les Spaghetti aux Coquillages

For 6

2½ pints/1½ litres mussels (discard any that are not tightly shut)

36 small carpet-shells (discard any that are not tightly shut)

2 tbs olive oil

4 cloves garlic, peeled

¼ pint/150 ml dry white wine

1 lb 2 oz/500 g spaghetti

2 oz/50 g butter

3 tbs chopped parsley

salt, pepper

1. Put the cleaned carpet-shells and scrubbed and bearded mussels into two different saucepans, cover, and boil over a high heat until the shells open. Discard any that refuse to open.

2. Heat the olive oil in a sauté pan. Just as it is beginning to smoke, put in the crushed garlic, lower the heat, and cook gently for 3 minutes, stirring all the time.

3. Pour 5 tablespoons each of the cooking liquids produced by the mussels and carpet-shells into the sauté pan. Add the white wine, bring to the boil, and reduce by half over a high heat.

4. Cook the spaghetti as indicated at the beginning of this chapter, making sure it remains decidedly *al dente*. Drain and put in a heated deep serving dish. Mix in the butter.

5. Shell the mussels and carpet-shells, and heat for 2 minutes in the sauce. Pour the sauce over the spaghetti, sprinkle with the chopped parsley, add salt (if necessary) and pepper, and mix well with two forks.

217 Baked Green Lasagne

Li Lasagna Verdi où Fourn / Les Lasagnes Vertes au Four

For 6

1 lb 2 oz/500 g lasagne	5 tbs dry white wine
5 tbs olive oil	1 pint/500 ml beef stock
1/2 lb/250 g raw ham	1/2 lb/250 g very ripe tomatoes
2 onions, peeled	1/2 lb/250 g chicken livers
2 carrots, peeled	1 pinch grated nutmeg
2 stalks celery	salt, pepper
3 oz/80 g butter	1/2 pint/250 ml double cream
7 oz/200 g minced beef	1/2 lb/250 g grated Parmesan
4 oz/125 g minced lean pork	

1. Cook the *lasagne* for 3 minutes in 6 quarts/6 litres of boiling water to which 3 tablespoons of the olive oil have been added (to prevent the *lasagne* from sticking together). Drain.

2. Chop the ham, onions, carrots, and celery as finely as possible. Melt 1 oz/30 g of the butter gently in a sauté pan. As soon as it stops foaming, add the chopped ingredients and cook for about 10 minutes over a medium heat, stirring often.

3. When the mixture begins to take colour, transfer to a thick-bottomed casserole. Heat 2 tablespoons of olive oil in the sauté pan and brown the minced beef and pork, stirring well with a wooden spoon so that no lumps form. Add the white wine, turn up the heat, and cook, still stirring, until all the liquid has evaporated.

4. Transfer the meat to the casserole, along with the beef stock and the peeled, seeded, coarsely chopped, and drained tomatoes. Bring to the boil, then turn down the heat, cover, and leave to simmer for 1 hour, stirring occasionally.

5. Meanwhile, melt 1 oz/30 g of the butter in the sauté pan and brown the chicken livers gently. Cut them into very small dice and add, along with the nutmeg, salt, and pepper, to the sauce in the casserole when it has been cooking for 50 minutes.

6. Butter a large deep gratin dish with the rest of the butter. Put in a 1-inch/2-cm layer of cooked *lasagne* and cover with some of the sauce, cream, and Parmesan (the exact amount will depend on how many layers of *lasagne* will fit into the dish). Repeat the process until all the *lasagne* is used up, and finish with a layer of sauce and cream. Sprinkle plenty of Parmesan on top.

7. Bake in a pre-heated moderate oven for between 15 and 30 minutes, depending on the temperature of the sauce when added to the *lasagne*. Turn up the heat 5 minutes before serving.

8. Baked green *lasagne* should not be unmoulded. It is cut into slices in its dish and served with a spoon or fish slice.

218 Gnocchi

Lu Gnocchi / Les Gnocchi

For 6

2 lb 3 oz/1 kg old, floury potatoes	¼ lb/100 g grated Parmesan
salt	2 oz/50 g butter
9 oz/250 g flour	pepper
1 egg	

1. Peel the potatoes and boil them in salted water.

2. When they are thoroughly cooked, purée them, then, while they are still hot, incorporate the flour and lightly beaten egg until a smooth paste is obtained. Leave for 30 minutes.

3. Divide the mixture into pieces the size of a tangerine and, on a floured board or marble-topped table, roll them out into sausage-like rolls of the thickness of a finger. Cut into pieces 1 inch/3 cm long.

4. With the thumb, gently dent the middles of the *gnocchi* (this helps them to cook properly).

5. Put the *gnocchi* in plenty of boiling water. When they float to the surface, they are done.

6. Drain thoroughly, put into a heated deep serving dish, and season with the Parmesan, dots of butter, and pepper.

● Other seasonings include *saoussoun* (No. 20), thinly sliced white truffles, sauce from a beef stew (No. 54), or the juice of roast veal.

219 Green Gnocchi

La 'Merda dé Can' / Les Gnocchi Verts

For 12

6½ lb/3 kg old, floury potatoes	2 tbs olive oil
2 lb/1 kg Swiss chard tops	salt, pepper
1¾ lb/800 g flour	¼ lb/100 g grated Parmesan
2 eggs	

1. Peel the potatoes and boil them in salted water.

2. Blanch the Swiss chard tops for 5 minutes in a large saucepan of salted boiling water.

3. Squeeze dry, chop finely, and leave to drain in a fine sieve.

4. When the potatoes are thoroughly cooked, purée them, then, while they are still hot, mix with the flour, the lightly beaten eggs, the Swiss chard tops, and the olive oil. Add a little salt and pepper.

5. When a firm consistency is obtained, leave for 30 minutes.

6. Cut the paste into ¾-inch/2-cm cubes and roll them into oblong shapes, pointed at both ends.

7. Cook for 5 to 10 minutes in plenty of slightly salted boiling water. When they float to the surface, they are done.

8. Drain well, sprinkle with the Parmesan, and serve with either *saoussoun* (No. 20) or the juice of roast chicken.

220 Polenta

La Poulenta / La Polente

For many years, *polenta* (maize flour boiled in salted water) was the staple food of the Italians. It is a healthy, invigorating food which is at its best when accompanied by high-quality roasting juices or a meat sauce, butter, and Parmesan. It is also very good with Corsican sausages such as *ficatelli*.

For6

3½ pints/2 litres meat stock, *or* half stock and half water, *or* 3½ pints/2 litres slightly salted water 1¼ lb/600 g *polenta*	¼ lb/100 g butter 5 oz/150 g grated Parmesan salt, pepper

1. Bring the liquid to the boil, pour in the *polenta*, and stir vigorously to prevent lumps from forming.

2. When the mixture is smoothly blended, turn down the heat very low and continue to cook the *polenta* very gently, stirring from time to time with a wooden spoon and scraping the bottom and sides of the saucepan.

3. The *polenta* will be cooked in about 20 to 30 minutes, when it comes away easily from the sides and bottom of the saucepan. It should be very thick in consistency.

4. Incorporate the butter, Parmesan, salt, and pepper, and serve.

● ● ●

221 Polenta Gratin

La Poulenta Broustoulit / La Polente au Gratin

For 6

3½ pints/2 litres meat stock, *or* half stock and half water, *or* 3½ pints/2 litres slightly salted water 1¼ lb/600 g *polenta*	4 tbs olive oil 2 oz/50 g butter salt, pepper 5 oz/150 g grated Parmesan

1. Cook the *polenta* as indicated in No. 220.

2. Pour on to a well-floured cloth so it forms a layer ¾ inch/2 cm thick. Roll the cloth into a sausage shape, and leave to cool.

3. Cut the *polenta* into slabs measuring 6 by 1½ inches/5 by 4 cm and arrange in a gratin dish. Pour the olive oil and melted butter over the *polenta*, season with salt and pepper, sprinkle with the Parmesan, and brown in the oven.

222 Family Polenta

La Poulenta dé Maïoun / La Polente de Ménage

For 6

3½ pints/2 litres meat stock, *or*
   half stock and half water, *or*
   3½ pints/2 litres slightly salted
   water
1¼ lb/600 g *polenta*
3 onions, peeled
2 tbs olive oil

1 pinch thyme
2 cloves garlic, peeled
6 very ripe tomatoes
2 tbs meat sauce *or* roasting juices
1 oz/25 g butter
salt, pepper

1. Cook the *polenta* as indicated in No. 220.

2. Pour on to a well-floured cloth so it forms a layer ¾ inch/2 cm thick. Roll the cloth into a sausage shape, and leave to cool.

3. Slice the onions finely and brown gently in the olive oil with the thyme and chopped garlic. When they have coloured slightly, add the peeled, seeded, coarsely chopped, and drained tomatoes. Simmer until the liquid has reduced by two thirds.

4. Add the meat sauce or roasting juices and stir in the butter a little at a time. Season with salt and pepper.

5. Cut the *polenta* into slabs measuring 6 by 1½ inches/15 by 4 cm, arrange in a buttered gratin dish, and brown slightly in a hot oven. Pour the sauce evenly over the *polenta* and cook for a further 5 minutes in the oven, turned low.

223 Roman Gnocchi

Lou Sémouloun a la Romana / Les Gnocchi à la Romaine

For 6

4 oz/100 g butter	5 oz/150 g fine semolina
salt, pepper	5 oz/150 g grated Parmesan
1 pinch nutmeg	1 egg
1¼ pints/750 ml milk	

1. Put 3 oz/80 g of the butter, some pepper and salt, and the grated nutmeg in the milk and bring to the boil. Pour in the semolina, whisking all the time, and cook for 3 to 4 minutes.

2. Remove the saucepan from the heat and, still whisking energetically, incorporate 4 oz/100 g of the Parmesan and the beaten egg. Pour the mixture into a flat buttered dish or tin in a layer about ½ inch/1 cm deep. To make an even layer, dip the fingers in cold water and pat the semolina flat.

3. When it is cold, cut into rounds with a cutter or a glass 2½ inches/6 cm in diameter, or into squares with a knife. In either case, the utensil needs to be floured after each operation.

4. Arrange the *gnocchi*, overlapping each other, in a buttered gratin dish, sprinkle with the rest of the Parmesan and the rest of the butter (melted), and brown in the oven.

224 Rice
Lou Ris / Le Riz

Situated as it is between the rice-producing regions of Piedmont and the
Camargue, the Comté de Nice has always been a big consumer of rice.
The most important thing about rice is that it should be cooked properly:
I know many people who used to hate rice dishes until they tasted them in
Italy, for instance, where they are often prepared with great skill.

Nowadays there are countless types of pre-treated, pre-cooked, and generally
pre-prepared rice, all of which have made the cook's task much easier. I would
not deny the practical advantages of such products, but for certain rice dishes
(when it is cooked Persian-style, for instance) the natural, untreated grain is the
only thing that will do.

There are four main methods of cooking rice:

Method 1
Gradually sprinkle 7 oz/200 g of rice into a large quantity of boiling salted
water. When it has cooked for 10 minutes, start testing the grains by biting
them. When they are tender but not mushy, and are well separated, drain the
rice, sprinkle with a little cold water, allow to drain again, and use as required.

Method 2
Heat 3 tablespoons of olive oil in a casserole, pour in 7 oz/200 g of rice and
stir with a wooden spoon. When the rice turns a milky colour, pour in two and
a half times its weight of liquid (i.e. 18 fl oz/500 ml), which can be meat stock,
fish stock, or water, depending on the final dish, and cook until the liquid has
been absorbed.

Method 3
Rice cooked Persian-style can be really superb if you can get hold of long
Camargue rice. Gradually sprinkle 7 oz/200 g of rice into a large quantity of
boiling salted water. When it has cooked for 10 minutes, rinse in plenty of hot
running water until almost all traces of starch have disappeared. Drain the rice
thoroughly and arrange in a casserole as follows: put a 1-inch/3-cm layer of
rice on the bottom, cover with a little salt and dots of butter, and repeat the
operation until all the rice is used up, ending with a layer of butter (about
2 oz/60 g of butter will be needed for 7 oz/200 g of rice). Cover and bake in a
medium oven for 25 minutes.

Method 4
The Chinese way of cooking rice results in its being snow-white, very well
cooked, but perfectly separated. Blanch the rice for 10 minutes in a large
quantity of slightly salted boiling water, rinse in plenty of hot running water,
place in the top of a steamer and cook for about 15 minutes more, or until the
rice is done. It can be kept warm in the steamer for anything up to 1 hour.

225 Rice with Young Broad Beans

Lou Ris aï Favéta / Le Riz aux Févettes

For 10

3 tbs olive oil
2 cloves garlic, peeled
1/4 lb/100 g onions, peeled
5 oz/150 g *petit salé* (see page xiii)

1 lb/500 g rice
2 lb/1 kg baby broad beans, shelled
2 oz/50 g butter
salt, pepper

1. Heat the olive oil in a casserole. Just as it is beginning to smoke, put in the finely sliced garlic and onion, and the diced *petit salé*.

2. When the ingredients are well browned, add the rice. As soon as it turns a milky colour, pour in two and a half times its weight of water (i.e. 2 pints/1¼ litres), and bring to the boil.

3. When the water boils, add the broad beans.

4. Cook very gently until all the liquid at the bottom of the casserole has been absorbed. Stir in the butter, cut in small pieces, adjust seasoning, and serve.

226 Rice Salad

Lou Ris en Salada / La Salade de Riz

For 6

8 tbs olive oil	tomato ketchup (optional)
11 oz/300 g rice	1/2 lb/200 g green peas, shelled
6 very ripe tomatoes	4 spring onions
2 lumps sugar	2 green peppers, seeded
1 tbs vinegar	2 oz/50 g black olives
salt, pepper	

1. Heat 4 tablespoons of the olive oil in a thick-bottomed saucepan, add the rice, and stir with a wooden spoon. When the rice turns a milky colour, pour in 1 1/4 pints/750 ml of water and cook until all the liquid has been absorbed.

2. Put the peeled, seeded, coarsely chopped, and drained tomatoes in another thick-bottomed saucepan with the sugar, bring to the boil, turn down the heat, and simmer gently.

3. In a large salad bowl, make a vinaigrette dressing with 4 tablespoons of olive oil, the vinegar, salt and pepper (add a dash of ketchup if desired).

4. Blanch the peas in boiling salted water for 5 minutes (3 minutes if they are frozen peas). Slice the onions and peppers.

5. When the tomatoes have reduced by half, let them cool, then put them in the salad bowl with the rice, onions, peppers, and olives. Mix thoroughly with the dressing. Serve chilled.

227 Risotto

Lou Risotou / Le Risotto

Risotto is, of course, an Italian dish; but the cooks of Nice have devised at least three characteristic versions of their own.

For 6

First version

3 quarts/3 litres mussels (discard any that are not tightly shut)	3/4 lb/300 g very ripe tomatoes
3 tbs olive oil	1 pinch saffron
3/4 lb/300 g rice	pepper

1. Bring about 1 pint/500 ml water. to the boil in a saucepan, then add the scrubbed and bearded mussels, cover, and cook over a high heat for 5 minutes, shaking frequently, until the mussels open. Discard any that refuse to open.

2. Heat the olive oil in a casserole. Just as it is beginning to smoke, put in the rice. When it turns a milky colour, add the peeled, seeded, coarsely chopped, and drained tomatoes, and pour in the mussels' cooking liquid (diluted with water if it is too salt). Add the saffron and plenty of pepper. Turn down the heat and leave the rice to absorb the liquid (do not stir).

3. After about 20 to 25 minutes, while there is still some liquid in the rice, add the mussels and cook for a further 5 to 10 minutes. Remove from heat, stir with a wooden spoon, and serve.

Second version

Replace the mussels by the same amount of live shrimps.

1. Bring 1½ pints/800 ml of well-salted water to the boil, and cook the shrimps in it for 1 minute (if the shrimps are already cooked, let them give flavour to the water by simmering them for 5 minutes in it and leaving to cool).

2. Proceed as in the first version, using the shrimps' cooking liquid to cook the rice in, and adding the shrimps instead of the mussels at the end.

Third version

Replace the mussels by 5 oz/150 g sultanas, soaked in water, 4 oz/100 g lightly roasted pine-nuts, 2 finely chopped spring onions, 2 oz/50 g black olives, and salt.

Proceed as in the first version, using 1½ pints/800 ml of salted water to cook the rice in, and adding the above ingredients at the end.

228 Mussel Pancakes

Lu Crespéou aï Musclé / Les Crêpes aux Moules

(Ed. note: These *crespéou* are very similar in name and in ingredients to the Italian *crespolini*.)

For 6

1 large onion, peeled	1/2 tsp baking powder
1 clove garlic, peeled	4 tbs olive oil
5 sprigs parsley	4 eggs and 2 egg yolks
2 quarts/2 litres mussels (discard any that are not tightly shut)	1/4 pint/150 ml milk
1/2 lb/250 g flour	2 oz/50 g butter
2 oz/50 g cornflour	1/2 pint/250 ml double cream
1/2 tsp salt	pepper
	7 oz/200 g grated Parmesan

1. Bring a little water to the boil in a large saucepan with the sliced onion, crushed garlic, and chopped parsley. Add the scrubbed and bearded mussels, cover, and cook over a high heat for 3 minutes, shaking frequently. Remove mussels with a perforated scoop, discarding any that refuse to open, and reduce the liquid for 20 minutes over a medium heat.

2. Shell the mussels and set aside in a bowl.

3. Put 6 oz/200 g of the flour, the cornflour, salt, baking powder, 3 tablespoons of olive oil, and 4 eggs into a bowl, and mix thoroughly. Gradually add the milk diluted with 1/4 pint/150 ml of water until a smooth batter is obtained.

4. Brush a thick-bottomed frying- or crêpe-pan lightly with olive oil, heat, and pour in a small amount of batter, tilting the pan in all directions so it is evenly covered. Cook over a fairly high heat until the underside of the pancake is light brown. Turn over and cook on the other side. Set aside in a dish in a low oven. Repeat the process till the batter is used up.

5. Make a white *roux* in a thick-bottomed saucepan with the rest of the flour and the butter. Pour in the mussels' hot cooking liquid (diluted with water if it is too salt), stirring all the time.

6. Put 2 egg yolks, the cream, pepper, and three quarters of the Parmesan into a bowl, and mix well. Add gradually to the sauce, away from the heat, whisking vigorously. Add the mussels and stir with a wooden spoon.

7. Pour 2 tablespoons of filling on to each pancake, roll up and arrange in an oiled gratin dish. Cover with the rest of the sauce and the remaining Parmesan, and brown in a hot oven.

● This dish, which can be varied by using baby sole instead of mussels, is a speciality of Saint-Jean-Cap-Ferrat, 11 kilometres along the coast from Nice.

229 Patties

Li Rissola / Les Rissoles

(Ed. note: A dish reminiscent of the Neapolitan speciality, *calzone*.)

For 6

1 lb 2 oz/500 g flour
salt
11 oz/300 g butter
1¾ lb/750 g filling (this may be the filling in No. 163, the sauce in No. 228, *or* the filling in No. 205, which may be varied by substituting for the beef stew an equivalent weight of diced chicken breasts and finely chopped *petit salé*
oil for deep frying

1. Put the flour on a marble-topped table or into a mixing bowl. Make a well and put in a pinch of salt, the warmed butter, and ¼ pint/150 ml of water. Blend well and roll out into a rectangle. Fold into three and leave for 1 hour.

2. Roll out into a layer ½ inch/1 cm thick and fold into three. Repeat this operation three times.

3. Roll out the pastry into a layer ⅛ inch/2 to 3 mm thick. With a glass or round cutter 3 to 4 inches/8 to 10 cm in diameter, cut into discs. Place 1 or 2 teaspoons of filling on each disc. Moisten the edges of the pastry with a brush dipped in water and fold up the sides of each disc to form a purse, pressing the top well together.

4. Slide the patties into hot oil and deep-fry until golden.

SWEETS, CAKES, AND PASTRIES

Dessert in Nice is usually referred to as *la frucha* (fruit) – hardly surprising in an area blessed with such abundance in this respect. In winter, our tables are laden with oranges, grapefruits, tangerines, clementines, kumquats, apples from Saint-Martin-de-Vesubie, walnuts from the Tende region, almonds, hazelnuts, and, of course, fruit bottled the previous summer. Summer brings cherries, strawberries, raspberries, redcurrants, apricots, plums, peaches, pears, jujubes, azaroles, pomegranates, medlars, arbutus-berries, fejoas, and kakis – a veritable explosion of colours, aromas, and tastes in the fruit basket.

However, there do exist a number of interesting Niçois pastries, the best-known of which is doubtless the Swiss-chard-top pie (No. 230).

230 Swiss-Chard-Top Pie
La Tourta ∂é Bléa / La Tourte ∂e Blette

For 16

The pastry

1 lb 2 oz/500 g flour	5 oz/150 g caster sugar
2 eggs	1 pinch salt
7 oz/200 g butter	

The filling

15 Swiss chard tops (young if possible)	1 tbs olive oil
	2 eggs
2 oz/50 g grated Parmesan	pepper
5 oz/150 g brown sugar	4 oz/100 g pine-nuts
2 fl oz/50 ml *grappa*	6 apples (Reinettes *or* Cox's Orange Pippins)
2 oz/50 g currants	
2 oz/50 g Malaga raisins	2 oz/50 g caster sugar
4 fl oz/120 ml rum	

1. Make a well in the flour. Beat 2 eggs and pour them into the well, and then add the softened butter, 5 oz/150 g of caster sugar, and salt.

2. Blend quickly with the hands, without kneading too much, and sprinkle a few drops of water if necessary over the dough. Set aside for at least an hour before rolling out.

3. Wash the Swiss chard tops thoroughly. Roll into cylinders and cut into strips 1/4 inch/5 mm wide with a sharp knife. Wash in several changes of water, until almost all traces of green have disappeared (this removes the bitterness of the leaves). Drain, then dry between two cloths.

4. Put the Parmesan, the brown sugar, the *grappa*, the currants and raisins, previously soaked in the rum, 1 tablespoon of olive oil, 2 beaten eggs, pepper, and the pine-nuts into a large bowl. Mix thoroughly, then add the Swiss chard tops and mix again.

5. Divide the pastry into two pieces. Roll out one piece until it is about 3/4 inch/2 cm larger all round than the pie tin (which should be between 12 and 16 inches/30 and 40 cm in diameter), and press lightly into the bottom of the tin.

6. Spread the filling over the bottom of the tin (it should be about 3/4 inch/ 2 cm thick), and pour in any liquid which may remain in the mixing bowl.

7. Cut the apples into slices and arrange on top of the filling.

8. Roll out the second piece of dough until it has the same diameter as the pie tin and lay on top. Pinch the two pieces of dough together all the way round the rim, and prick the top with a fork. Bake in a hot oven until the top of the pie is slightly brown.

9. Remove from oven, sprinkle with 2 oz/50 g of caster sugar, and leave to cool to room temperature.

● This pie may be kept for several days in a cool place.

● (Ed. note: It requires some bravery to use Parmesan in a sweet pie, and the result is novel to say the least; but Jacques Médecin insists that it is used in the authentic version of Nice's most celebrated dessert. Any misgivings you have can be allayed by following the version given by other authorities, in which 2 oz/50 g of grated mature Gouda – a much milder cheese – replaces the Parmesan.)

231 Christmas Bread
La Grissa dé Caléna / Le Pain de Noël

For 10

5 oz/150 g sugar
14 oz/400 g flour
2 fl oz/50 ml rum
5 oz/150 g seedless raisins
2 fl oz/50 ml orange-blossom water
2 oz/50 g pine-nuts
grated rind of 1 lemon

1 tsp aniseed
2 oz/50 g crystallized citron peel
3 oz/75 g butter
6 tbs olive oil
1/2 tsp baking powder
9 oz/250 g bread dough (for recipe,
   see page 40)

1. Put into a large mixing bowl the sugar, flour, rum, raisins (previously soaked in the orange-blossom water), the pine-nuts, lemon rind, aniseed, finely chopped citron peel, melted butter, and 5 tablespoons warmed olive oil. Mix well until a smooth paste is obtained, then add the baking powder and bread dough.

2. Mix thoroughly with a wooden spoon, but do not knead. Turn on to an oiled baking sheet and mould the mixture into a thick disc that is slightly higher in the middle.

3. Cover with a damp cloth and leave to rise at kitchen temperature for 8 hours.

4. Make incisions in the disc as indicated in Figure 1 and fold over the flaps towards the centre, carefully interleaving them as shown in Figure 2.

5. Put into a hot oven for 15 minutes, then turn the heat down to medium and bake for 1 hour. If, in the course of baking, the bread seems to be turning too brown, open the oven door for a minute or two. Then continue to bake as before.

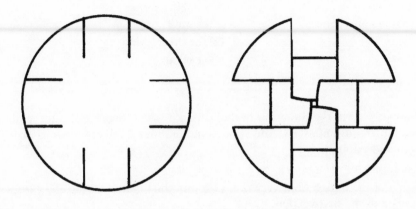

Figure 1   *Figure 2*

232 Ganses

Li Gansa / Les Ganses

Mardi Gras in Nice, when the city's well-known *Carnaval* takes place, would be unthinkable without this delicious Niçois version of doughnuts. When carefully made – and I insist on the word carefully – *ganses* not only make a light sweet course, but also go well with morning coffee or tea.

There exist several ways of making *ganses*. Here are two of them, one compact and almost biscuit-like, the other featherlight.

First version

....

9 oz/250 g flour   1 pinch salt
3 oz/75 g sugar   oil for deep-frying
2 egg yolks   icing sugar
4 tbs orange-blossom water

....

1. Make a well in the flour, put in the sugar, egg yolks, orange-blossom water, salt, and a few drops of cold water, and mix well until a smooth dough is obtained.

2. Let it rest for 1 hour in a cool place.

3. Break the dough into walnut-sized pieces, and roll them out until very thin (1½ mm thick).

4. With a pastry cutter, cut the dough into strips measuring ¾ inch/2 cm wide and 6 to 8 inches/15 to 20 cm long. Tie the strips into loose knots, or make a slit in the middle along most of their length.

5. Drop the *ganses* into very hot oil and fry until golden, turning over once during cooking. Drain and toss immediately in icing sugar.

Second version

....

9 oz/250 g flour   4 oz/120 g butter
½ tsp baking powder   2 tbs milk
3 tbs sugar   oil for deep-frying
1 pinch salt   icing sugar
2 eggs

....

1. Make a well in the flour, put in the baking powder, sugar, salt, eggs, and softened butter, and mix well. Add enough milk (about 2 tablespoons) to make a smooth, light dough.

2. Let it rest for 30 minutes.

3. Roll out the dough until very thin (1½ mm thick), and cut out the *ganses* as described in the first version.

4. Drop the *ganses* into very hot oil and fry until golden, turning over once during cooking. Drain and toss immediately in icing sugar.

233 Fougassette

La Fougassetta / La Fougassette

For 6

¼ oz/10 g yeast	2 eggs and 2 egg yolks
1 lb 2 oz/500 g flour	salt
1 tbs orange-blossom water	7 tbs olive oil
5 oz/160 g sugar	

1. Mix the yeast and half of the flour with ¼ pint/150 ml of water. Make a ball, put into a mixing bowl, and leave to rise for 3 hours.

2. Make a well in the rest of the flour, and put in the orange-blossom water, sugar, eggs, and a large pinch of salt. Add ¼ pint/150 ml of water, mix well, and incorporate into the dough that has risen. Knead the dough by folding it over itself repeatedly, adding the olive oil little by little.

3. Put the dough into a mixing bowl and leave for another 5 hours.

4. With the dough, make little balls about the size of a small peach, then leave for another 30 minutes. Roll each ball out into an oval shape about ¾ inch/2 cm thick, then leave for another 30 minutes. Cut four or five slits crosswise in each *fougassette*, opening them well so they do not close up during baking.

5. Bake on a baking sheet in a medium oven for 15 minutes.

234 Frangipane

La Frangipana / La Frangipane

This is a puff pastry dessert with an almond custard filling.

For 10

The pastry

1 lb 2 oz/500 g flour	1 lb 2 oz/500 g butter
2 tsp salt	

1. Make a well in the flour. Dilute the salt in 9 fl oz/250 ml of cold water and pour a little into the well. Mix thoroughly and go on adding the salted water until you obtain a dough mixture, which should be very pliable.

2. Form the mixture into a ball, sprinkle lightly with flour, and leave in a cool place for 30 minutes.

3. Put the butter into a mixing bowl and knead thoroughly until of spreading consistency.

4. Spread the dough out on a well-floured board or marble-topped table and form into a rectangle about 3/4 inch/2 cm thick. Spread the butter over the middle of the dough to make a rectangular shape covering about one third of its surface. Fold the edges of the dough over the butter as though closing an envelope.

5. Sprinkle with flour and roll out the pastry as evenly as possible, without exerting too much pressure (which would squeeze out the butter).

6. Fold the dough in three and put in the refrigerator for 20 minutes or so.

7. Flour the top and bottom of the dough lightly, roll out, and fold in three. Repeat this operation two or three times more, leaving an interval of 20 minutes each time. Refrigerate for 2 hours.

● Very good results, with infinitely less labour, can be obtained with the frozen puff pastry.

The almond cream

3 1/2 oz/100 g sugar	1/2 vanilla pod
3 1/2 oz/100 g flour	2 oz/50 g butter
2 eggs and 3 egg yolks	30 almonds (including 2 or 3 bitter
18 fl oz/500 ml milk	almonds)

1. Put the sugar and flour in a thick-bottomed saucepan, mix, and incorporate the eggs and egg yolks. Heat the milk and vanilla pod to almost boiling point, then pour very gradually over the mixture. Stir until a smooth consistency is obtained.

2. Cook over a low heat, stirring all the time with a wooden spoon or

whisk, until thick. Away from the heat, beat in the butter, cut into small dice. Keep stirring as the cream cools to stop a skin forming on the surface.

3. Put 2 or 3 tablespoons of the cream into a mortar, add the almonds, and pound to a smooth paste (alternatively, pulverize them, without the cream, in a liquidizer). Add little by little to the rest of the cream.

4. Roll the pastry out into two rectangular sheets and dry them one after the other in a very low oven for 5 minutes. Spread one of the sheets with the almond cream, lay the other on top, glaze with beaten egg, and bake in a preheated oven (425°F/220°C, gas mark 7) for about 50 minutes.

• • •

235 Sweet Patties
Li Rissola / Les Rissoles Sucrées

These are made in exactly the same way as savoury patties (No. 229), except that the filling used is the almond cream described in No. 234.

• • •

236 Black Nougat
Lou Nougat Négré / Le Nougat Noir

2 lb/1 kg honey	1 tbs orange-blossom water
2 lb/1 kg lightly roasted almonds	2 sheets of rice paper

1. Put the honey into a thick-bottomed saucepan and bring slowly to the boil over a gentle heat, stirring all the time with a wooden spoon.

2. When the honey has begun to boil vigorously, add the almonds and orange-blossom water. Keep stirring.

3. When the mixture turns brown and the almonds begin to sizzle, remove the saucepan from the heat and continue stirring for several minutes. Then cover the bottom of an oiled baking tin with a sheet of rice paper, and pour in the nougat.

4. Cover with another sheet of rice paper and a board with a weight on top. Leave to cool completely before turning out.

237 Biscottins
Lu Biscutin / Les Biscottins

8 oz/250 g sugar	1 tbs orange-blossom water
12 oz/375 g flour	

1. Put the sugar in a saucepan with 4 fl oz/100 ml of water, stir, and heat until a transparent syrup is obtained.

2. Make a well in the flour on a board or marble-topped table, and pour in the syrup. Add the orange-blossom water. Knead into a fairly thick dough.

3. Roll the dough into little balls the size of a large hazelnut. Arrange them on a buttered baking sheet, sprinkle with a little water, and bake in a very hot oven until light brown.

• • •

238 Raisin Fritters
Li Bignéta d'Asébic / Les Beignets aux Raisins Secs

1 lb 2 oz/500 g flour	raisins, *or* currants
2 tbs olive oil	7 fl oz/200 ml rum
2 eggs, separated	1/2 oz/15 g sugar
salt	1 tbs orange-blossom water
2 medium-sized apples	oil for deep-frying
11 oz/300 g sultanas, raisins, Malaga	sugar for sprinkling

1. Put the flour in a mixing bowl and make a well. Pour in 2 tablespoons of olive oil, 2 egg yolks, a pinch of salt, and 1/2 pint/300 ml of water. Mix until a smooth and fairly liquid batter is obtained.

2. Dice the apples and put them in a bowl with the raisins, previously soaked in rum, the sugar, and the orange-blossom water. Mix thoroughly.

3. Beat 2 egg whites until stiff, and fold into the batter. Heat the frying oil until just smoking. Scoop up a tablespoon of batter, take a large pinch of apples and raisins, roll them in the batter, and drop into the hot oil.

4. When the fritters turn golden, remove, drain, and sprinkle with sugar.

239 Shavings
Li Bofa / Les Copeaux

---

4 oz/100 g sugar
2 eggs
1 tbs orange-blossom water

4 oz/100 g flour
1 tsp butter

---

1. Put the sugar and the beaten eggs into a mixing bowl, and mix, though not too thoroughly. Add the orange-blossom water and flour, and mix until a smooth dough is obtained (it should not, however, be kneaded for more than a minute).

2. Smear a baking sheet with the butter. Put the dough in a pastry bag, and squeeze out strips about ½ inch/1 cm wide and 4 to 5 inches/10 to 12 cm long on to the baking sheet, leaving a space of 1 inch/2 to 3 cm between each strip.

3. Bake in a hot oven for 4 to 5 minutes. If your oven has a glass door, watch the biscuits carefully. As soon as they are nicely browned, transfer the baking sheet from the oven on to the open oven door (if it opens downwards) and roll the biscuits quickly in a spiral round a stick or cylinder the thickness of a broom handle. This must be done with great speed, otherwise the biscuits will lose their pliability. As soon as each biscuit is twisted into shape, transfer to a cool surface, so it does not collapse.

• • •

240 Aniseed Cakes
Lu Pan d'Anisi / Les Pains d'Anis

---

1 lb 2 oz/500 g flour
1 lb 2 oz/500 g sugar
4 egg whites

1 oz/25 g aniseed
salt

---

1. Put the flour, sugar, egg whites, aniseed, and a pinch of salt into a bowl, and mix until a dough is obtained. Roll out into a layer ¼ inch/5 mm thick.

2. With a pastry-cutter, cut out discs 1 inch/3 cm in diameter. Arrange on a buttered baking sheet and bake in a low oven until light brown.

241 Pine-Nut Biscuits
Lu Bescuech aï Pignoun / Les Biscuits aux Pignons

1/2 lb/250 g almonds, peeled	2 1/4 lb/1 kg sugar
3/4 lb/300 g pine-nuts	8 egg whites

---

1. Pulverize the almonds and all but 2 oz/50 g of the pine-nuts in a mortar or, preferably, in a grinder.

2. Put in a large bowl with the sugar, and mix well. Gradually whisk in the egg whites.

3. Arrange tablespoons of the mixture on a buttered baking sheet. Decorate each heap with 6 pine-nuts. Sprinkle with a very little water and bake in a low oven until light brown.

● ● ●

242 Almond Fritters
Li Bignéta dé Péna / Les Beignets d'Amande

---

7 oz/200 g flour	4 oz/100 g ground almonds
14 oz/400 g sugar	1 oz/30 g butter
salt	oil for deep frying
6 eggs and 10 egg yolks	fine breadcrumbs
35 fl oz/1 litre milk	

---

1. Put the flour, 12 oz/350 g of the sugar, and a small pinch of salt into a thick-bottomed saucepan. Stirring all the time, add first 4 beaten eggs, then the 10 egg yolks.

2. Stir 5 fl oz/150 ml of the milk into the ground almonds until a smooth paste is obtained, then add this to the mixture in the saucepan. Mix well.

3. Bring the rest of the milk to the boil, and pour slowly into the saucepan stirring all the time with a wooden spoon. Put over a gentle heat and thicken the cream, beating with a whisk.

4. When the cream is fairly thick, retnove from heat and pour into a lightly buttered, large shallow flat dish. Pat the surface flat with moistened fingers, cover with a thin layer of melted butter, and leave to cool.

5. Cut the almond cream into lozenge shapes measuring 1 inch/3 cm on each side. Heat the oil until it is just beginning to smoke. Dip each lozenge into a bowl containing 2 beaten eggs, then coat with breadcrumbs and drop into the oil.

6. Remove when brown, drain, sprinkle with the remaining sugar, and serve on a napkin.

243 Lemon Tart

La Tourta dé Limoun / La Tarte au Citron

For 6

The pastry

4 oz/125 g butter	salt
8 oz/250 g flour	1 egg yolk

1. Put the softened butter, the flour, and a pinch of salt in a bowl, and blend rapidly with the fingers until the pieces are the size of rolled oats. Add the egg yolk and a tablespoon of chilled water, and knead until you can form a smooth-surfaced ball (it may be necessary to add a tablespoon or two more water). Set aside for 1 hour in a cool place.

2. Butter the inside of a tart tin and sprinkle lightly with flour. Roll out the pastry and line the tin with it. Prick its entire surface with a fork.

3. Partially bake the pastry in the oven for 20 minutes, and set aside.

The cream

4 eggs	2 lemons
7 oz/20 g sugar	1 tsp cornflour

1. Separate the yolks and whites of the eggs. Put the yolks in a bowl with half the sugar and beat vigorously until creamy and light yellow in colour. Grate the rind of the lemons into the mixture, then add their juice and the cornflour, beating all the time with a wooden spatula.

2. Cook the cream very gently in a double saucepan, stirring it until it begins to get thick. This operation may take from 10 to 20 minutes.

3. Beat the egg whites until stiff, adding the rest of the sugar gradually as you do so. Fold carefully into the cream, one spoonful at a time.

4. Fill the pastry shell with this mixture and bake in a hot oven for 15 minutes. The surface of the tart should be slightly brown. The filling will sag slightly when the tart is removed from the oven: this is normal.

● A similar tart can be made with oranges: the filling consists of a *crème patissière* made of 4 oz/125 g of sugar, 3 egg yolks, 1 oz/30 g of cornflour, ½ pint/250 ml of milk, and 2 tablespoons of curaçao, mixed with 5 crystallized oranges, cut into dice, and the rind of 2 fresh oranges.

244 Échaudés
Lu Chaudet Dur / Les Échaudés

Échaudés are ring-shaped pastries about 6 inches/15 cm in diameter.
The best ones to be found in the Comté de Nice used to be made in La Turbie,
at the foot of Augustus' trophy.

There are two types of *Échaudés* – what one might call the 'tourist' version,
made with bread dough, and a more traditional, much harder product
altogether, which only the strong in tooth are advised to tackle. It is this second
recipe which I give here.

1 lb 2 oz/500 g sugar	2 tbs orange-blossom water
1 lb 9 oz/700 g flour	2 oz/50 g aniseed

1. Melt the sugar with a little water in a saucepan until a transparent syrup
is obtained. Make a well in the flour, pour in the syrup, and mix energetically.

2. Add the orange-blossom water and the aniseed. Knead the dough for half
a minute or so, then roll it into long sausage shapes ¾ inch/2 cm across.
Form into rings 6 inches/15 cm in diameter.

3. Arrange the rings on a buttered baking sheet, brush them with a little
water, and bake in a hot oven until brown.

• • •

245 Sweet Panisses
Li Panissa Dous / Les Panisses Sucrées

This is simply the sweet version of the *panisses* described in No. 50.
Either follow that recipe from the very beginning, substituting a sprinkling of
sugar for salt and pepper just before serving, or, if the *panisses* have already
been deep-fried and allowed to get cold, reheat them in a medium oven for
30 minutes, sprinkle with sugar, and serve.

• • •

246 Rice with Pine-Nuts
Lou Ris aï Pignoun / Le Riz aux Pignons

This is a variety of rice pudding that used to be made with fresh ewe's milk.
If ewe's milk is unavailable the pudding has can be made with cow's milk.

For 10

4 oz/100 g mixed crystallized fruit (which should include, at least, oranges, peaches *or* apricots, pears, and cherries)	8 oz/250 g sugar
	1 oz/30 g butter
	1 vanilla pod
	1¼ pints/700 ml milk
4 tbs *grappa*	5 egg yolks
1 tbs olive oil	8 oz/250 g pine-nuts
8 oz/250 g long-grained rice	18 fl oz/500 ml double cream

1. Cut the crystallized fruit into small dice, put in a bowl with the *grappa*, mix, and leave to macerate.

2. Smear the inside of a 4 pint/2 litre charlotte mould with olive oil.

3. Bring 4 pints/2 litres of water to the boil in a large saucepan, pour in the rice, and cook for 5 minutes. Transfer the rice to a large strainer and wash in plenty of warm running water.

4. Put 4 tablespoons of sugar, the butter, the vanilla pod, and ½ pint/250 ml of the milk in a double boiler, and heat over a medium flame, stirring from time to time to melt the sugar. When tiny bubbles begin to appear, add the rice, cover, and cook gently for 30 minutes. If the liquid seems to be evaporating too quickly, add a spoonful or two of hot milk.

5. Taste the rice often. By the time it is cooked, the milk ought, in theory, to have been completely absorbed. If it has not, strain the rice. Remove the vanilla pod.

6. Heat the rest of the milk in a large saucepan over a medium heat. As soon as it begins to boil, set aside.

7. Put the egg yolks and the rest of the sugar in a thick-bottomed saucepan and beat until creamy. Pour in the hot milk, whisking vigorously until the mixture is smooth. Put over a low heat and cook until the custard begins to thicken. It is necessary to stir all the time and to be very careful not to let the liquid boil; otherwise it will separate.

8. Put 1 teaspoon of olive oil into a heavy frying pan, and heat until just beginning to smoke. Add the pine-nuts, shaking and stirring all the time so they brown uniformly. Transfer to a bowl.

9. Put the custard through a conical sieve (*chinois*) into a mixing bowl, then stir in the crystallized fruit, the *grappa*, the pine-nuts, and, without hurrying, the rice. Leave to cool.

10. When this mixture has cooled, beat the double cream until stiff, fold into the rice mixture, pour into the charlotte mould, and refrigerate until firm (i.e. 8 to 10 hours).

11. Unmould the pudding by dipping the mould for 1 second into boiling hot water, putting a plate over the open end, and turning upside down. If desired, the pudding may be decorated with a few pine-nuts.

247 Semolina Pudding with Crystallized Fruit

La Sémoula aï Frucha Counfichiadi
La Semoule aux Fruits Confits

For 8

2 pints/1 litre milk	parts of oranges, peaches *or*
5 oz/50 g sugar	apricots, plums, pears, and
½ vanilla pod	cherries)
2 oz/50 g semolina	1 tsp cold milk
2 eggs	1 tbs olive oil
4 oz/100 g crystallized fruit (which	icing sugar
should include, at least, equal	

1. Heat the milk slowly with the 5 oz/150 g sugar and vanilla pod.

2. Just as it is coming to the boil, remove the vanilla pod and pour in the semolina. Cook for 5 minutes, whisking all the time.

3. Beat the eggs in a bowl with the crystallized fruit, cut into small dice, and 1 teaspoon of cold milk.

4. Add to the semolina, beating vigorously. Pour the mixture on to an oiled flat ovenproof dish and sprinkle with icing sugar. Put the dish in a roasting pan containing a little water and place in a hot oven until brown.

● This pudding can be made in exactly the same way with tapioca taking the place of semolina.

248 Rice Soufflé
Lou Ris Boufat / Le Soufflé de Riz

For 6

4 oz/100 g rice	3 oz/75 g sugar
salt	rind of 1 lemon
1 pint/500 ml milk	5 eggs, separated
1 oz/25 g butter	1 oz/25 g cornflour

1. Cook the rice in 2 pints/1 litre of salted boiling water for 8 minutes, drain, and wash in plenty of warm running water.

2. Heat the milk in a saucepan with three quarters of the butter, the sugar, and the grated lemon rind. Add the rice and cook until tender.

3. When it is quite cold, stir in 5 egg yolks and the cornflour.

4. Smear a soufflé mould with the rest of the butter and sprinkle with a little flour. Prepare a *bain-marie* that can be put in the oven.

5. Beat 5 egg whites until stiff, fold them into the rice mixture, pour into the soufflé mould, and bake in the *bain-marie* in a hot oven for about 30 minutes.

● This soufflé can be served with apricot sauce, egg custard, or *sabayon* (the French version of the Italian *zabaglione*), which is the most traditional accompaniment in Nice. The recipe for *sabayon* follows (No. 249).

249 Sabayon

Lou Sabaïoun / Le Sabayon

This dish, which comes originally from Piedmont, is made exclusively with Marsala in Italy. However, when *sabayon* moved to Nice, other flavourings were tried, first fortified muscat wine, from Languedoc, then sherry, port, and Madeira.

For 6

6 egg yolks	½ pint/250 ml Marsala, port, sherry,
3 oz/80 g sugar	Madeira, *or* muscat wine

1. Whisk the egg yolks and sugar in a bowl until creamy.

2. Stir in the wine and transfer to a very thick-bottomed stainless steel or enamelled saucepan. Place over a low heat and whisk constantly until the *sabayon* turns to a firm, thick froth.

3. Pour into cups or glasses and chill.

● *Sabayon* can accompany puddings and sweet soufflés.

250 Iced Oranges, Tangerines, and Lemons

Lu Pourtugale, li Mandarina, é lu Limoun Gélat
Les Oranges, les Mandarines, et les Citrons Glacés

For 6

about 16 oranges, tangerines, *or* lemons	1 lb/450 g sugar
	2 egg whites

1. Take 6 of the fruits you have chosen (if possible, they should still have a stalk and a leaf), and slice a lid, about 1½ inches/4 cm across, off the top. With a grapefruit knife and spoon, remove the pulp and put the shells in the refrigerator.

2. Extract the juice from the fruit pulp. Squeeze the juice out of as many fruits of the same kind as is necessary to make up 1 pint/500 ml in all (about 10).

3. Put 2 teaspoons of grated rind in 1 pint/500 ml of water along with the sugar. Stir until the sugar is dissolved. (If you are in a hurry, you may dissolve the sugar over a gentle heat – the liquid must not boil; but it must have cooled completely before you tackle the next step.)

4. Mix together the fruit juice, the rind and dissolved sugar, and the egg whites, beaten stiff.

5. Put through a fine sieve and freeze in an ice-cream maker.

6. When the mixture is firm, fill the fruit shells so they are slightly overflowing, put on the lids and freeze until needed.

PRESERVES

251 Salted Cucumbers
Lu Cougoumbré / Les Concombres

For a 2½-pint/1½-litre jar

3¼ lb/1½ kg small cucumbers (3-5 inches/12 cm long)	tarragon
	fennel
oak leaves	coriander seeds
cherry leaves	salt

1. Wash the cucumbers, which should be of more or less equal size.

2. Put a layer of oak leaves, cherry leaves, tarragon, fennel, and a few coriander seeds on the bottom of a 2½ pint/1½ litre preserving jar. Cover with a layer of cucumbers. Repeat the operation until the jar is filled, finishing with a layer of leaves.

3. Boil enough water to immerse the contents of the jar and add 2½ oz/ 60 g of salt for each 2 pints/1 litre of water. Stir until dissolved and leave to cool completely. Pour into the jar until filled, seal securely, and keep in a cool place.

● The cucumbers will be ready for eating 1 month later.

252 Marinated Artichokes

Lu Archicota en Samoira / Les Artichauts en Marinade

100 tiny globe artichokes	18 spring onions
(see page x)	2 bay leaves
14 lemons	4 sprigs thyme
2 pints/1 litre dry white wine	2 sprigs fennel
1 pint/500 ml olive oil	2 cloves garlic
2 tbs coarsely ground pepper	salt

1. Trim the artichokes and set aside in a bowl containing plenty of water and the juice of 2 lemons.

2. Put into a very large saucepan 2 pints/1 litre of water, the white wine, olive oil, pepper, the juice of 12 lemons, the sliced spring onions (including the green stem), bay leaves, thyme, fennel, garlic (unpeeled), and a very large pinch of salt. Boil for 20 minutes.

3. Drain the artichokes well, then transfer quickly to the boiling marinade. Bring back to the boil and cook over a fierce heat until the vegetables are done. The cooking liquid should just cover the artichokes; if too much of it evaporates, top up with boiling water.

4. Arrange the artichokes in jars and cover with their cooking liquid (without the herbs). Seal securely and sterilize for 10 minutes.

● This recipe, for artichokes, maybe applied to a wide variety of other vegetables, either separately or mixed. The preserve may also be flavoured in a number of different ways (with curry powder, saffron, tomato, paprika, caraway seed, and so on).

253 Gherkins

Lu Cougoumbret / Les Cornichons

3 lb/1 kg small gherkins	1 sprig tarragon
salt	1 sprig thyme
1½ pints/750 ml vinegar	1 bay leaf
6 spring onions	4 shallots, peeled
3 cloves garlic, peeled	

1. Wash the gherkins thoroughly and put in a large bowl, sprinkle with salt, and leave for 48 hours, turning them over from time to time.

2. Drain the gherkins and cover with boiling vinegar. Allow to cool and leave for 24 hours. Do not be alarmed if the gherkins turn yellowish.

3. Drain the vinegar off into a saucepan, bring to the boil, add the gherkins, bring back to the boil, then remove the gherkins.

4. Pack the gherkins into jars with the spring onions, cut into ¾-inch/2-cm lengths, the very coarsely chopped garlic, the tarragon, the thyme, the bay leaf broken into small pieces, and the sliced shallots. Cover with the vinegar used to blanch the gherkins and seal well.

● The gherkins will be ready for eating 20 days after bottling.

● If you intend to keep the gherkins for a longer period, it is advisable, before bottling, to mix the vinegar with the same amount of cold boiled water which has been salted with the equivalent of 2½ oz/60 g of salt per 2 pints/ 1 litre.

● A healthier way of preparing gherkins (they do not look so good) is simply to put them straight in jars after step 1 along with their flavourings and cover with boiling vinegar.

254 (Black) Niçois Olives
Li Oùliva (Négré) dé Nissa / Les Olives (Noires) de Nice

Niçois olives	wild fennel
salt	

1. Soak the olives in water for 12 days, changing the water every day.

2. Prepare enough brine to cover the amount of olives you wish to preserve: put coarse sea salt into water (4 oz/100 g of salt per 2 pints/1 litre), boil for 5 minutes, covered, and leave to cool.

3. Put the olives into the brine along with the wild fennel (garden fennel will do, though it does not have the same flavour), and leave for about 3 weeks. Make sure the olives remain covered with liquid, otherwise add more brine made in the way described in step 2, once it has completely cooled.

4. As the oil in the olives will have formed little grey patches, skim the surface of the brine, then put the olives into jars and cover with the brine they have been soaking in. If this is not enough, make some more brine (again, using 4 oz/100 g of salt per 2 pints/1 litre of water) and pour into the jars. Seal securely.

● ● ●

255 Tarragon
L'Estragoun / L'Estragon

Although there has been much improvement in recent years in the quality of dried herbs available on the market, the following traditional method of preserving tarragon does, I think keep the flavour more intact than drying.

tarragon	salt

1. Select some particularly healthy-looking sprigs of tarragon, wash in running water, and blanch in boiling water for 1 minute. Transfer immediately back to cold running water.

2. Put them in small heat-proof bottles or jars with cold boiled water, salted with 4 oz/100 g of salt per 2 pints/1 litre of water, seal, and boil for 3 minutes.

256 Peppers in Vinegar

Lu Pébroun où Vinaügré / Les Poivrons au Vinaigre

---

4 lb/2 kg red *or* yellow peppers   salt
2 pints/1 litre vinegar

---

1. Wash the peppers thoroughly, cut in half, remove the stem and seeds, sprinkle with salt, and leave on kitchen tissue in a cool place for 4 days.

2. Rinse in a bowl full of vinegar, then put into jars, cover with vinegar, and seal.

● This method can also be used to preserve hot capsicums, except that they are left whole.

● ● ●

257 Tomato Pulp

Lu Toùmati Councassadi / Les Tomates Concassées

This is one of the most important preserves for the Niçois cook: when, in mid-winter, one of the many local dishes requiring tomatoes is being prepared, the broaching of a jar of tomato pulp lets a ray of sunshine into the kitchen.

---

11 lb/5 kg very ripe tomatoes   ¼ pint/150 ml lemon juice

---

1. Blanch the tomatoes for a few seconds in boiling water, then peel, seed, chop, and pack them tightly into jars. Leave for 1 or 2 hours.

2. Pour off the liquid that will have risen to the surface, fill up the jars with more peeled, seeded, and chopped tomatoes and the lemon juice to the level indicated for sterilizing, and stir well.

3. Seal the jars and sterilize for 1 hour.

● ● ●

258 Pistou Preserve

Lou Pistou en Counserva / Le Pistou en Conserve

Basil has a very short summer season, so *pistou* preserve is particularly useful for flavouring soup, pasta, and so on at other times of the year. Make the *pistou* as indicated in No. 7, pack very carefully and tightly into small jars (no air pockets should remain), cover with a layer of olive oil, seal, and keep in a very cool place.

259 Salted Anchovies

Li Amploua où Saou / Les Anchois au Sel

For a 2¹/₂-pint/1¹/₂ litre jar

4¹/₂ lb/2 kg fresh anchovies	peppercorns
about 3 lb/1¹/₂ kg medium-coarse	cloves
sea salt	bay leaves

1. Remove the heads of the anchovies, gut and clean them, and place for 24 hours between layers of sea salt (about 1 lb/500 g).

2. Put some sea salt in the bottom of a jar, and arrange a row of anchovies on top, head to tail, and bellies facing down. Cover with 10 peppercorns, 3 cloves, and ¹/₂ bay leaf. Put in another layer of salt, anchovies, and peppercorns, and repeat the operation until the jar is filled. Finish with a layer of salt, peppercorns, 3 cloves, and ¹/₂ bay leaf.

3. Place a rust-proof jam-jar lid that fits neatly *inside* the top of the preserving jar on top of the anchovies, and weigh down with a large pebble (not a cast-iron weight, which would corrode). Leave in a cool place for a week.

4. Press down on the pebble, the oil which rises to the surface should be meticulously removed with a spoon, otherwise it will go rancid.

5. Remove the pebble and lid, and top up with a little salt if necessary. Seal the jar and store in a cool, dark place.

260 Salt Fish Paste

Lou Pissala / La Purée de Poissons Salés

Authentic *pissala* is made with *palaia* (small fry) of sardines and anchovies. Because of the difficulty in obtaining *palaia*, there is an increasing tendency to make *pissala* with fully-grown anchovies. I give both recipes, though no self-respecting connoisseur would touch anything but the first.

First version

4 lb/2 kg *palaia*	5 bay leaves
1 lb/500 g sea salt	5 pinches thyme
15 cloves	2 tbs olive oil
50 peppercorns	

1. Remove the heads of the *palaia*, and gut them.

2. In a bowl or pot, which should be neither too wide nor too large, put a layer of fish, a layer of salt, 3 cloves, 10 peppercorns, 1 bay leaf, and 1 pinch thyme. Repeat the operation until the receptacle is full, finishing with a layer of salt and flavourings.

3. Put in a cool and dust-free place for a week.

4. Remove with a spoon any oil that has risen to the surface, then stir the fish thoroughly with a wooden spoon. Every day for a month, remove the oil and stir, making sure that the paste at the bottom of the receptacle gets circulated.

5. Put the fish through a fine sieve, which will remove scales, bones, and flavourings, and pack into a jar. Cover with a thin layer of olive oil. The *pissala* is ready for eating. Make sure that there is always a layer of olive oil after use, adding more if necessary.

● *Pissala*, which is much appreciated by the people of Nice, is used to flavour a wide range of dishes (hors-d'oeuvres, fish, cold meat), as well as cocktail biscuits. It is also a useful ingredient for anchovy butter (No. 29) and *pissaladière* (No. 48).

Second version

2 lb/1 kg salted anchovies	3 bay leaves
9 cloves	3 pinches thyme
30 peppercorns	1 tbs olive oil

1. Soak the salted anchovies in cold running water for at least 12 hours.

2. Proceed as in steps 2, 3, and 5 of the first version (minus the salt).

261 Halved Apricots
Lu Abrico a Mitan / Les Abricots en Moitiés

apricots	sugar

1. Use unbruised, slightly unripe apricots. Slit them open and remove the stones.
2. Pack the apricots into jars and cover with sugar syrup (1 lb 2 oz/500 g of sugar per 1³/4 pints/1 litre of water).
3. Seal and sterilize for 30 minutes.
● Extra flavour can be obtained by breaking open the stones and adding the halved kernels to the apricots before sterilizing.

● ● ●

262 Cherries
Li Cérieüa / Les Cerises

cherries	sugar

1. Remove the cherry stalks, and wash the fruit carefully.
2. Pack the cherries into jars and cover with sugar syrup (1 lb 2 oz/500 g of sugar per 1³/4 pints1 litre of water).
3. Seal and sterilize for 20 minutes.

263 Cherries in Grappa*
Li Cérieïa a la Branda / Les Cerises à la Branda

2 lb/1 kg cherries	9 oz/250 g sugar
4 cloves	2¼ pints/1¼ litres *grappa*
1 stick cinnamon	

1. Shorten the cherry stalks, and wash the fruit carefully. Put in a large bowl with the spices.

2. Melt the sugar in a little water over a low heat. Remove from heat, acid the *grappa*, and leave to cool.

3. Add to the cherries in the bowl. Distribute the contents of the bowl evenly between the number of jars you wish to fill (the cherries should come up to within 1 inch/3 cm of the top, and be covered with liquid).

4. Seal the jars, leave in sunlight for a few days, and store.

* See A Note on Drinks, page 217.

• • •

264 Strawberry Compote
La Coumposta dé Maïoussa / La Compote de Fraises

2 lb/1 kg strawberries	1½ lb/700 g sugar

1. Hull the strawberries and wash if necessary. Drain and put in a bowl with the sugar. Shake until well covered with sugar.

2. Transfer strawberries and sugar delicately to jars. Seal and sterilize for 20 minutes.

265 Halved Peaches
Lu Pessegué a Mitan / Les Pêches en Moitiés

yellow peaches   sugar

1. Peel the peaches, which should be unblemished and slightly unripe, cut in half, and remove the stones.
2. Pack the peach halves into jars, cut side down, and cover with sugar syrup (1 lb 2 oz/500 g of sugar per 1³/4 pints/1 litre of water).
3. Seal and sterilize for 30 minutes.
● Whole peaches can also be preserved in this way, using a syrup made of 2¹/4 lb/1 kg sugar per 1³/4 pints/1 litre of water. But it is not a very practical system, as only a very few peaches can fit into each jar.

● ● ●

266 Pears
Li Péra / Les Poires

firm pears   sugar
lemon juice

1. Peel the pears, halve or quarter them, core them, and put them in a bowl of water containing plenty of lemon juice (to stop them going brown).
2. Drain, pack into jars, and cover with sugar syrup (1 lb 2 oz/500 g of sugar per 1³/4 pints/1 litre of water).
3. Seal and sterilize for 20 minutes.

● ● ●

267 Apples
Lu Poun / Les Pommes

apples   sugar
lemon juice

Proceed exactly as with pears (No. 266).

268 Perdrigon Plums
Li Perdigouna / Les Prunes Perdrigon

firm, unblemished plums	sugar

1. Shorten the plum stalks. Pierce each fruit in four or five places with a pin and leave to soak for 4 hours in running water.
2. Pack into jars and cover with sugar syrup (1 lb 2 oz/500 g of sugar per 1¾ pints/1 litre of water).
3. Seal and sterilize for 30 minutes.

• • •

269 Fruit Juices
Lu Jus dé Frucha / Les Jus de Fruits

fruit (strawberries, raspberries, blackcurrants, apricots, blackberries, redcurrants, etc.)	sugar

1. Liquidize the fruit and strain through a fine sieve. Measure the resulting liquid and add 7 oz/200 g of sugar to each 1¾ pints/1 litre. Stir until dissolved.
2. Put in jars, seal, and sterilize for 30 minutes.

• • •

270 Whole Strawberries, Raspberries, and Blackberries
Li Maïoussa, li Frambouosa, é li Armoura Entié
Les Fraises, les Framboises, et les Mûres Entières

strawberries, raspberries, and blackberries	sugar

1. Choose slightly unripe and, if possible, unblemished fruit. Hull.
2. Pack into jars and cover with sugar syrup (1 lb 11 oz/750 g of sugar per 1¾ pints/1 litre of water).
3. Seal and sterilize for 10 minutes.

271 Lemon or Orange Jelly

La Géladina dé Limoun o dé Pourtugale
La Gelée de Citron ou d'Orange

The jellies and jams made in the Comté de Nice are basically the same as those made in other French provinces, at least as far as the recipes are concerned. The only difference is often the quality and freshness of the fruit used. But this recipe for lemon or orange jelly and the three recipes which follow (Nos. 272, 273, and 274) are specifically Niçois.

4 lb/2 kg Reinette apples	2¾ lb/1,200 g sugar
2 lb/1 kg Calville apples	6 lemons *or* oranges

1. Wash the apples very carefully, but do not peel or core them. Quarter, put in 7 pints/4 litres of water, and simmer till soft, prodding from time to time with a wooden spoon.

2. Put the pulp through a jelly bag.

3. Boil the sugar with 1 pint/600 ml of water until a bit of syrup dropped into cold water can be formed into a ball between the fingers. Add the juice of the apples, the juice of 6 oranges or lemons plus the pared rinds of 3 oranges or lemons, and bring to the boil.

4. After 3 minutes' boiling, remove from heat, take out the rind, and pot.

5. Allow to cool, and cover.

● ● ●

272 Violet Jelly

La Géladina aï Viouléta / La Gelée de Violettes

4 lb/2 kg Reinette apples	sugar
2 lb/1 kg Calville apples	½ lb/250 g violet petals

1. Wash the apples very carefully, but do not peel or core them. Quarter them, put in 7 pints/4 litres of water, and simmer till soft, prodding from time to time with a wooden spoon.

2. Put the pulp through a jelly bag.

3. Measure the resulting liquid and add 1¼ lb/600 g of sugar to each 1¾ pints/1 litre. Dissolve.

4. Boil the liquid for 5 minutes, add the violet petals, and, after a minute or two, test for setting.

5. As soon as the setting point is reached, remove pan from heat, skim jelly, pot, allow to cool, and cover.

273 Tomato Jam

La Counfitura dé Toùmati / La Confiture de Tomates

fleshy, very ripe and unblemished tomatoes	sugar vanilla pod

1. Peel the tomatoes, cut in half crosswise, remove pips, and purée.

2. Weigh the resulting pulp and add 1½ lb/700 g of sugar to each 2 lb/1 kg.

3. Bring the mixture slowly to the boil in a large saucepan, after adding 1 or more vanilla pods (1 pod to every 6½ lb/3 kg). Stir from time to time with a wooden spoon, making sure that the jam is not sticking to the bottom of the saucepan.

4. The jam is cooked when a small drop of it, cooled and held between the fingers, feels slightly tacky.

5. Remove from heat, take out the vanilla pod(s), pot, and leave to cool. Lay waxed circles of paper on the jam in each pot, and cover.

• • •

274 Fig Jam

La Counfitura dé Bélouna / La Confiture de Figues

4 lb/1¾ kg fresh figs 2¾ lb/1¼ kg sugar	½ vanilla pod

1. Trim the figs and peel off their outer skin.

2. Heat the sugar and 1¼ pints/750 ml of water in a large saucepan. As soon as the syrup begins to boil, add the figs one by one, so that boiling continues without stopping. Put in the vanilla pod.

3. Simmer uncovered over the lowest heat possible for 5 hours.

4. Pot, making sure the fruit is covered by syrup, leave to cool, and cover.

A NOTE ON CHEESES

Brous
Lou Brous / Le Brous

This explosive mixture is made of clotted milk, from either the cow, the goat, or the ewe, and often from a combination of all three: the cheese is put into jars, each layer alternating with a layer of chopped garlic, pepper, and local *marc* (see page 217); the jars are then closed.

In the high mountain valley of La Tinée, *brous* is eaten when it begins to crawl with maggots: the latter are given their marching orders as soon as the cheese is spread on burning-hot toast.

Curds
Lou Caïet / Le Caillé

This is quite simply fresh goat cheese. It is usually marinated in olive oil for a few days, sometimes with additional flavouring, then eaten with pieces of bread dipped in the oil.

Rouré Cheese
Lou Tomou dé Rouré / La Tome de Rouré

The village of Rouré, perched high above the valley of La Tinée, produces this quite exceptional cheese, one of the finest to be found anywhere in the French Alps. It is made from the unskimmed milk of cows which have been sent up into mountain pastures during the summer. The only trouble is that it is in very short supply.

Fromage Blanc
Lou Blanc / Le Fromage Blanc

In Nice, *fromage blanc* is much appreciated mixed with chopped chives, salt, pepper, and a few drops of olive oil. Another flavouring consists of some diced green pepper and one or two chopped basil leaves.

215

Brousse

La Broussa / La Brousse

There are several ways of eating this wonderfully aromatic ewe's cheese: with sugar and orange-blossom water, sugar and *grappa*, or sugar and black coffee.

Personally, however, I prefer *brousse* on its own. When I was a boy, peasant girls used to come down from La Brigue to sell the cheese in Nice. Their wicker trays, held horizontal by a ribbon round their necks, were piled high with tiny heart-shaped baskets containing the precious, delicately flavoured cheese.

Sometimes the *brousse* was not eaten up in time – it is a fresh, unsalted cheese that does not keep for very long – so it was put, along with a sprig of thyme, a bay leaf, and some ground pepper, to marinate in a bowl of slightly salted water which had previously been boiled and allowed to cool. In time, if turned over each day, the cheese gradually came to taste as distinctive and as strong as Roquefort.

A NOTE ON DRINKS

Wine

Nice is, without any doubt, the only French city which can claim to possess, within the boundaries of its commune, vineyards enjoying *appellation contrôlée*. The wine is called Bellet.

If you are visiting the Côte d'Azur, I do urge you to go up to the very attractive 'village within the walls', Saint-Romain-de-Bellet, perched above the vineyards that sweep down, at times very steeply, to the River Var.

A few decades ago, carnation growers had designs on the quietly declining vineyards of Bellet. The Bagnis family, who own Château de Crémat, needed plenty of courage and faith in themselves, at a time of apparent crisis, to 'relaunch' the wine: it was immediately recognized for the top-class product it is by wine experts all over the world, and more especially in France.

Because the Bagnis family held out, other wine-growers returned to work the vineyards of Bellet. The pebbly soil brings out the very best in the grape varieties used there – Grenache, Cinsault, Rolle, Clairette, and others; and the smoothness, body, and bouquet of the resulting wine, whether red, white, or rosé, makes it a worthy accompaniment to any course of a meal, whether hors-d'oeuvre, fish, meat, cheese, or dessert.

Bellet's area of production (a mere 70 hectares) is now protected by *appellation contrôlée* legislation. Those who appreciate the wine will be delighted to hear that more and more vines are being planted on the hills within that area.

True, Bellet is rather an expensive wine. But this, I can assure you, is only because the vineyards are tiny; and as the wine they produce is completely unadulterated only a very few bottles of it are available.

Branda

This is a locally produced *marc* (grape spirit). The closest equivalent to it found in Britain is the Italian *grappa*, which has been indicated in recipes calling for *branda*.

Grata-Quéca

Grata-quéca, which is served at the end of a meal – usually supper – instead of coffee, cannot really be called a drink, a sweet, or an ice. Yet it is all of them rolled into one: crushed ice doused in fruit syrup. Depending on the time of day and year, the syrup may be mint, peach, apricot, raspberry, strawberry, or pomegranate.

MEASUREMENTS AND TEMPERATURES

Solid Measures

British
16 oz = 1 lb

Metric
1000 grams (g) = 1 kilogram (kg)

Approximate equivalents

British	*Metric*
1 lb (16 oz)	450-500 g
½ lb (8 oz)	225-250 g
¼ lb (4 oz)	100-125 g
1 oz	25 g

Metric	*British*
1 kg (1000 g)	2 lb 3 oz
½ kg (500 g)	1 lb 2 oz
¼ kg (250 g)	9 oz
100 g	4 oz

Temperature Equivalents for Oven Thermostat Markings

Degrees Fahrenheit	*Gas Mark*	*Degrees Centigrade*	*Heat of Oven*
225	¼	110	Very cool
250	½	120	Very cool
275	1	140	Cool
300	2	150	Cool
325	3	160	Moderate
350	4	180	Moderate
375	5	190	Fairly hot
400	6	200	Fairly hot
425	7	220	Hot
450	8	230	Very hot
475	9	240	Very hot

Liquid Measures

British

1 quart	=	2 pints	=	40 fl oz
1 pint	=	2 cups	=	20 fl oz
½ pint	=	1 cup	=	10 fl oz
¼ pint	=	8 tablespoons	=	5 fl oz
		1 tablespoon	=	just over ½ fl oz
		1 dessertspoon	=	⅓ fl oz
		1 teaspoon	=	⅙ fl oz

Metric

1 litre = 10 decilitres (dl) = 100 centilitres (cl) = 1000 millilitres (ml)

American

1 quart	=	2 pints	=	32 fl oz
1 pint	=	2 cups	=	16 fl oz
		1 cup	=	8 fl oz
		1 tablespoon	=	⅓ fl oz
		1 teaspoon	=	⅙ fl oz

Approximate equivalents

British	Metric	Metric	British
1 quart	1.1 litre	1 litre	35 fl oz
1 pint	600 ml	½ litre (500ml)	18 fl oz
½ pint	300 ml	¼ litre (250 ml)	9 fl oz
¼ pint	150 ml	100 ml	4 fl oz
1 tablespoon	15 ml		
1 dessertspoon	10 ml		
1 teaspoon	5 ml		

British	American	American	British
1 quart	2½ pints	1 quart	1½ pints plus 3 tbs (32 fl oz)
1 pint	1¼ pints		
½ pint	10 fl oz (1¼ cups)	1 pint	¾ pint plus 2 tbs (16 fl oz)
¼ pint	5 fl oz		
1 tablespoon	1½ tablespoons	1 cup	½ pint minus 2 tbs (8 fl oz)
1 dessertspoon	1 tablespoon		
1 teaspoon	⅙ fl oz		

INDEX